THE YOGĀCĀRA IDEALISM

THE YOGĀCĀRA IDEALISM

Ashok Kumar Chatterjee

MOTILAL BANARSIDASS
Delhi :: Varanasi :: Patna

Head office : Bunglow Road, Jawahar Nagar, Delhi-7
Branches : 1. Chowk, Varanasi (U. P.)
2. Ashok Rajpath, Patna (Bihar)

ISBN O 8426 O742 O

First edition published by Banaras Hindu University, 1962
Second revised edition : 1975
Price : Rs. 50.00

Printed in India :
At Bhargava Bhushan Press, Varanasi, and Published by Sundarlal Jain
For Motilal Banarsidass, Chowk, Varanasi (U. P.)
14/4–75

CONTENTS

			Page
Foreword	..	..	vii
Preface	..	..	ix
Preface to Second Edition	..	..	xv
Abbreviations	..	..	xvii
Ch. I A Historical Introduction	..	..	1
Ch. II The Development of the Yogācāra	..	..	24
Ch. III Refutation of Realism	..	..	45
Ch. IV Some Objections Answered	..	..	73
Ch. V The Three Vijñānas	..	..	87
Ch. VI Dharma Theory in the Yogācāra	..	..	108
Ch. VII The Yogācāra Conception of the Absolute		..	126
Ch. VIII The Yogācāra Discipline	..	..	157
Ch. IX The Concept of the Tathāgata	..	..	169
Ch. X The Yogācāra and Some Other Forms of Absolutism			178
Ch. XI The Yogācāra and Some Other Forms of Idealism			204
Glossary	..	..	231
Index	..	..	233

FOREWORD

The Yogācāra-Vijñānavāda Idealism was the last great creative synthesis of Buddhism and its position in that tradition is comparable to that of the Advaita Vedānta in the orthodox Hindu tradition. It is perhaps the only original epistemological idealism to be formulated on the Indian soil. Its impact on the other systems of thought was tremendous. Even those philosophies that were completely out of line with idealism, like the Nyāya, the Mīmāṁsā and Jainism, had to reckon with it. Considering the important role played by the Yogācāra Idealism in Buddhism and in Indian philosophical and religious thought in general, it is surprising that there had been no full or reliable expositions of this philosophy. This gap in our knowledge is admirably filled by the present work of Dr. Chatterjee.

The author deals with the Yogācāra-Vijñānavāda in all its aspects and bearings, historically, analytically and comparatively. The first two chapters of the book show, with great clarity and sufficient detail, the origin and development of the Yogācāra idealism as an outcome of those fruitful and dynamic ideas associated with the previous schools of Buddhism, especially with the Sautrāntika and the Mādhyamika. The originality of the Yogācāra synthesis of Buddhist teachings has been clearly brought out, and the individual contribution made by the philosophers of this school, such as Asanga, Vasubandhu, Sthiramati, Dignāga, Dharmakīrti and Śāntarakṣita, has received adequate attention.

The subsequent chapters, which form the core of the work, represent a constructive and critical exposition of the Yogācāra metaphysics, its idealism and absolutism as well as its spiritual discipline. Dr. Chatterjee has utilised nearly all the sources available on the subject and has given a faithful and persuasive account of this system of thought. He has not hesitated to go behind the literal meaning of the texts to extract their real significance. There is a measure of risk in such a venture, and at some places one might choose to disagree with the author's interpretation. However, the duty of a scholar is not just to reproduce literally, but to re-interpret and to re-construct his theme.

Comparison of the Yogācāra with other forms of idealism and absolutism, Indian as well as European, has been undertaken in the last two chapters of the work. This serves to bring out the affinities and distinctions which are only too often blurred. These comparative studies are among the best specimens of the author's keen analysis and lucid exposition.

I cannot help feeling that the work of Dr. Chatterjee would have gained considerably more in comprehension and authoritativeness if the Yogācāra texts in Chinese and Tibetan or their translations in French had been made use of more fully. I have no manner of doubt, however, that the work of Dr. Chatterjee, even as it stands, will prove a valuable and outstanding contribution to our understanding of a very important phase of Indian thought. It is an excellent piece of philosophical writing, both with regard to the range of problems covered and the delightful manner of presentation. There is hardly any dull or unstimulating page in a work of 230 pages.

It is a matter of personal gratification to me that the line of thought nitiated by me in dealing with the basic philosophy of Buddhism in my study of the Mādhyamika system (*The Central Philosophy of Buddhism*, George Allen & Unwin, London, 1955) has been largely accepted and carried out by my student and friend, Dr. Ashok Kumar Chatterjee. His study of the Yogācāra Idealism may well be considered as a sequel to my book on the Mādhyamika Absolutism which together constitute the revolutionary Mahāyāna movement.

T. R. V. Murti

PREFACE

An attempt is here made to expound the metaphysics of the Yogācāra school of Buddhism and to analyse its logical implications. It may not be rash to think that little apology is needed for making such an attempt. The expository literature on the Yogācāra system is plentiful, but unfortunately, not adequate. Scholarly studies on the subject from the historical point of view are not lacking. There is hardly any work, however, which treats of the system as an original contribution to philosophy. At best, it is construed as a phase in the historical development of Buddhism. The account of the Yogācāra philosophy given in the standard histories of Indian thought is necessarily all too meagre. The details cannot be discussed with sufficient fulness within the limited space in such works. Treatises devoted entirely to the exposition of Buddhism fare no better. The analysis is sometimes positively misleading. The Yogācāra is described merely as idealism. For a correct appraisement of the system it is very necessary to remember that it is a form of absolutism. This is the central problem in the Yogācāra philosophy—the problem of effecting a logical synthesis between idealism and absolutism. The Yogācāra is wise enough to perceive that idealism, when pressed, yields an absolutism by the sheer dynamism of its own inner logic. This point needs bringing out with sufficient deductive clarity. In the existing accounts this point is not utterly lacking, but it is hardly given that attention and emphasis which it demands. The late Stcherbatsky was a notable exception which only proves the general statement.

Other constructive details also of the system have not been fully analysed. In the present essay I have simply tried to present a more or less complete picture of the system, to collect the scattered details into a coherent connected picture and to size it up, not merely as a phase of Buddhism, but rather as an original and constructive philosophy. Completeness has been with me more an ideal than an actual achievement. I have neither the soundness of scholarship nor the maturity of judgment required for this. Certain omissions are however deliberate. The first chapter professes to be a historical introduction to the Yogācāra metaphysics, but history, in its popular sense of chronology of dates and events, will not be found there. Not that such a chronological study is uninteresting or unimportant ; it is simply that in a morphological analysis of any metaphysics, chronology of dates and events is absolutely beside the point. In the present essay I have attempted to show that the Yogācāra philosophy is a logical elaboration of the basic epistemological pattern of Buddhism. The first chapter is a history of the gradual development of the fundamental logic of Buddhism, culminating in the Yogācāra idealism. The omission of actual chronological details appeared excusable, and is deliberate.

For the same reason, minor doctrinal differences, if any, between various Yogācāra ācāryas, have not been discussed. I have taken Vasubandhu's *Vijñaptimātratāsiddhi* as the basic work on the system. Other texts are consulted only as throwing light on the problems raised in that treatise. The other omission is regarding the insufficient space devoted to the 8th and 9th chapters, dealing with the discipline and the religion of the Yogācāra system. In a strictly metaphysical essay, they could very well be deleted. I have said a few words only for the sake of completeness. Here also the shifting of emphasis away from these problems appeared to be justifiable, though I do not know how far this point of view is really justified. All that I ask is to have the essay judged purely on its merits as a philosophical analysis, and not as a piece of historical survey.

As regards the plan of the essay, the first two chapters are more or less historical. The first chapter discusses how the Yogācāra school emerged out of the inner dynamism inherent in Buddhism from the very outset. The second chapter is devoted to the important ācāryas, texts, sub-schools, and other such minor details. These two chapters are in no way integrally related with what follows.

The third and fourth chapters analyse the epistemological basis of the system. The third is concerned with the refutation of the category of the objective, and in the fourth realistic arguments are considered from the Yogācāra standpoint. The fifth chapter sets forth the elaboration of the Yogācāra idealism as a constructive metaphysics, and attempts to show how consciousness, the sole reality, is actually diversified into the multi-dimensional forms of the so-called empirical world. The sixth chapter is again a concession to the ideal of completeness. It deals with the Dharma-theory, a doctrine of central interest in entire Buddhism, as adapted by the Yogācāra.

The seventh chapter attempts to analyse the Yogācāra metaphysics as a form of absolutism. This problem can certainly be said to represent the very heart of the system. All the other details are to be understood as leading upto this logical climax. To this chapter is added a section on the doctrine of Three Truths.

The last two chapters are comparative and, as such, do not materially add to the understanding of the system. They are included in order to make clear the spiritual affinities and differences between the Yogācāra and other allied schools of idealism and absolutism. For this purpose, Berkeley and Hegel are selected as representing different forms of idealism. I had intended to add a section on Leibnitz too, but had to refrain from doing so because of considerations of space. A section on Gentile is added however as an appendix to that on Hegel. The Advaita Vedānta and the Mādhyamika are chosen as two other definitive forms of absolutism.

A few words may be said about the use of the term 'idealism' in the present essay. Idealism is so ambiguous a term and is employed in metaphysics in so many totally different senses, that its use might lead to gross misunderstanding unless it is defined with great precision at the very outset. Some scholars choose to understand it in a very loose manner. Prof S. N. Dasgupta, for example, says,[1] "I shall call any theory idealistic which asserts that 'Reality is spiritual'. . . . Idealism is not committed to any particular kind of epistemological doctrine. . .the concern of the idealist is with regard to the assertion of the nature of reality, and it is not difficult to conceive that there should be an idealism which is largely in agreement with some forms of realism in the field of epistemology but may yet be thoroughgoing idealism." I venture to think that epistemology is a more primary discipline than ontology, and idealism therefore should essentially be understood in an epistemological sense. Any theory of reality presupposes a theory of knowledge by which it is determined. Nothing can be asserted about the nature of reality unless certain assumptions are tacitly made regarding the nature of knowledge. Prof. Dasgupta's contention that idealism is committed to the doctrine "Reality is spiritual" would include as idealistic systems like those of Rāmānuja and Nimbārka, while exclude systems like that of Kant. This appears to me as something of an anomaly. The use of the term in the history of Western

1. Indian Idealism, p. 25.

philosophy would also show that idealism is primarily an epistemological doctrine. Kant, for instance, in the famous section on "Refutation of Idealism", does not seek to refute any theory of reality being spiritual or otherwise. The controversy raised by the Neo-Realists and the Critical Realists is purely an epistemological one.

Idealism as an epistemological doctrine means that knowledge is constructive. It does not reveal ; it creates. Even this, however, is not free from ambiguity. Any metaphysics which makes a distinction between appearance and reality, accepts the creativity of the subjective in some form or other. In this sense, Kant, the Sautrāntika, and the Advaita Vedāntin, would all be idealists. Idealism, in the strictest sense of the term, connotes three important things, viz. (a) knowledge is creative; (b) there is nothing given in knowledge ; and (c) the creative knowledge is itself real. Though Kant, the Sautrāntika, and the Advaita Vedānta, accept the first proposition, viz., the creativity of the subjective, they are also committed to a doctrine of the thing-in-itself, which is not made or unmade by being known. These systems are idealistic, but are not pure forms of idealism. For the Mādhyamika, there is no thing-in-itself ; he accepts the second proposition as well. But he thinks that the creative knowledge also is only appearance; it is the denial of all metaphysics, including idealism. My contention is that the Yogācāra alone represents idealism in its strict sense in Indian philosophy. In the Advaita Vedānta the reality of the given, which is not known but is the implicate of all knowledge, is scrupulously maintained and as such, it is not idealism.

The system is named 'Yogācāra' in preference to the more well-known appellation 'Vijñānavāda' merely for the sake of drawing a convenient distinction. The school of Dignāga and Dharmakīrti occupies a peculiar position. They essentially accept the doctrine of Vijñaptimātratā, and the unreality of the object. When they enter into logical discussions however they endorse the Sautrāntika standpoint of something being given in knowledge. The name 'Vijñānavāda' can be reserved for this school and the pure idealism of Maitreya, Asanga and Vasubandhu be called Yogācāra. The entire system may be called, as is actually done by some scholars and historians, the system of Yogācāra-Vijñānavāda.

Mention might also be made of the standpoint adopted in the essay. I am not an idealist. I believe that no speculative metaphysics can stand the corrosive test of criticism, and idealism is no exception. The Yogācāra is just the illustration of a great pattern of metaphysics, but it is no better than other possible patterns. The only solution of the Antinomies of Reason appears to be the Mādhyamika dialectic. Speculation is not the correct method of metaphysics and must be superseded by criticism. The Yogācāra system, as a speculative metaphysics, is dogmatic. Its redeeming feature is however that it is not merely an idealism; it is essentially an absolutism. It represents one of the alternative approaches to the Absolute, conforming to the form of absolutism set once for all by the Mādhyamika.

The shortcomings and defects in the essay are legion. They can be excused only by the justifiability of an attempt at such an exposition, and not by any positive achievement. Of orginality I can claim little. I am not presenting a novel metaphysics. I dare to hope however that there may be found some novelty of presentation and the raising of some problems which are generally slurred over.

I do not know how to express my indebtedness and gratitude to my revered teacher, Professor T.R.V. Murti. Whatever little I know of philosophy, I have learnt at his feet. The defects in the essay would have been infinitely greater, had not the entire essay been thoroughly revised by him with loving care. Those that are still lurking are only due to my inherent limitations. His great work, "The Central Philosophy of Buddhism", forms the theoretical basis and background of the present essay. It is in fact only a continuation and further elaboration of some of the problems raised in that book.

A. K. Chatterjee

PREFACE TO THE SECOND EDITION

The first edition of this book was published in the Darsana Series, Banaras Hindu University, 1962, with a Foreword by Prof. T. R. V. Murti who was then the General Editor of the Series. Much research work has appeared in print since then—textual, exegetic and critical. Texts have been brought out in many new editions, while original work has been done, mainly by Japanese scholars. To utilise all that material would have meant writing a completely new book. I have not however seen anything which would make me revise the standpoint adopted here, though some details might need modification here and there. A careful rereading of the basic sources convinces me that any deviation from the line of interpretation adopted by me is misinformed, not warranted by the tradition itself. I might have been mistaken in my attempt to reconstruct the system, but that, I think, does not affect the soundness of the general perspective. I have not therefore made any alteration in the text, apart from correcting minor errors. I am grateful to Messrs Motilal Banarsidass for bringing out this edition.

A. K. Chatterjee

LIST OF ABBREVIATIONS

BCA	..	Bodhicaryāvatāra by Śāntideva (Bib. Ind.)
BCAP	..	Bodhicaryāvatārapañjikā by Prajñākaramati (Bib. Ind.)
BSSB	..	Brahmasūtra Śāṅkarabhāṣya (Nirṇayasāgar)
CPB	..	The Central Philosophy of Buddhism, by Prof. T. R. V. Murti, Allen & Unwin, 1955.
HB	..	Buston's History of Buddhism, Tr. by Obermiller (Heidelberg 1931).
HIL	..	History of Indian Literature by Winternitz Vol. II (Calcutta University 1933).
LAS	..	Laṅkāvatārasūtra, ed. B. Nanjio, Kyoto 1923.
MA	..	Madhyamakāvatāra by Candrakīrti, Ch. VI (incomplete) restored by Aiyaswami Sastri (Journal of Oriental Research, Madras, 1929 ff).
MK	..	Mādhyamikakārikās by Nāgārjuna (Bib. Bud. IV).
MKV	..	Mādhyamikakārikāvṛtti by Candrakīrti (Bib. Bud. IV).
MSA	..	Mahāyānasūtrālaṅkāra by Asaṅga, ed. S. Levi, Paris.
MVSBT	..	Madhyāntavibhāga-sūtrabhāṣyaṭīkā by Sthiramati, Part I, ed. V. Bhattacharya and G. Tucci (Luzac & Co., 1932).
NB	..	Nyāyasūtrabhāṣya by Vātsyāyana (Vizianagaram Sanskrit Series).
NK	..	Nyāyakandalī by Śrīdhara (Vizianagaram Sanskrit Series).
NM	..	Nyāyamañjarī by Jayanta (Vizianagaram Sanskrit Series).
NS	..	Nyāyasūtra by Gotama.
NV	..	Nyāyavārttika by Udyotakara (Vizianagaram Sanskrit Series).
PV	..	Pramāṇavārttika by Dharmakīrti, ed. R. Sāṅkṛtyāyana (Journal of Bihar and Orissa Research Society, XXIV-XXV, Patna).
PVA	..	Pramāṇavārttikālaṅkāra by Prajñākaragupta, ed. R. Sāṅkṛtyāyana, Patna.

SV	..	Ślokavārttika by Kumārila (Chowkhamba Sanskrit Series).
TS	..	Tattvasaṅgraha by Śāntarakṣita, 2 Vols. (Gaekwad Oriental Series).
TSN	..	Trisvabhāvanirdeśa by Vasubandhu ed. S. Mukhopadhyaya, Viśvabhāratī.
TSP	..	Tattvasaṅgrahapañjikā by Kamalaśīla (Gaekwad Oriental Series).
VMS	..	Vijñaptimātratāsiddhi by Vasubandhu, ed. S. Levi, Paris.
VMS(JBORS)		Vijñaptimātratāsiddhi by Hsüan Tsang, partially reconstructed by R. Sāṅkṛtyāyana (Journal of Bihar and Orissa Research Society, XIX-XX, Patna).
VSM	..	Vedāntasiddhāntamuktāvalī by Prakāśānanda, Banaras.

(Other works consulted are referred to in full)

CHAPTER I

A HISTORICAL INTRODUCTION

Subjectivity is the key-note of Buddhism. From the very outset Buddhism had been subjectivistic and critical.[1] A sceptical attitude was always maintained regarding the reality of the whole of experience. Unifying categories like substantiality, universality, wholeness, etc., were rejected. The significance of these categories in empirical experience can certainly not be denied. Thus the initial postulation in Buddhism is the distinction between what obtains in reality and what appears empirically. The discovery of the subjective nature of certain aspects of experience was a great achievement which revolutionised, not only the subsequent development of Buddhism, but the trend of entire Indian philosophy.

A content is said to be subjective, when it is merely in thought, and has no grounding in external reality. Subjectivity thus entails a constructive mechanism of thought. This is the basic concept in Buddhism which sharply distinguishes it from all realistic theories of knowledge. The history of Buddhism is to be read as the gradual deepening of this consciousness of the subjective, beginning from a more or less realistic metaphysics to full-fledged idealism.[2] But even the earliest phase of Buddhism was not realism in its technical sense. The reason for calling it realistic will appear subsequently.

In spite of the perplexing abundance of schools and sub-schools in the history of Buddhism, some phases having distinct metaphysical

---

1. "The Buddhiṣt metaphysics from the very start partook of the Humean and the Kantian." CPB, p. 57.

2. It is not, however, maintained that Buddhism was idealistic from the very beginning. Cf, the views of Franke, Kern, Walleser and Rhys Davids, discussed in Keith's *Buddhist Philosophy*, pp. 47-56. This is a gross misunderstanding of Pali Buddhism. Keith himself does not reach a definite conclusion regarding the relationship between idealism and Buddhism.

leanings can broadly be distinguished. These are mainly three, described by historians like Buston and others as the three Dharmacakrapravarttanas, viz., the realistic phase, the critical phase, and the idealistic phase. Buddhism is thus not one system but a matrix of systems, comprising as it does three great philosophies along with their satellites, viz., realism, criticism, and idealism.[3] The seed of idealism was latent from the very outset, i.e., in the discovery of the subjective, which initiated a new tradition in Indian philosophy.

A. Sarvāstivāda, along with its sister schools, constitutes the early realistic phase of Buddhism. The name 'Sarvāstivāda' is significant, but is somewhat misleading. When Buddha said that everything exists (sarvam asti), he meant that all the elements of existence (dharmas)[4] are real. The wholes (pudgalas) however are unreal (prajñaptisat). The distinction between appearance and reality has already been drawn.

At first the 'pudgala' referred only to the ego, the mysterious 'subject' or 'self', lurking behind the discrete mental states (skandhas). Only the latter were accepted as real and the supposed unity behind them was explained away as a construction. The so-called unity is not that of a substance, but is rather a unity manifested in the continuity of a stream changing incessantly (dhārāvat). This was the so-called subjective classification of dharmas. This logic was later on applied to all 'wholes', i.e., all objects, physical as well as mental. This is the so-called objective classification. The perception of a whole, identical and permanent amidst change and difference, is the work of constructive imagination (kalpanā). This postulation of a whole was called satkāyadṛṣṭi, the imposition of a pudgala upon the real dharmas.

The negative or critical attitude thus operates even in the earliest phase. It is still called realistic because dharmas are accepted as objectively real. Though construction is possible on the basis of the dharmas, these latter are independent of construction and are free from any trace of subjectivity. The theory of dharmas is, therefore, realistic. But it

---

3. For an exposition of the three phases see Stcherbatsky, *Buddhist Logic*, Vol. I, pp. 3-14; Obermiller's *The Doctrtne of Prajñāpāramitā*, pp. 91-100; CPB, pp. 1-2, and pp. 66 ff.

4. Regarding the meaning of this elusive term, see Stcherbatsky's fine exposition in his *Central Conception of Buddhism*, pp. 4-6; Cf. also p. 42.

is to be distinguished from naive realism which unquestioningly accepts the reality of a content of perception just as it appears. For the Sarvāstivādin, the pudgala, though appearing in knowledge, is yet imaginary, subjective. The theory combines the elements of criticism as well as of realism, and is best termed as 'critical realism'.

The allied school of Theravāda presents a peculiar problem. Though the texts ordinarily supposed to be the authentic canons of original Buddhism are in Pāli and belong to this school, little mention is made of them in any of the subsequent schools. When the later schools subject the early realistic phase to criticism, they invariably refer to Sarvāstivāda or the Vaibhāṣika. Whatever truth there might be in the contention that the Pāli texts represent the original teaching of Buddha, there is little doubt that Theravāda exerted little or no influence in the subsequent development of Buddhism.[5] The philosophy of Theravāda is surprisingly akin to that of Sarvāstivāda, so that, from this point of view even, Theravāda does not present a new system, meriting study for its own sake. The interest in this school remains antiquarian. It prevails, however, in Ceylon, Burma and other parts of southern Asia.

In the Sarvāstivāda, doctrines are stated dogmatically, with no attempt at their rational defence. This is remedied in the Sautrāntika school. This is not so much a new philosophy as the analysis of the implications of the Sarvāstivāda realism. The Sautrāntika must be understood as Sarvāstivāda itself, aware of its own logical basis. They are not two schools, but two phases of the same metaphysical pattern. The critical spirit, characteristic of all Buddhism, gets intensified here. Certain dharmas of dubious status, accepted by the early schools, are deleted by the Sautrāntika.[6] Problems of a purely logical nature are raised and discussed threadbare, in conformity with the basic metaphysics of critical realism. But, though the realistic pattern is retained, the transition is yet very fundamental and is fraught with far-reaching consequences. The statement can be hazarded that, without the Sautrāntika, there would have been no Mahāyāna philosophy.

---

5. Cf. Mcgovern's *A Manual of Buddhist Philosophy*, pp. 16-17.
6. Cf. *The Central Conception of Buddhism*, pp. 41-43.

In his metaphysics the Sautrāntika maintains three theses.[7] Everything is transient and perishing (anitya); everything is devoid of selfhood or substantiality (anātma); everything is discrete and unique (svalakṣaṇa). The first militates against permanence and endurance of things; the second precludes all unity and substantiality and wholeness; the third does away with the reality of universals.

I. A real thing, according to the Sautrāntika logic, cannot be permanent. The criterion of reality is efficiency (artha-kriyā-kāritva). If a thing is to be real, it must have some causal determination; it must have some bearing or relevance to the other existents. A sky-lotus or a barren woman's son are not the links in any causal series and are, therefore, not real. An utterly unproductive thing is unreal. A real thing must make itself felt.

To have efficiency is to change. An efficient permanence is a contradiction in terms. It might be held that the permanent is not something having eternal duration; it endures only so long as the effect is not produced, after which it is destroyed. But it is either in the nature of a thing to be destroyed or it is not. If the latter, it can never be destroyed; but if it is its very nature to perish, it will die the next moment it is born. Then again a permanent entity is one which never changes its nature. Otherwise it will not retain its identity for two consecutive moments. But if it is eternally unchanging it can never pass from an unproductive state to a productive one. If it is unproductive at first it will never produce anything; if it is productive from the very outset, it will never cease producing. If it does anything contrary to this rule it cannot really be permanent. Dharmakīrti urges[8] that objects cannot be permanent. If they were, the knowledge of the present would by itself give rise to the knowledge of the entire future, there being no change, no novelty. And relative permanence is still more indefensible. If a thing changes at all, it must change incessantly. The real is momentary.

II. The substance and the whole are unintelligible categories. Whatever the senses perceive is a discrete sense-datum. If the substance also were to be perceived, it can be perceived only through some sense.

---

7. On these points see *Six Buddhist Nyāya Tracts*; TS; Stcherbatsky, *Buddhist Logic*, Vol. 1; and Satkari Mukherjee, *Buddhist Philosophy of Universal Flux*.

8. PV, II, 421.

But the eye perceives only a colour, never a colour *and* a substance. The ear hears a sound, but nothing else. The substance, therefore, is only a name which is given to a collection of sense-data; the latter are all really particular and discrete. There is no blue *object* apart from the blue. Logically also, the concept of the substance is indefensible. If the substance is something different from the attributes, how are the two related to one another ? The apple is sweet as well as smooth. But is one half of it sweet and the other half smooth ? It is no longer one then, and is not an *object* at all. But if the whole of it is both, these two aspects cannot be related to each other. So far as the apple is sweet, it repels other attributes. But it is also smooth, i.e., not sweet, at the same time. This is evidently a contradiction.

The same consideration can be applied against the reality of the whole as well. What is the whole over and above the parts ? When the parts are all separated, is something left over ? How does the whole exist ? Does it exist wholly in each of the parts or only partially ? If the former, it would be exhausted in one part which would be superfluous. But if it exists only partially in the parts, then it is only an unneceesary duplication of the parts themselves, and the distinction between one whole and many parts can no longer be maintained. Moreover, if the parts have contradictory attributes, which attribute should be ascribed to the whole ? It must possess both, but contradictories cannot be reconciled in the bosom of the same entity. The whole, like the substance, is a mere construct, imposed on the discrete parts.

III. The concept of the universal also is subject to the same criticism. If things are different, nothing is found identical in them. The universal is supposed to be present in all its particulars. But how can one thing be identically present in different places, and still remain one ? Does it exist by parts ? If not, the existence of one universal in different particulars cannot be explained. If it exists by parts, it cannot be known till all its particulars are known—an impossible task. How is the universal cognised ? Senses cognise only sensedata; but the universal is not a sense-datum. When a thing is produced, how does the universal enter into it ? Where was it before the production of this particular ? Did it come out of another particular, which would then be devoid of any universal, unless it had two ? When and where does it go away when a particular is destroyed ? Can the universal exist without inhering in the particulars ? The five fingers are perceived, but never the sixth, viz., fingerhood. The universal is only a thought-construct, a vikalpa. Only the particular is given. The real is unique and discrete (svalakṣaṇa).

The Sautrāntika puts the Anātma tradition on a logical basis. A thorough-going Analytic is expounded, more or less on the Kantian lines. The distinction between the thing-in-itself, the objectively given and the thought-construct, the work of the *a priori*, is relentlessly drawn, with the full consciousness of all the implications of this metaphysics. It is not that one detached element in experience is accidentally subjective; it is rather that all experience is a synthesis obtained by superimposing the *a priori* categories on the given. All empirical experience, therefore, is necessarily conditioned by the subjective. Even the bare act of naming a thing is not possible without construing it as an object, a whole of parts, a particular belonging to a class, in short, without thought-construction (kalpanā). Unity, substantiality and universality are all the work of the *a priori*; they are transcendental functions of the subjective.

The stabilisation of the pattern of the Sautrāntika metaphysics entailed a detailed analysis of the constitution of empirical knowledge. On the one hand there is the thing-in-itself, viz., the particular and unique dharmas, a momentary and incessant flow of unrelated reals; on the other hand there are the relations read into them by constructive imagination (kalpanā). A relation is a subjective construction, an *a priori* category. This analysis, well-known to us in its Kantian form, is undertaken by the Sautrāntika. Knowledge can be traced to two sources, belonging to entirely different levels, viz., the thing-in-itself on the one hand which is objectively given and the transcendental categories of synthesis on the other, which are *a priori* functions of the subjective. Intuition of the pure given is pratyakṣa according to the Sautrāntika. Manipulation of the universal, which is a creature of the subjective, is anumāna. All knowledge is exhausted by these two pramāṇas, there being no third kind. This pramāṇavāda is the original contribution of the Sautrāntika; the critical or the destructive work is merely the elucidation of the implications of pudgalanairātmya.

The historical importance of the Sautrāntika school is very great, as it is this metaphysics which paved the way for the later Mahāyānistic developments in the history of Buddhism. The transition, from a philosophical point of view, from the realistic Hīnayāna to the absolutistic and idealistic Mahāyāna was made possible by the Sautrāntika analysis of experience. The Sautrāntika prepared the way of the Mādhyamika on the one hand and the Yogācāra on the other, and is, in a sense, the parting of the ways.

B. Subjectivity, the *a priori* character of which had been demonstrated by the Sautrāntika, receives a still deeper interpretation in the Mādhyamika philosophy. The scope of subjectivity is infinitely widened by demolishing the category of difference as well. The Sautrāntika had established a kind of nominalism. The unifying categories like identity, permanence, universality, wholeness, substantiality, these were all shown to be merely conceptual, lacking an objective basis. The Mādhyamika completes the dialectical movement of criticism; he urges, with great logical cogency and rigour, that difference fares no better. Identity and difference are purely relative categories. One derives all the significance that one has only in and through the other.

The Sautrāntika had refuted the reality of the pudgala, but had maintained that of the dharmas. The pudgala was a thought-construct projected upon the real dharmas which alone existed objectively. A dharma was the ultimate existent and was a unique particular. The list of dharmas included 75 in the Sarvāstivāda, but was cut down to 43 by the Sautrāntika. The Mādhyamika continues this critical process to its logical extreme and refuses to accept the reality of the dharmas even. If an object is nothing apart from its various aspects, nor are the aspects to be arbitrarily grouped together without an objective basis. The subject is not a predicate-less unity. The predicates on the other hand are not independently real ; they are not floating universals but can exist only within the context of the subject. The Mādhyamika Dialectic is simply the analysis of this relativity of thought. Thought cannot take a stand on the category of particularity and difference, after demolishing its contrary. All thought is relative ; pick a hole at any point and the entire structure collapses. And this relativity is not peculiar to any one fragment or one aspect of thought; it infects thought or Reason as such.

This point is pressed with great dialectical skill in connection with every traditional problem of metaphysics. It can be illustrated in the case of the two most important ones, viz., the problem of causation and the problem of self.

Like any other relation, causality[9] implies two things, viz., relation and distinction. The effect must be related to the cause; otherwise the

9. CPB, pp. 132 ff.

cause would not be relevant to the effect. The latter must at the same time be distinguished from its cause, or there would be no transition, no novelty. Neither of these two aspects of causation can ever be dispensed with, and yet they are mutually irreconcilable. Different metaphysics try either to explain one aspect away or effect some sort of impotent compromise.

The causal relation may be understood as one of difference. This is done in a radical way by Hume and the Sautrāntika, and by the Nyāya-Vaiśeṣika in a qualified way. The basic argument of this metaphysics is that without distinction there is no causation. If the effect is nothing new, what is it then that has been produced ? There is indeed no relation at all without a distinction between the two terms which sustain it. A thing cannot be related to itself. The causal relation would lapse along with the denial of the causal distinction. Nothing new would ever be produced. A thing would eternally be what it is, with the result that the universe would be reduced to a monotony of bare unchanging elements.

As contrasted with this there is the other metaphysics, represented by the Sānkhya and the Advaita Vedānta, which stress the relational aspect of causation. The effect must be the effect *of* a cause. The cause must bear upon its effect. Unless the two are related one would not be the cause of the other. An identity, or rather a continuity, is to be traced between the cause and the effect. Without this minimum identity between them, the two terms would utterly fall asunder. There would be no cause at all, or everything would be the cause of everything, the lack of relation being available everywhere.

The Mādhyamika points[10] out that these two points of view are absolutely irreconcilable, and that neither position can yet be completely given up. The concept of causation is inherently unintelligible; all the speculative devices to render it intelligible are riddled with insoluble antinomies. Pure identity or pure difference does not explain causation; they explain it away. Causation requires both at same time, and this is a logical impossibility. It is therefore only a figment of constructive imagination, and is purely subjective. It is not that one aspect is subjectively constructed while the other is real. Within the context of

10. Cf. MK, Ch. 1, *Pratyaya-parīkṣā*.

empirical experience one cannot be had without the other (parasparāpekṣikī siddhiḥ na tu svābhāvikī); identity and difference are relative to one another and are both equally subjective.

A similar impasse confronts us when we come to the problem of self.[11] Our empirical experience has two distinguishable aspects, viz., change and continuity. Experience is a stream of consciousness, a succession of fleeting states, perishing every moment. On the other hand, this stream somehow coheres around an identical centre, which appropriates and holds together the various discrete moments. Different metaphysics take one or the other of these aspects as the pattern of explanation ; the Mādhyamika shows that the other aspect stubbornly refuses to be explanined away.

Change or succession in experience cannot be denied. Experience is, as Hume found out, a "bundle of different perceptions." Whenever Hume strives to discover his innermost self, he invariably stumbles on some particular perception or other. The identical and unchanging self is only an ideal construction. The Sautrāntika also arrives at the same conclusion. The pudgala is a projection of kalpanā, it being only an assemblage of discrete skandha-moments. Only the dharmas are objectively real; identity or continuity is an illusion.

The Ātma-metaphysics, on the other side, stresses this continuity permeating our entire experience. Experience is not merely a series of discrete moments. They must all be gathered togther into an individual consciousness. A perception is not a solitary unit; it is always the perception *of a person*. Particular ideas are not sufficient to constitute a fully articulated experience; without a form imparting unity and determinateness to the ideas they would not adhere to a single stream, a form which Kant names the Transcendental Unity of Apperception. A self is therefore posited to serve the function of an identical reference of the various mental states. This motive can be seen underlying the analysis of experience in all the Brāhmanical systems.

The Mādhyamika simply brings to light[12] the essential relativity of both these factors of experience. One is not intelligible without the other. The assertion of change presupposes the awareness of change, which awareness therefore must be distinguished from the change it-

11. CPB, p. 205.

12. MK, Ch. XXVII; CPB, pp. 136 ff.

self (yeṣu vyāvarttamāneṣu yad anuvarttate tat tebhyo bhinnam). Change requires an unchanging perspective, without which the affirmation of change remains dogmatic. Personal identity and memory are inexplicable on the hypothesis of pure difference. Pure identity on the other hand fares no better. To affirm identity we must be able to trace the continuity of the identical content between different contexts. There must have been some change in order to make possible the assertion of the pervading identity. A non-relational identity cannot be affirmed. Pure identity can never be made relevant to change. Even to know change as change, identity must come down from its high pedestal of perpetual monotony. Absolute identity cannot serve the function of knowing change, for which it is posited; it has no means of noting the change, as succession plays no part in its being. At the same time change cannot be known without identity, and there is no means of making consistent these two concepts, viz., change cannot be known without identity and identity cannot know change. This is the bankruptcy of all speculative metaphysics.

All this is only to illustrate the universality of the subjective. Every category of thought is infected with relativity and is therefore void of reality (nissabhāva). As such it is purely imaginary, is subjective. In early Buddhism only one aspect of experience was subjective; difference, change and particularity were objectively real. The Mādhyamika however repudiates the reality of all experience, all thought-categories. The whole is unreal (pudgalanairātmya); the discrete and momentary elements on which the whole is supposed to have been superimposed are no less unreal (dharmanairātmya), as they become meaningless without the whole. Sarvāstivāda accepted as many as 75 dharmas; the Sautrāntika accepted only 43 and rejected the rest as subjective; for the Mādhyamika, even the remaining ones are subjective, by the extension of the same logic. Subjectivity is another name of relativity. If a thing were objective and real, it would be able to exist by itself; it must not be in need of being understood through something else.[13] But nothing is found in thought which is not relative; everything is relative to everything else. Relativity is the mark of the unreal, of the subjective. The Mādhyamika concludes that our entire experience is purely subjective;

13. Cf. MK, X, 10.

things have only an apparent existence (saṃvṛti); in reality they are imaginary (kalpita) and subjective.

C. This wholesale rejection of all experience as illusory appeared to be an extreme position and could not be maintained for long. Speculation is an inveterate demand of human reason and its silence, when criticism reveals its inner fissures, is only transient. The denial by the Mādhyamika of all metaphysics seemed to be an unqualified nihilism and a barren scepticism, and we have the 'Third Swinging of the Wheel," represented by the Yogācāra idealism. This was a return to speculation and to constructive metaphysics, and was, in this respect, spiritually akin to the Sarvāstivāda and the Sautrāntika.

The Yogācāra also takes his cue from the Sautrāntika, which thus plays a pivotal transitional role. The Sautrāntika had stressed the subjective factor in all experience. There is no experience into the constitution of which subjectivity does not enter. The Yogācāra endorsed this analysis, but to him the acceptance of subjectivity by the Sautrāntika appeared to be only half-hearted. Coming as it did in the wake of the Mādhyamika, the Yogācāra looked at the critical realism of the Sautrāntika as an illogical compromise between realism and criticism. Criticism meant to him giving up realism altogether. If the number of dharmas could be cut down from 75 to 43, and the rest relegated to the realm of the subjective, the process may as well be continued to its logical finish, and the last trace of a thing-in-itself be wiped off.

Thus far the Yogācāra accepted the Mādhyamika criticism of the Sautrāntika position. He also advocated dharmaśūnyatā. His revolt against the extremism of the Mādhyamika centres around the interpretation of subjectivity.[14] For the Mādhyamika subjectivity creates unreality and is itself unreal ; the Yogācāra however contends that subjectivity, though the source of unreality, is real. The demand of speculation is to reach the ground of all phenomena. The Mādhyamika showed that this demand can never be met within Reason, as Reason by its very nature leads to insoluble antinomies. The Yogācāra, as a speculative metaphysics, could not rest satisfied with such a purely negative result. The Sautrāntika and the Mādhyamika were both critical, and had demonstrated the subjective character of phenomena. This insight into the nature of experience was not lost by the Yogācāra. He also

---

14. CPB, pp. 104 ff.

maintained the unreality of phenomena. But, unlike the Mādhyamika, he urged that phenomena, though unreal, must be rooted in some reality. A groundless appearance is uninteligible.[15] This ground cannot be anything objective ; the concept of objectivity was effectively demolished by the Sautrāntika and the Mādhyamika, and could not be resuscitated again. The alternative left to the Yogācāra was to hold that subjectivity is in itself real ; only its objective projections are unreal. Consciousness is the only reality. Everything that appears in experience is only within experience ; it is some form of consciousness or other. The appearance of a form of consciousness as something objective and independent is illusory. Every thing is subjective, though appearing as something different. This appearance is unreal; its essence however, as a mode of subjective existence, is real. For the Sautrāntika subjectivity is purely epistemic ; the ultimately real is the unique particular which exists objectively and independently. For the Mādhyamika, nothing is independent. The subject and the object are entirely correlative to each other, and are both only subjective. Subjectivity is conceptual and lacks any real basis. The Yogācāra declines the notion of objectivity, but the subjective becomes ontological ; it really exists, while the objective does not.

The Yogācāra is thus the culmination of Buddhism, arrived at by a gradual reinterpretation and successive reorientation of its central concept of subjectivity. And it is the Sautrāntika which makes this reorientation possible, by establashing subjectivity on a logical basis and by unfolding various implications of this position. The content on which subjectivity makes its construction is still there, but the scope of the subjective becomes so enormous as to threaten to engulf that shadow of a thing-in-itself. The next step is obviously to dispense altogether with the ghostly content, and the Yogācāra, emboldened by the Mādhyamika criticism of the unstable position of the Sautrāntika, takes this next step. The thing-in-itself is itself a projection of the subjective, the most primal projection out of which the entire empirical experience evolves. Whenever in the history of philosophy criticism makes a distinction between the subjective and its content, the former invariably tends to get inflated and to swallow its content completely. This comedy was played out in the development of British empiricism. Locke held that the material

15. VMS, p. 16

substance is not what actually appears in knowledge, but that it is shrouded by the so-called 'secondary qualities,' which are subjective creations. The result is that the material substance becomes merely an 'I-know-not-what' and Berkeley had little difficulty in showing up the inherent instability of the logic of empiricism. The same comedy was played out, though after an infinitely larger pattern, in the development of German idealism. Kant thought that the real object, the thing-in-itself, never appears in knowledge. Knowledge is determined by certain trancendental functions, viz., the *a priori* categories of understanding. The *known* object is therefore a synthesis of these subjective categories and the thing-in-itself to which thought cannot penetrate. Fichte, and after him, Hegel, strove to abolish this dualism. If the categorised content is all that we know, the assertion of an unknown thing-in-itself is dogmatic to the extreme. Criticism paves the way for idealism by reducing the object to a precarious existence and by extending the scope and importance of subjectivity.

The emergence of the Yogācāra idealism was made possible by the Sautrāntika emphasis on the subjective constitution of experience. The Yogācāra simply equates subjectivity with the whole of experience, so that creative Will becomes the sole reality. But the Sautrāntika contributed to the evolution of the Yogācāra in another and more specific way. His analysis of the problem of perception was the specific factor which led to the rise of idealism.[16]

Perception is the direct intuition of the object. It is very easily the basis of all knowledge, all other pramāṇas being dependent on it. Without perception knowledge would lack a starting-point ; it would have a floating character, as it is this pramāṇa that knowledge ultimately falls back upon. If therefore any metaphysics fails to explain perceptual knowledge, it rings its own death-knell. Metaphysics cannot dictate to experience; it can only try to interpret it.

The perceptual relation requires at least two terms, if complications are avoided. Perception means cognition of an object by a subject. Were there only the object, there would be facts but no experience of facts. And this assertion itself presupposes experience. The subject therefore must be taken for granted. Knowledge cannot be transcend-

---

16. Cf. Keith's *Buddhist Philosophy,* pp. 161-162. *The Central Conception of Buddhism,* pp. 54-65.

ed. The object of knowledge however does not enjoy the same indisputable status. That something appears in knowledge and confronts the subject is certainly not to be denied. But whether it is a term independent of the relation in which alone it is found, or it is exhausted in that relation itself, is an open question. If it is, we have a realistic theory of perception; if not, we have full-fledged idealism.

Early Buddhism was, as already seen, realistic. Though the subjective factor in the constitution of experience was recognised, the reality of the object existing independently was maintained. The pattern is closely akin to that of the Kantian Analytic. Kant also detects the presence of the *a priori* in experience. But experience is not all *a priori*; there is an irreducible element of the given, the thing-in-itself, without which no experience would be possible. There is however a very important distinction between these two theories of knowledge. Kant believes that the thing-in-itself is never known as it is. Whenever it is given to knowledge, it is necessarily refracted through the categories of Understanding, so that what we know is always a categorised object, and never the pure given. The possibility of our ever transcending these categories in empirical knowledge is not visualised by Kant. "Intellectual Intuition" is impossible, at least for human beings. The Sautrāntika however holds that intuition of the pure given is possible. There is one kind of knowledge where the bare object in all its particularity and uniqueness is cognised, without the operation of any subjective construction.

The logic for the acceptance of this kind of cognition of the pure given is very cogent. For the Sautrāntika, as also for Kant, knowledge has a two-fold root, viz., the given and the construction. This distinction itself is not possible unless the given is also cognised without construction. Were the constructed object all that we ever could know, we would not even have the suspicion of there being any construction at all. Or, if the fact of illusion awakened us to its function, we would go to the other extreme and deny any element of the given. That something is given and something constructed can be affirmed only when both are known in isolation. Moreover, the Sautrāntika asserts that the particular alone is given and that the universal is a construction (nāmajātyādi-yojanā kalpanā); this knowledge also cannot be had *a priori* or by mere logic. We must *know* that the particualar lone is given which must therefore be immediately perceived.

This cognition of the pure given is termed Perception[17] in the Sautrāntika theory of knowledge. The knowledge of the constructed universal is the other pramāṇa which is accepted, known as Inference. This conception of the two pramāṇas is radically different from that held in other systems of Indian Philosophy. There is also another fundamental difference between the Sautrāntika and other systems. For the Sautrāntika, the content of perception can never be inferred and vice versa. This is technically known as pramāṇaviplavavāda, as opposed to the orthodox view of pramāṇasamplavavāda.

Perception, according to the Sautrāntika, is this cognition of the ultimately real dharmas. These dharmas are not static; they are undergoing incessant change. No dharma endures for any duration of time. It is absolutely momentary (kṣaṇika). But here arises a grave complication. If the object is momentary, the cognition of it is no less so. There is no abiding self behind the various mental states. These states are all that are found on the dissection of a personality and they are fleeting, momentary. But if the object and its cognition are both momentary, perception becomes an inexplicable riddle. Perception is a process in which the mind, whatever it might be, somehow comes into contact with the object through the various sense-organs, and the resultant is the perceptual knowledge, viz., the cognition of the object. This whole process cannot take place in one moment. Granting even that the process itself is a series of moments, the object must at least endure till the process is completed.[18] One moment cannot possibly know another moment, since, by the time it reaches the latter, both are dead. Supposing that the cognition-moment leaves its impression and efficiency on the succeeding moment, the moment to be cognised is no longer there. If another moment has emerged in its stead, the knowledge is not of the first moment; and if one moment cannot be known, it is difficult to imagine how any subsequent moment can be known, the original predicament remaining unaltered. Ultimately nothing can ever be known. This is the impasse to which early Buddhism is inevitably led by its hypothesis of radical momentariness of things.

In this hypothesis the germ of idealism is already latent. Early Buddhism is critical realism. Being realism, it is committed to accept-

---

17. Cf. *Nyāyabindu*, I ; PV, II, 123.

18. varttamānālambanagrahaṇe ca kṣaṇabhaṅgabādhaḥ, MVSBT, p. 21.

ing something absolutely given; being critical as well, the given is not supposed to be just what appears in knowledge. Permanence and stability is denied to the given; it is momentary. Being momentary, the given cannot enter into any causal relation to knowledge ; the hypothesis fails to explain knowedge for which purpose alone it was posited.

The object is supposed to be the cause (ālambana-pratyaya) of its knowledge. Its cognition is causally determined by its being given to knowledge. Causality however entails a determinate temporal sequence. The cause, as Kant demonstrated, cannot be related to the effect in any order; it must invariably precede the latter. The object therefore must be antecedent to its cognition to which it is supposed to stand in the causal relation.[19] But, being momentary, it will perish by the time its cognition is produced.[20] Knowledge cannot reach a momentary object.[21] We have therefore the paradox that there appears in knowledge something which is no longer existent.[22] But a past moment is, according to the Sautrāntika, unreal. The content of perception is thus unreal from the objective point of view, having no objective counterpart. This is idealism. Since knowledge is that of a non-existent object,[23] the latter may very well be dispensed with. If the content is cognised even when it is no longer existent, then everything past and future will be the content of knowledge.[24]

Perception of a real object and the momentariness of that object are thus mutually irreconcilable. The object precedes knowledge and must also endure, if the pitfal of idealism is to be avoided, till the completion of the knowledge-process. This endurance militates against the Buddhist hypothesis of momentariness. Theravāda here offers a very ingenious subterfuge.[25] According to the Theravāda analysis the full process of cognition takes 17 moments. Since realism requires that the object

19. PV, II, 247.

20. Cf. *Abhidharmakośa*, I, 43.

21. kṣaṇasya jñānena prāpayitum aśakyatvāt, *Nyāyabinduṭīkā*, p. 16.

22. na avidyamānasya svarūpeṇa darśanam, hetutvena ca jñānāt pūrvatvam. pūrvatve ca kṣaṇikatayā na jñānakāle astitā. PVA, p. 108.

23. yadārthas tadā na jñānam yadā jñānam tadā nārtha iti kuto vyaṅgyavyañjakabhāvas tayoḥ, PV, p. 243.

24. MVSBT, p. 21 ; PV, II, 418-419.

25. Cf. *Abhidhammatthasamgaho*, IV, 8.

should endure throughout this process, Theravāda boldly declares that one object-moment is equivalent to 17 cognition-moments. Both are momentary, but the speed of the perishing of the object is slowed down 17 times, so that, for the purposes of knowledge, it is relatively stable. The stability of the object is secured without absolutely giving up its ultimate momentariness. This device can succeed however only at the cost of logic. Logic cannot tolerate such discrimination in the treatment of the subject and the object. Their respective momentarinesses cannot be measured by disparate standards. If the object can survive for 17 moments, it may as well do so till infinity. We cannot thus play fast and loose with the hypothesis of momentariness, paying lip-service to it and giving it up when it suits our convenience.

The Sarvāstivāda and the Sautrāntika are aware of these difficulties. Their theory is not that the object precedes its cognition ; otherwise the proposition that knowledge cognises something non-existent and unreal cannot be refuted, and that would be playing into the hands of the idealist. In the Sarvāstivāda, the object is not the cause, in the ordinarily accepted sense of the term, of its cognition. The two are rather flashed together simultaneously. In any case of knowledge, three distinct elements appear simultaneously. Causality, in the sense of a determinate temporal sequence, is not to be found there. A perceptual knowledge is generated by a contact (sparśa)[26] of three things, viz., an objective dharma (ālambana), a sense-activity (indriyavikāra), and a moment of pure consciousness (vijñāna). There is no actual contact between these three, each dharma being unique (svalakṣaṇa). There is contact only in the sense that the three appear simultaneously (trikasaṅnipāta). Because of this contact, a moment of consciousness emerges bearing the form of an object-moment. This is all that is meant by the causality of the object ; it is not a dead antecedent, but lives at the same moment as its cognition does. In this way perception of a real (existent) and objective dharma is sought to be reconciled with the momentariness of that dharma.

The reconciliation is however only apparent ; the inner logical contradiction still remains. The object is no longer the cause of its cognition; its emergence is merely the occasion for the emergence of its cognition-moment. These two parallel emergences are simultaneous.

26. *The Central Conception of Buddhism*, p. 55.

Contact is not interaction, but only this simultaneity. But, whether the object is a cause or an occasion, there is no doubt that it determines the cognition-form, and that without its existence the latter also would not be. No relation of determination can subsist however without a temporal order. Simultaneity is not a sufficient ground for determination.[27] Occasionalism is theoretically unintelligible. In Western philosophy a God was always there to fall back upon in the last resort; *deus ex machina* was the solution of all insoluble problems. Sarvāstivāda did not have even this last resort of dogmatic philosophy.

If two moments are simultaneous, one cannot be supposed to determine the other. Or, if determination is still insisted upon, there is no reason why it should not be construed the other way round. Cognition and the object are both simultaneous. It is difficult to conceive why the former should be determined by the latter, instead of itself determining it.[28] Simultaneity may as much be an argument for idealism as for realism. The object-moment loses its causal efficiency, as two simultaneous moments cannot be causally related to each other. And if it determines cognition even without being related to it, cognition would then be determined by everything whatsoever, the lack of any relation to cognition being common to all things.[29] The ālambana-pratyaya, so long as it is consistently held to be momentary, cannot explain its perception, since there is no way of relating the two. Cognition therefore, in the absence of any external determination, acquires this from the preceding moment of cognition itself. The samanantarapratyaya is the fundamental condition of perception.[30] A real ālambana, being unrelated, is superfluous. The ālambana-pratyaya means simply that cognition arises having the form of an external object. This

27. samānakālayoś ca hetuphalatvāyogāt, *Abhisamayālaṅkārāloka*, p. 381.

28. Sarvāstivāda holds that there is a peculiar relation known as "Sārūpya" between consciousness and object, which determines that consciousness should "grasp" the latter and not otherwise. This is however "a confession of ignorance." *Central Conception*, p. 56; 64.

29. atha yadaiva asti tadaiva grahaṇam, hetubhāvam antareṇāpi..na samānakālasya hetutā tathā apratīteḥ. asambaddhagrahaṇe ca sarvam eva gṛhyeta. PVA, p. 108.

30. PV, II, 323.

appearance of the semblance of an object is the form of consciousness itself; there is no real ālambana. This is idealism, born out of the inherent lack of coherence in the account of perception given in early Buddhism. The contradiction becomes more explicit in the Sautrāntika, as it is here that the hypothesis of momentariness is fully analysed in all its implications. The Yogācāra philosophy is the logical outcome.

It can now be seen how the Yogācāra is only the extreme development of the logic implicit in Buddhism even from the very outset. The discovery of the subjective is the great achievement of Buddhist epistemology. The Sautrāntika undertook the task of clarifying the implications of such a position. This clarification made explicit the inner contradiction of a half-hearted acceptance of the subjective. Idealism is an attepmpt to remove the contradiction by giving up the dualistic theory of knowledge. Moreover, the Sautrāntika analysis had shown the inexplicability of perception, as being inconsistent with its theory of momentariness. Idealism again tries to solve the riddle by making perception independent of anything given.

Here arises an interesting problem of historical speculation. The Yogācāra is directly the result of the attempt to remove the inconsistencies of the Sautrāntika position. The Mādhayamika is another similar attempt, though with radically different results. The Sautrāntika thus occupies a central position in the history of Buddhism. The problem is as to whether the emergence of the Yogācāra school would have been possible even without the mediation of the Mādhyamika. As a matter of fact, the Mādhyamika intervened between the Sautrāntika and the Yogācāra. The speculative possibility is however there : is the Yogācāra school the last phase of Buddhism because of a merely historical coincidence or is the development a matter of logical sequence as well ? The Mādhyamika is a very extreme position, and it is generally expected that the extremes should come last. The Sautrāntika and the Yogācāra are both speculative systems and are spiritually akin; the Mādhyamika is the champion of pure criticism entailing the rejection of all metaphysics. It appears to be an accidental episode between two speculative philosophies. Is it really so, or is the Mādhyamika a necessary step in the logical development of idealism ?

It has been seen that the Sautrāntika theory of knowledge is unstable. The least tampering with the integrity of the object opens the door to idealism. Subjectivity, once accepted in any form, refuses to be limited to any single aspect of experience ; it threatens so to swell as to engulf everything foreign to it within its corrosive fold. Give up rank realism, and there is no stopping anywhere short of idealism. The Yogācāra is therefore the natural sequence to the Sautrāntika logic ; the intervention of the Mādhyamika is an accident which could have been dispensed with. The Sautrāntika prepared the ground for the emergence of idealism also in another important respect ; his analysis exposed the unintelligibility of perception, as inconsistent with the Buddhist logic. All these considerations tend to prove that the transition from the critical realism of the Sautrāntika to the Yogācāra idealism is a logical and a natural one, and that it does not stand in any necessity of being mediated by the Mādhyamika criticism.

But this is not the whole story. The Yogācāra is not merely idealism, but also absolutism. The system cannot be sized up unless this latter aspect also is taken into consideration. And the transition from mere idealism to absolutism is made possible by the Mādhyamika dialectic. The contradiction inherent in the Sautrāntika position would have yielded an idealism and it did so. The concept of the given is utterly unintelligible and has to be given up. But the insight that the subject and the object are correlative categories and that one cannot be had without the other is a legacy of the Mādhyamika. The subject cannot be obtained in its purity. In isolation from the object, it becomes the Inexpressible (śūnya). Absolutism cannot be reached except through a dialectical approach, and this norm is established by the Mādhyamika by inexorable logic. The Yogācāra, as a dogmatic metaphysics, has a speculative bias in favour of the subject, but is at the same time aware that idealism cannot be a final position. Pure subject ceases to be subject at all ; it becomes something non-conceptual. This awareness is dialectical, and compels the Yogācāra to transcend mere idealism. This then is the part the Mādhyamika plays in the evolution of the Yogācāra system. Idealism it could have been even without the Mādhyamika, by the sheer dyanamism of the Sautrāntika logic itself, but it would have stopped at that. It would not have occurred to it to take the further step to absolutism, but for the fact that there was the Mādhyamika criticism to which idealism provided no answer.

It is thus seen that the two-fold character of the Yogācāra system is to be traced to two different influences. Idealism is the result of the attempt to remove the incompleteness of the Sautrāntika logic and epistemology. Idealism passes into absolutism due to the pressure exerted by the Mādhyamika dialectic. But in spite of all this evolution the Yogācāra remains true to the essential spirit of Buddhism. The development takes place within the fold of Buddhism of which the Yogācāra remains only a phase to the last, though a most important one. The central concepts of Buddhism are radically modified, but never discarded. This point can be illustrated by considering the development of some of the basic doctrines of Buddhism, such as Śūnyatā, Pratītyasamutpāda and Madhyamā Pratipad.

Śūnyatā can easily be supposed to be the most central doctrine in entire Buddhism. It does not connote however one single meaning acceptable to all the schools. Different schools construe it in different ways. Early Hīnayāna Buddhism understood śūnyatā to mean merely pudgala-śūnyatā. The substance and the whole are unreal fictions ; they are void of reality (śūnya). The dharmas however are real (aśūnya) existents. The Mādhyamika deepened the conception of śūnyatā. Unreality or essencelessness is not confined to any particular aspect of experience; experience itself in all its entirety is unreal and void (śūnya). It has no real existence. Peculiarly enough, the term connotes, not only unreality, but also reality. Reality is śūnya, being inexpressible through concepts (dṛṣṭiśūnyatvāt). For the Yogācāra also, whatever appears to confront experience is unreal (śūnya). There is nothing other than consciousness. Consciousness itself is not however śūnya. It has an ontological existence. Śūnyatā pertains therefore only to its mode of appearance[31] as something objective. Consciousness is infected by the correlative categories of the object fand the subject. This infection alone is unreal (grāhadvayaśūnyatā).

Pratītyasamutpāda is also a basic doctrine of Buddhism, but its interpretations vary widely in the different schools. At first it referred to the theory that all the elements (nidānas) in the Wheel of Existence, beginning with Avidyā and ending with jarāmaraṇa, are causally conditioned. Pratītyasamutpāda was the theory of causation only in its moral aspect. Later on the interest shifted from ethics to logic. The theory of dharmas (dharmasaṅketa) along with that of momentariness (kṣaṇikatva) was elaborated. Pratītyasamutpāda then meant the law of

31. MVSBT, p. 12, 13.

causation as applied to the realm of dharmas, the sole existents.[32] It was purged of its ethical implications. Since there is no real continuity between one dharma and another, causal relation in its ordinary sense cannot be had between them. The cause is only an occasion depending on which the effect happens (asmin sati idam bhavati). The dharma-moments are subject to this law of dependent origination. Pratītya-samutpāda is the law of their rigorous temporal sequence. The Mādhyamika exposes the hollowness of this view of causation; without a real relation causality cannot obtain. Since the effect depends on the cause for its emergence, it cannot be real by itself. Everything depends on everything else; nothing then is intrinsically real (pratītya yad yad bhavati na hi tāvat tad eva tat). Pratītyasamutpāda does not mean temporal sequence, but this essential dependence of things (parasparasāpekṣatva), and consequently their unreality (śūnyatā or niḥsvabhāvatā). The Yogācāra however accepts the reality of consciousness. The object is unreal, but the moments of consciousness are real. The original interpretation of pratītyasamutpāda, viz., causation as temporal sequence, is again restored to it, but with the important modification that it is no longer applicable to the world of objective dharmas; its jurisdiction is limited to the moments of consciousness. One moment of consciousness emerges because of the preceding one, even in the absence of a real continuity between them. Pratītyasamutpāda is again the mark of reality[33] and not, as in the Mādhyamika, the mark of the unreal. The moments of consciousness, as governed by this law, are real.

Madhyamā Pratipad is another concept of paramount importance in Buddhism. Every school represents itself as the middle course, steering clear between two extreme positions. Even the extremest metaphysics tries to represent itself as the avoiding of a still more extreme one. This is an essential characteristic of Buddhist philosophy. The Hīnayāna Buddhism depicted itself as the middle course between the two extremes of śāśvatavāda and ucchedavāda. If things are eternally unchanging and immutable, one cannot strive to attain a better morality. All change, for better or for worse, is ruled out, and the development of a moral life becomes an impossibility. Eternalism is one extreme to be avoided.

---

32. Cf. *The Central Conception of Buddhism*, p. 28.

33. vijñānam punaḥ pratītyasamutpannatvād dravyato' stīti, VMS, p. 16.

But nihilism, the other extreme, is no less so. If anything perishes without a reisdue and nothing endures, then no effort is of any avail. All striving is futile and morality is again rendered inexplicable. Morality requires change and, at the same time, a rigorous law of causation. This is secured by the theory of dharmas along with pratītyasamutpāda. This then is the madhyamā pratipad. The Mādhyamika claims to be the middle position. The two extremes to be avoided are ātmavāda, with the logic of identity, and anātmavāda, with the logic of difference. The substance and the modes being entirely relative to each other, one cannot be exalted as the reality and the other brushed aside as appearance. Every metaphysics falls either in the one or the other pattern and the middle course is therefore refraining from any metaphysics (dṛṣṭi) whatsoever. We cannot take any conceptual attitude towards the real. The basic attitudes are affirmation and negation (astīti nāstīti ubhe'pi antā). The Real is the Inexpressible where all concepts are silenced (paramārthas tu āryāṇām tūṣṇīmbhāvaḥ). This silence, by getting rid of all concepts and by refraining from indulging in any speculative metaphysics, is the madhyamā pratipad. The extreme positions feared by the Yogācāra are realism on the one hand and nihilism or scepticism[33] on the other. The object is real and exists like the subject : this is one extreme, represented by the realistic Sarvāstivāda. The subject isunreal and non-existent like the object : this is the other extreme, represented by the Mādhyamika[34]. The middle position is idealism. The object is unreal and is a fiction of the subjective; the subject however is real and the sole reality. Rejection of the reality of the object and maintaining that of consciousness—this is the madhyamā pratipad[35]. The appearances are unreal (yacchūnyam tad asat); but that which appears is real (yena śūnyam tad sat).

---

33. Cf. MSA, p. 60.

34. athavā vijñānavad vijñeyam api dravyata eveti kecin manyante. vijñeyavad vijñānam api samvṛtita eva na paramārthata (iti anye). iti asya dviprakārasya api ekāntavādasya pratiṣedhārthaḥ prakaraṇārambhaḥ. VMS, p. 15; also MVSBT, p. 13.

35. VMS, pp. 15-16 ; MVSBT, p. 9,14.

Chapter II

THE DEVELOPMENT OF THE YOGĀCĀRA

The Yogācāra is the development of the logic of Buddhist thought. The object is not as it appears, and cannot be of any service to knowledge. It is therefore unreal. Consciousness is the sole reality. The object is only a mode of consciousness. Its appearance as though something objective and external is the Transcendental illusion, because of which consciousness is bifurcated into the subject-object duality. Consciousness is creative and its creativity is governed by the illusory idea of the object. Reality is to be viewed as a Will or an Idea. This creativity is manifested at different levels of consciousness. The idealistic explanation of the empirical world is made possible by the hypothesis of the three strata of consciousness, viz. Ālaya-vijñāna, Kliṣṭa Manas, and the Pravṛtti-vijñānas. Everything that exists is exhausted in these three. They are however not the ultimate form of consciousness. The evolution of consciousness takes place because of the Transcendental Illusion of objectivity. When the object is realised to be illusory its sublation is followed by the dissolution of the subject as well. No special effort is needed for the negation of the subject; it evaporates out of its own accord, there being nothing to know. Consciousness, as thus freed of the false duality of subject and object, is the Absolute. This is the ultimate reality, the essence of everything (dharmāṇām dharmatā).

These are the principal tenets of the Yogācāra idealism. The question as to how far they represent the real teaching of Buddha is an insoluble one. There are several considerations which must be taken into account while dealing with this very difficult problem. First, there is the disconcerting fact that Buddha himself wrote nothing. His teachings were all oral sermons, delivered to different people on different occasions. The exact import of these sermons depended, therefore, on the particular context in which they were delivered. Since he was not writing an abstruse metaphysical treatise, but was interested in leading the suffering folk to their spiritual freedom, he could not afford to make fine distinctions. Moreover, the sermons themselves were not prepared beforehand, but were delivered on the spur of the moment, sometimes simply as answers to questions put by some layman. He had to modulate his statements in order to suit the understanding of the person addressed. The interpretation of his utterances also depended on the intellectual equipment of the listeners. It is rash therefore to hold that Buddha preached any particular philosophy.

There is another grave difficulty that even his pupils did not immediately record his utterances. The necessity to record them arose decades later when controversy as to the exact meaning of the master had already arisen. Every school made the claim to represent the true teaching of Buddha. All the schools made their own version of the Canon so that there is no version which is free from careful editing from a particular point of view.[1] The primary interest was not so much to sift the real teaching as to give authenticity to their own views. And moreover, after the lapse of so many decades, it was impossible to distinguish between the authentic and the spurious.

The Mahāyāna emerged out of this hectic controversy. It was a revolt against the narrow-mindedness of the earlier schools. Peculiarly enough, the Mahāyāna schools claimed to resuscitate the real spirit of Buddha's teachings, the spirit which was said to have been obscured by the Hīnayānistic aberrations. This claim cannot be denied to the Mahāyāna merely on the ground of its coming later into the arena, since, by the time the Hīnayānistic schools themselves arose, the original sayings were all mixed up with the later interpolations made by partisan editors. In spite of this however there remains a kernel amidst the later elaborations, the authenticity of which cannot be denied. That Buddha did preach the doctrine of dharmas, variously arranged and classified into skandhas, dhātus and āyatanas, is not challenged even by the most monistic schools of Mahāyāna, the evidence for its being original being too patent. The break however between Hīnayāna and Mahāyāna was so violent and so complete that the latter had to take refuge in the doctrine of two kinds of utterances by Buddha, viz., the nītārtha and the neyārtha. There are certain statements which are true only of the

1. HB, Vol. II, p. 101.

empirical world and are not to be understood literally. These are neyārtha and are equivalent to samvṛti. There are other statements which speak of the ultimate truth (paramārtha). These were not delivered to the ordinary people (pṛthagjana), being too deep for their comprehension. This contention of the Mahāyānists is not to be summarily dismissed, since it is known that Buddha had to appeal to the understanding of the person he addressed, and could not therefore always express his innermost convictions. Later on, when Mahāyāna itself was split up into the Mādhyamika and the Yogācāra schools, this distinction between the neyārtha and nītārtha utterances came as a handy weapon of controversy. When the Yogācāra cited sūtras to testify that Buddha taught the sole reality of consciousness, the Mādhyamika could dismiss it by construing it as having only a conventional significance.[2] This much is clear that no school ever contended that a particular theory was *not* advocated by Buddha. This can only mean that no one was sure of his actual teachings.

The problem gets still further complicated by the characteristic dogma, mentioned at very many places in the Mahāyāna canons, that there is no doctrine which has been proclaimed by Buddha. "Between that night during which the Tathāgata attained to enlightenment and the night during which he will be completely extinguished, in that time not one syllable was spoken by the Tathāgata, and he will not speak a single syllable; the Buddha word is a non-word."[3]. Different constructions can be put on this paradoxical statement. Since there was no certainty that Buddha actually uttered a particular view, the Mahāyānists tried to brush aside all fruitless controversy regarding this by making this peculiar construction. Or it might refer to Buddha's unwillingness to discuss the ultimate problems (avyākṛta) which lead to insoluble antinomies of Reason. He therefore kept silent about such problems. A literal interpretation of this statement is certainly not justifiable.

All these considerations tend to prove that no school can claim to represent the original teaching of the Master. They all belong to one spiritual genus however, viz., to the nairātmyavāda tradition. This tradition is unmistakably different from the Upaniṣadic one, and is the

2. HB, Vol. II, p. 54 ; BCA, p. 484 ; MKV, p. 276.

3. LAS, pp. 142 ff.

common measure of all schools of Buddhism. In this tradition, however, no school can claim authenticity, in the absence of any recorded statement of Buddha, merely on the ground of temporal priority. There is no means of settling the doctrinal differences in favour of any one school. The canons themselves, as we have seen, belonged to particular schools.

We thus see that the fact that there is not the slightest trace of idealism in the Hīnayānistic canons, and the fact on the other hand that the Yogācāra quoted in his favour certain sūtras, supposed to have been delivered by Buddha—these facts do not lead to any definite conclusion. From our point of view, however, it is a matter of little importance whether idealism was actually taught by Buddha, or whether it is only a later elaboration. We have only to see whether idealism does logically follow from the premises of the early Buddhism or not; this has already been discussed in the last Chapter.

The origin of the Yogācāra system is, therefore, shrouded in obscurity. Of the "nine Dharmas" accepted as canonical by the Mahāyāna, *Laṅkāvatāra* or *Saddharma* etc., *Laṅkāvatāra-Sūtra* alone distinctly contains idealistic teachings.[4] It teaches the sole reality of consciousness and denies the reality of the external world. Winternitz says, "In the form in which we have it, the work is either a very careless compilation, or it has suffered very badly in coming down to us; moreover, it consists of portions which belong to various periods."[5]

"With Ch. II, which has no connection whatsoever with chapter I Mahāmati begins to ply Buddha with a long series of over 100 questions; these questions bear on all the details of the doctrine, on release, on Ālaya, manovijñāna and other main notions of the Vijñānavāda, on Śūnyatā, enlightenment etc.....The main portion of Chapter II-VII is entirely philosophic in content, and actually treats of the whole system of the Buddhist doctrine, mainly from the standpoint of the Vijñānavāda. ....Chapter IV treats of the ten bhūmis....The whole of the chapter X is a long philosophical treatise in 884 verses. In this case, too, the doctrines put forth are those of the Vijñānavāda. It is, however, expressly

4. ed. B. Nanjio, Kyoto, 1923.

5. That it is a compilation also appears from Buston's statement that out of 36000 ślokas, originally contained in the LAS, only 3600 have survived. HB, Vol. II, p. 169.

emphasised again and again, that phenomena are unreal like a *fata morgana*, an illusion, a delusion. As in the *Gauḍapādīyakārikās*, this work (V. 443) also illustrates the nonreality of the world by the simile of the circle of fire, which originates when a burning stick is twirled round. Again and again we come across the instances of the "horn of a hare," the "ring-like apparitions before the shut eyes," and similar fictions and delusions of the senses, which are intended to show that everything is only illusion and that nothing is real, not even release[6] (V. 623)."

"We could infer that Chapter X was written not long before 513 A. D. The philosophy of the Vijñānavāda, which is taught in all the parts of the *Laṅkāvatāra*, coincides with the doctrines of Maitreya-nātha, Asaṅga, and the *Mahāyāna Śraddhotpāda,* which may be ascribed to the 4th cent. A. D. at the earliest. It is, therefore, probable that the *Laṅkāvatārasūtra,* even in its earliest form, was not in existence more than 50 or, at its very most, 100 years before 443 A. D."[7]

Then there is the *Buddha-avataṅsaka Sūtra* which comprises two works: (a) *Daśabhūmikasūtras* and (b) *Gaṇḍavyūhasūtra.* The first, known as *Daśabhūmaka* or *Daśabhūmīśvara*[8] as well, is also found as an independent work. "The subject-matter of this work is a discourse on the ten steps (daśabhūmi) by which Buddhahood may be attained. The *Daśabhūmaka* is the most important work which treats of this doctrine."[9] *Gaṇḍa-vyūha Sūtra*[10] is the other part of *Avatamsaka.*

Some other Yogācāra sūtras are (1) *Sandhinirmocanasūtra,*[11] explaining

---

6. Cf. also D. T. Suzuki's *The Laṅkāvatāra Sūtra*, 1932, and *Studies in the Laṅkāvatāra Sūtra*, 1930.

7. HIL, pp. 333-337.

8. The Sanskrit text is edited by J. Rahder, Leuven, 1926. It is also edited by R. Kondo, Tokyo, 1930. The seventh Chapter is separately published in *Acta Orientalia,* IV, 1925, along with an English Translation. Cf. also Poussin in *Le Museon*, 1907-11 ; in ERE, II, p. 743 and VIII, pp. 329. ff.

9. HII, pp. 327-328.

10. The Sanskrit text is edited by D. T. Suzuki and H. Idzumi, Kyoto, 1934-1936.

11. The Sanskrit text is not available. Cf. E. Lamotte, *Liexplication des Mysteres*, Louvain, 1935.

the hidden intentions of Buddha (sandhi=abhiprāya), and (2) *Ghanavyūhasūtra.*[12]

A work which has given rise to a lot of controversy is the *Mahāyāna Śraddhotpādaśāstra*, attributed to the great Aśvaghoṣa, the author of *Buddhacarita*. As such, Suzuki places its date not later than the first century of the Christian era.[13] He thinks that Aśvaghoṣa was one of the principal actors who practically initiated the great spiritual and intellectual movement of Mahāyāna in India,[14] and that this work is one of the foundations of the Mahāyāna. It anticipates both the Mādhyamika and the Yogācāra systems.[15]

The work appears to be an attempt at a synthesis of the two Mahāyāṇistic schools. "Aśvaghoṣa's system is in all essential points the same as the Mādhyamika's, but it accepts the theory of an "All-conserving mind" (ālayavijñāna), as a stage in the evolution of "Suchness" (tathatā) in which consciousness is awakened."[16]

This tends to throw doubt on its belonging to so early a date as Suzuki imagines. A synthesis is a reconciliation of two rival points of view, when their doctrinal divergence becomes very acute. It is attempted when the two doctrines are sufficiently developed, as indeed they are found in the work. Anyway it cannot be treated as an anticipation of the Mahāyāna, because such a work would have presented a state of affairs where the differences have not as yet emerged. Suzuki unfortunately treats Mahāyāna as a unity,[17] which might be true from a religious point of view, but is certainly not true of the great philosophies of Mahāyāna.

There are other strong grounds for rejecting the authenticity of this work. Writes Winternitz, "A work which attempted a synthesis of the teachings of the Mādhyamika and Vijñānavāda schools is the *Mahāyāna-Śraddhotpāda*. It is attributed to Aśvaghoṣa, but cannot possibly have been written by the poet of the *Buddhacarita*. It must remain an open question whether it was attributed to the great poet with a view to securing a greater reputation for the book, or whether there was an Aśva-

12. The Sanskrit text is not available.
13. *The Awakening of Faith*, p. 17.
14. Ibid, p. 42.
15. Ibid, p. 43.
16. *The Conception of Buddhist Nirvāṇa*, p. 32.
17. Cf. his *Outlines of Mahāyāna Buddhism*.

ghoṣa II in about the 8th cent. A.D. who wrote this philosophical work, which gives evidence of an advanced stage of development of Mahāyāna philosophy. The work has come down only in two Chinese versions.[18] It is entirely unknown in Sanskrit,[19] and is not quoted either by the great masters of the Mahāyāna or their commentators."[20] It is however much studied in Japan, even at the present day. "In a biography of Hsuan-Tsang, it is said that he translated it from *Chinese into Sanskrit*."[21] In a footnote he adds, "This account would speak in favour of the view, held by a few Japanese scholars, especially S. Munakami, that it is a Chinese, and not a Sanskrit work. There was a heated controversy on this question in Japan."[22]

He adds further on, "The whole extremely complicated problem of the authenticity of the *Mahāyānaśraddhotpādaśāstra* has been fully discussed by Paul Demieville[23] ....He sees no reason to deny the Indian origin of the work which (he thinks) must be later than the *Laṅkāvatāra,* but earlier than Asanga and Vasubandhu. Else it would be difficult to explain why they are never quoted in the work.[24] On the other hand it is strange that the work, so famous in China and Japan, is never attended to in any Sanskrit text, nor in any Chinese or Tibetan translations of Buddhist Sanskrit works."[25]

Two sharply demarcated phases can be distnguished in the evolution of the Yogācāra system. "The Yogācāra school is divided into

---

18. D. T. Suzuki has translated it into English, after the second Chinese version : *Aśvaghoṣa's Discourse on the Awakening of Faith in the Mahāyāna,* Chicago 1900. See also T. Richard, *The New Testament of Higher Buddhism*, pp. 37-125. On Aśvaghoṣa's system, see Sogen's *Systems of Buddhist Thought*, pp. 252 ff.

19. It does not appear to be known in Tibet either. Buston makes no mention of this work.

20. HIL, pp. 361-362.

21. HIL, p. 362.

22. See *Eastern Buddhist*, I, 1921, pp. 88, 103 ff.

23. *Extrait du Bulletin de la Maison Franco-Japonaise*, Tome II, No. 2, Tokyo, 1929.

24. Nor is this quoted in their works; but here M. Demieville sees no problem.

25. HIL, p. 633.

the ancient one, or the followers of Āryāsanga, and the new one, or the followers of Dignāga. The first established their idealistic views on a new interpretation of the old Abhidharma. Āryāsanga himself composed a Mahāyānistic Abhidharma (*Abhidharma-Samuccaya*) where the number of elements is increased from 75 to 100. The ālayavijñāna is here a new element....However it is not the Absolute."[26] "In the system of Dignāga the old Abhidharma is forsaken altogether[27] and replaced by logic and epistemology. Dignāga started with the reform of the Brahmanical logic (Nyāya) and adopted it to the Buddhist ideas. His analysis of cognition resulted in the conception of an extreme concrete and individual (svalakṣaṇa), the root, or, so to say, the differential of cognition, a point-instant (kṣaṇa) in which existence and cognition, object and subject, coalesce."[28]

Hitherto it has usually been thought that the founder of the Yogācāra school was Asaṅga or Āryāsaṅga.[29] Considerable evidence has, however, been accumulating in favour of the view, gradually forcing itself into acceptance, that the real founder of the system was Maitreya or Maitreyanātha. The tradition is that five of his works were revealed to Asaṅga by Maitreya in the Tuṣita heaven[30] and this would imply that Maitreya was a mythical character,[31] rather than a historical personage. It now appears however, that he was a historical person, the teacher of Asaṅga, and the real founder of the Yogācāra school.[32]

---

26. *The Conception of Buddhist Nirvāṇa*, p. 32.
27. HB, Vol. I, p. 45.
28. Ibid, p. 35.
29. Cf. ibid, p. 31.
30. HB, Vol. II, p. 139.

31. Cf. Obermiller : *The Sublime Science of the Great Vehicle to Salvation* (*Acta Orientalia*, Vol. IX), 1931, p. 92.

32. Cf. Harprasad Sastri in IHQ, I, 1925, p. 465 ff. He places Maitreya between 150 and 265 A.D. ; H. Ui, *Maitreya as an Historical Personage*, Lanman Studies ; G. Tucci, *On some Aspects of the Doctrines of Maitreya (nātha) and Asanga*, Calcutta, 1930 ; also JASB, N.S. XXVI, 1930, 9, 125, ff.

According to Buston[33] the works of Maitreya are five, viz., (1) *Mahāyānasūtrālankāra,*[34] (2) *Madhyāntavibhanga,*[35] (3) *Dharmadharmatāvighanga,*[36] (4) *Uttaratantra*[37] and (5) *Abhisamayālankāra.*[38] Winternitz says, "At all events, the *Abhisamayālankāra-Kārikās* are certainly the work of Maitreyanātha. In all probability, the text of *Mahāyānasūtrālankāra*, which is composed of memorial verses (kārikās), which was discovered by S. Levi, and attributed to Asaṅga by the same scholar, is also the work of Maitreyanātha." In a footnote he continues, "H. Ui has made it seem very probable that Maitreyanātha, and not Asaṅga, was the author of the *Mahāyānasūtrālankāra*. . . . In the work itself Asaṅga

---

33. HB, Vol. I, p. 53; Cf. also Obermiller, op. cit.. He gives a summary analysis of all these works, pp. 83-90.

34. The Sanskrit text with commentary is edited by S. Levi (as being the work of Asaṅga), Paris, 1907. Its Chapters have been surveyed in *Acta Orientalia*, IX, 1931, pp. 84-86. There is a French translation by S. Levi.

35. The Sanskrit text, with the bhāṣya and ṭikā, is edited by S. Yamaguchi, Nagoya, 1934. The first chapter is edited by Tucci and V. Bhattacharya, Calcutta, 1932. The first chapter is translated into English by D. L. Friedmann, Utrecht, 1937, and by Stcherbatsky, BB, XXX, 1936. Cf. IHQ, IX, p. 1019 ff ; MCB, V, p. 271 ff.

36. There is no edition of this work. Obermiler gives a summary analysis in his translation of the *Uttaratantra*, *Acta Orientalia*, Vol. IX, 1931.

37. There is no Sanskrit edition. It is translated from Tibetan into English by E. Obermiller, *The Sublime Science of the Great Vehicle of Salvation*, being a manual of Buddhist Monism, the work of Ārya Maitreya with a commentary by Āryāsaṅga, *Acta Orientalia*, Vol. IX, 1931, pp. 81-306.

38. The Sanskrit Kārikās are edited by Stcherbatsky and Obermiller, BB, XXII, Leningrad, Vol. I, 1929. Cf. E. Obermiller, *The Doctrine of Prajñāpāramitā*, *Acta Orientalia*, Leiden, XI, 1933, pp. 1-133 ; 334-354. Obermiller has also published an analysis of the same, *Acta Orientalia*, I, 1933, pp. 106; II, 1936, pp. 275; III, 1943, pp. 404; IV. Cf. Tucci, *Aspects*. Haribhadra's *Āloka*, which is at once a commentary on the *Abhisamāyālaṅkāra* and the *Aṣṭasāhasrikā*, has been published by Wogihara, Tokyo, 1932-5, and by G. Tucci, GOS, 62, Baroda, 1932.

is not mentioned as the author. According to S. Levi, both the Kārikās and the commentary are the work of Asaṅga. H. Ui shows that Vasubandhu is the author of the commentary."[39] "H. Ui says[40] that it is still a question whether the authorship of the commentary belongs to Asaṅga or to Vasubandhu. He ascribes to Maitreya the works : *Yogācāra-bhūmi*, *Yogavighangaśāstra* (now lost), *Mahāyānasūtrālankāra*, *Madhyāntavibhanga*, *Vajracchedikā-Pāramitāśāstra*, and *Abhisamayālankāra*. Tucci thinks that he was the author of six works, including the *Mahāyānasūtrālankāra* and the *Yogācāra-bhūmiśāstrs*. He is of opinion that Maitreya is the author of the Kārikās of all the six works ,while Asaṅga, his chief pupil, wrote the commentaries on them....As the commentary on the *Abhisamayālankāra* is ascribed to Asaṅga, and as both text and commentary must have been composed by the same author, Obermiller inclines to the opinion that all the five treatises which show a great resemblance with each other as regards style, though they are written from different points of view, were written by Asaṅga, and that the tradition of Asaṅga having heard them from Maitreya in the Tuṣita Heaven is only meant to give a divine sanction to the works."[41]

The names of the two brothers Asaṅga and Vasubandhu loom large in the history of the Yogācāra system. Asaṅga was the pupil of Maitreya, but his name has become more famous than that of his teacher. "Asaṅga, more properly Vasubandhu Asaṅga, is the eldest of three brothers, who were born as the sons of a Brahman of the Kauśika family in Puruṣapura (the present-day Peshawar) in the extreme north-west of

---

39. HIL, pp. 353-4.

40. *Maitreya as an Historical Personage*, p. 99.

41. HIL, pp. 630-1. Obermiller thinks that there are only two alternatives; either Asaṅga (granting that he was the author of the works attributed to Maitreya) changed his views or he wrote according to different stand-points. *The Sublime Science*, pp. 94-46. He thinks that the latter view is more plausible. *Uttaratantra* and *Abhisamayālaṅkāra* are Mādhyamika works (pp. 83, 88-9). The *Madhyāntavibhaṅga* and *Dharmadharmatāvibhaṅga* are special interpretations of *Sandhinirmocanasūtra*, a Yogācāra canonical text (p. 86). Also *The Doctrine of Prajñāpārmitā*, pp. 99-100. Cf. also Stcherbatsky, *Nirvāṇa*, p. 34 and also the footnote 1. therein. Stcherbatky also appears to doubt the historicity of Maitreya.

India (now Pakistan). They probably lived in the 4th century, and were all three originally adherents of the *Sarvāstivāda* school. The youngest was not prominent in literature."[42]

His most important work is the *Yogācāra-Bhūmiśāstra.*[43] Winternitz thinks that it is the work of Maitreyanātha. "(It) is among the works which are supposed to have been revealed to Asaṅga by the mythical Maitreya;[44] probably however it is one of Maitreyanātha's works. It is a prose work after the style of the Abhidharma texts. The *Bodhisattva-bhūmi*[45] is the 15th of the 17 steps taught in this large work; the last step is that in which no trace of the karman remains....The Tibetans attribute the *Yogācārabhūmiśāstra* to Asaṅga."[46]

Besides this great work, Buston mentions two summary works of Asaṅga,[47] viz.,(1) the *Abhidharmasamuccaya*[48] and (2) *Mahāyāna saṃgraha.*[49]

---

42. HIL, pp. 355-6

43. Buston mentions the *Yogacaryābhūmi* as the great work of Asaṅga. It is in five volumes which are briefly described by him, HB, I, pp. 654-56. It appears to be the same as *Yogācāra-bhūmiśāstra.* The Sanskrit manuscript has recently been brought from Tibet by Rāhul Sānkṛtyāyana and is being edited by V. Bhattacharya.

44. HB, II, p. 139.

45. The Sanskrit text has been edited by U. Wogihara, Leipzig, 1908, and again, with text, synopsis, and dissertation, Tokyo, 1130-6. It is edited by J. Rahder in the Appendix to his edition of the *Daśa-bhūmisūtra*, Leuven, 1926. It is also published by W. Geiger in *Studia Indo-Iranica* 1931, pp. 20-38. French and English summary and notes etc., are published by C. Bendall and de la Vallee-Poussin : *Sommaire et notes, Le Museon*, N. S. VI, 1905, pp. 38-52 (Chs. 1-2); VII, 1906, pp. 213-230 (Chs. 3-4); XII, 1911, pp. 155-191 (Chs. 5-8). There is no edition of the larger work. The chapter on ātmavāda is published in *Dr. C. Kunhan Raja Presentation Volume*, 1946, pp. 29-37. There is a survey of the chapters in ZDMG, 1908, p. 91.

46. HIL, p. 435.

47. HB, I, 56.

48. The Sanskrit text is edited by Prahlad Pradhan, *Viśva Bhāratī Studies*, 12, 1950.

49. There is no Sanskrit edition. Cf. E. Lamotte : *Le Somme du grand vehicule d' Asaṅga*, II, 1938. Also MCB, III (1934-5), pp. 169-255.

He also mentions the following : *Tattvaviniścaya*, the commentary on the *Uttaratantra*, the commentary on the *Sandhinirmocanasūtra* and other works.[50] Winternitz mentions[51] the following works as those of Asaṅga, which have come down only in Chinese translations; *Mahāyānasamparigraha* translated by Paramārtha (563 A.D.) ; *Prakaraṇa-Āryavācā-Mahāyānā-bhidharma-Samgītī-śāstra*, translated by Hsuan-Tsang (625 A.D.); and a commentary on the *Vajracchedikā*, translated by Dharmagupta (590-516 A.D.).

Certain Tantric works also have been supposed to be the works of Asaṅga. "One Sādhanā (No. 151) is attributed to Asaṅga. It is scarcely feasible, however, that Asaṅga himself should already have written Tantric works, though there seems to be a historical connection between the Yogācāra school and the rise of the Vajrayāna."[52] "Tārānātha says that Tantrism was handed down by secret means from the time of Asaṅga until the time of Dharmakīrti and B. Bhattacharya believes[53] that Asaṅga actually had something to do with the rise of the Vajrayāna. It seems to me that Tārānātha's statement is accounted for by the mere fact that adherents of the Vajrayāna had an interest in ascribing a great antiquity to their doctrines."[54] "The Nāgārjuna who is mentioned as the author of Sādhanas and numerous Tantric works, is not the founder of the Mādhyamika system, but a teacher, who probably lived about the middle of the seventh century."[55] G. Tucci also[56] is of opinion that the Tantras go back to the times of Asaṅga (4th century A.D.). Dr. B. Bhattacharya would ascribe *Guhyasamājatantra*[57] to Asaṅga, but his arguments are very weak indeed....No real Tantra can be proved to have existed before the 7th century A.D.....All we can say is that some of the elements of Tantrism are already found in earlier works.[58]

---

50. HB, II, p. 140.
51. HIL, p. 355.
52. HIL, p. 392.
53. IHQ, III, p. 736 ff, and Introduction to *Sādhanamālā*, II, pp. XXIII ff, XXVII ff.
54. HIL, p. 392, footnote.
55. HIL, p. 392-3.
56. JASB, XXVI, 1930, p. 129 ff.
57. GOS, No. 53, Baroda 1931; Introduction : pp. XXXIV ff.
58. HIL, pp. 634-5.

Vasubandhu is the central figure in the Yogācāra system, and one of the most prominent figures in the entire history of Buddhism. He was the younger brother of Asaṅga, and lived in the 4th century A.D.[59] The Indian monk Paramārtha (499-569 A.D.) compiled a biography of Vasubandhu in which that of his brother Asaṅga is also included.[60] It is however more remarkable for its account of magic and miracles than for historical accuracy. The Tibetan account, as given by Tāranātha, is still more fantastic. Vasubandhu combined great critical acumen and insight with astonishing erudition.

His activity falls into two well-defined periods. At first he was a Sautrāntika, and wrote works from the Hīnayāna point of view. During the latter part of his life he was converted to the Mahāyāna by his brother and teacher Asaṅga. His great classic on idealism belongs to this period.

His most famous work of the earlier period is the great *Abhidharmakośa,* one of the greatest works in entire Buddhist literature, so long thought lost in Sanskrit, is now awaiting publication. We know only

59. N. Peri, *A propos de la date de Vasabandhu*, BEFEO, XI, 1911, nos. 3-4, argues in favour of this date. J. Takakusu, JRAS, 1905, pp. 33 ff., had placed him between 420 and 500 A.D., but later on, JRAS, 1914, p. 1013 ff., placed him at an earlier date. Wogihara, *Bodhisattvabhūmi*, p. 16, places Vasubandhu between 390 and 470 A.D., and Asanga between 375 and 500 A.D., but in ERE, XII, 1921, p. 595 f., he states 420-500 as the period of Vasubandhu's life. It appears, however, that there were two Vasubandhus both of whom dealt with Abhidharma. This view was supported by sound arguments by T. Kimura. The question of Vasubandhu's date has been discussed by J. Takausu, T. Kimura, and G. Ono in *Lanman Studies*, pp. 79 ff., 89 ff., 93 f. They agree in assigning Vasubandhu to the 5th century A.D. T. Kimura speaks here also of two Vasubandhus. The sources, on which N. Peri relies, are declared by Takakusu to be spurious. On the other hand, H. Ui, *Lanman Studies*, p. 101 f., gives the following dates : Maitreya 270-350 A.D.; Asanga 310-390 A.D.; Vasubandhu 320-400 A.D. ; which Takakusu considers too early by 100 years. (The references are from HIL, pp. 355-6 ; 631-2). Cf. also Foreword to TS, p. LXVI.

60. It has been translated from the Chinese by J. Takakusu, 1904.

the commentary on it by *Yaśomitra*,[61] and its Tibetan and Chinese versions. "The *Abhidharmakośa* treats, in 600 memorial verses (kārikās) together with the author's own commentary (bhāṣya), of the entire field of ontology, psychology, cosmology, ethics and the doctrine of salvation. The last chapter, which is given either as chapter IX or as an appendix to chapter VIII, and which is not composed of memorial verses, treats of the Buddhist doctrine of the soul (denial of a permanent soul), and is directed against the Pudgalātmavādins, those who believe in a permanent soul. Though the *Abhidharmakośa* is written from the standpoint of the Sarvāstivāda, it is nevertheless an authority for *all* schools of Buddhism. We can learn far more from the Kośa with its commentary about the dogmatics of the ancient Buddhist schools than from any other work, and it affords us a sidelight upon the debates between the Vaibhāṣikas and the Sautrāntikas. Moreover, the work is rich in quotations from the earlier literature." [62]

"There is a book of sayings, thoroughly Hīnayānist in character, extant only in Tibetan and ascribed to Vasubandhu, called the *Gāthāsamgraha*[63], with a brilliant commentary." "A similar work is *Śīlaparikathā*[64],

---

61. The entire text of *Abhidharmakośovyākhyā* is edited by U. Wogihara, Tokyo. The first Kośasthāna is edited by S. Levi and Stcherbastsky, BB, XXI, 1918. The second Kośasthāna is edited by V. Wogihara, Th. Stcherbatsky, and E. Obermiller, BB, 1931. The Tibetan version of the Kārikās and the Bhāṣya has been edited by Stcherbatsky in BB, XX, 1917, 1930. Poussin has translated the Sanskrit text of the Vyākhyā, 1930, making use of the Tibetan and Chinese versions, into French. This has again been translated into Hindi by Ācāyra Narendra Deva, and two Kośasthānas are already published from Hindustani Academy, Allahabad. Rāhul Sānkṛtyāyana has collected the scattered fragments of the Kośa embedded in Poussin's translation and published them from Vidyapith, Banaras. The Appendix to the eighth chapter is translated by Stcherbatsky, *The Soul Theory of the Buddhists*, Bulletin de l'Academ. des Sciences de Russie, Petrograd, 1919, pp. 824 ff, 937 ff.

62. HIL, pp. 357-8.

63. Cf. A. Schiefner, *Melanges Asiatiques*, VIII, St. Petersburg, 1878, p. 559 ff.

64. See Anatha Natha Basu in IHQ, VII, 1931, p. 28 ff.

a moral treatise of all verses, which is ascribed to Vasubandhu and preserved in the Tibetan Tanjur only."[65]

Vasubandhu wrote a special work, the *Paramārthasaptati*, in order to refute the Sāṅkhya philosophy. This work, the Sanskrit original of which is lost, seems to be a confutation of Īśvarakṛṣṇa's *Sāṅkhyasaptati*. Strange to say, the Chinese also ascribe a commentary on Īśvarakṛṣṇa's work to Vasubandhu.[66]

When he was converted to the Mahāyāna, he regretted his calumniation of the Mahāyāna so deeply that he wanted to cut off his tongue[67]. But Asaṅga advised him to employ his tongue in expounding the Mahāyāna. Vasubandhu wrote therefore a large number of commentaries on Mahāyānasūtras, on the *Saddharma Puṇḍarīka*, the *Mahāparinirvāṇa-sūtra* and the *Vajracchedikā-Prajñāpāramitā*. Buston thinks that he also wrote a very large commentary on the *Śatasāhasrikā*, the *Pañcaviṅśati-sāhasrikā* and the *Aṣṭādaśasāhasrikā*[68], expounding the Prajñāpāramitās from the stand-point of the Yogācāra system.

Buston mentions eight treatises by Vasubandhu on idealism[69]. The first and most important of these are the two classical treatises, the *Viṅśatikā* and the *Triṅśikā*, comprising together the great *Vijñaptimātratā-siddhi*[70]. This is the complete and definitive text on the Yogācāra idealism.

---

65. HIL, pp. 358, 632.
66. HIL, p. 359.
67. HB, II, p. 143.
68. HB, I, pp. 52-3.
69. HB, I, pp. 56-57; Cf. also II, p. 144.
70. The Sanskrit original of these two treatises, the *Vimśatikā* with the author's commentary and the *Trimśikā* with Sthiramati's commentary, were discovered by S. Levi and edited by him for the first time, Paris, 1925. The *Vimśatikā* with the author's commentary has been translated into French from the Tibetan by Poussin, *Le Museon*, 1921, pp. 53-90; also S. Levi, *Materiaux pour l'Etude du Systeme Vijñaptimātratā*, 1932, pp. 43-49; 61-623. For English translation, cf. Hamilton, *Journal of American Oriental Society*, XIII, 1938. In German, cf. Kitayama, *Metaphysik des Buddhismus*, 1934, pp. 234-69. Cf. Hamilton, *Buddhist Idealism* (thesis), Chicago, 1929. A good summary is given by S. N. Dasgupta, IHQ, IV, 1928, pp. 36-43.

The category of the objective is refuted with great dialectical skill, and the sole reality of consciousness vindicated. Vasubandhu has also written a commentary on the *Viṅśatikā*. The other six works mentioned by Buston are the *Pañcaskandha-prakaraṇa*[71], *Vyākhyāyukti*, the *Karmasiddhi-prakaraṇa*[72] and the three commentaries on the *Māhayānasūtrālaṅkāra*, the *Pratītya-samutpādasūtra*[73] and the *Madhyāntavibhaṅga*.[74] He wrote many other commentaries including those on the *Daśa-bhūmikāsūtra*, *Mahāyānasaṅgraha*, *Dharmadharmatāvibhaṅga*, *Akṣayamatinirdeśa*, *Gayāśīrṣa*, *Sanmukhadhāraṇī*, *Caturdharmaka*, etc.

One important tract, *Trisvabhāvanirdeśa*[75], is not mentioned by Buston. Winternitz also makes no reference to it. It consists of 38 verses, elucidating the doctrine of the three Truths, viz., parikalpita, paratantra, and pariniṣpanna.

H. R. Rangswamy Ayengar[76] and G. Tucci[77] have proved that the

---

There were as many as ten different commentaries on the *Triṁśikā*. These were translated by Hsuan Tsang who melted them down to one work, chiefly relying on Dharmapāla. This has been rendered into French by Poussin : *La Siddhi de Hsūan Tsang*, two volumes, Paris, 1928-30. Cf. H. Ui, *The Vaiśeṣika Philosophy*, London, 1917, p. 2. Some portions of it have been restored into Sanskrit by Rāhul Sānkṛtyāyana, JBORS, XIX, XX. Ācārya Narendra Deva has contributed a brief summary in Hindi in *Sampurnanand Commenmoration Volume*. Cf. also JAOS, 51, 1931, pp. 291-308; S. Lindquist, *Siddhi and Abhiññā*, Upsala, 1935; Demieville, BEFEO, 27, pp. 283-98.

71. Cf. *The Pañcaskandhaka by Vasubandhu and its commentary by Sthiramati*, *Annals of Bhandarkar Oriental Research Institute*, XVIII, 1936-7, pp. 276-86.

72. Cf. *Le Traite de l'acte de Vasubandhu*, MCB, IV, 1935-6, pp. 151-263.

73. A fragment of the Sanskrit text of the commentary on this has been published by G. Tucci in JRAS, 1930, p. 611 ff.

74. Cf. Stcherbatsky in *Le Muséon*, N. S., VI, 1905, p. 44 ff.

75. The Sanskrit text is edited in MCB, II, pp. 146-61, and also by S. Mukhopadhyaya, Viśvabhāratī, 1939.

76. JBORS, XII, 1926, p. 587 ff; IHQ, V, 1929, p. 81 ff.

77. IHQ, IV, 1928, p. 630 ff.

Vādavidhi also is a work of Vasubandhu, and not of Dharmakīrti as Keith[78], following S. C. Vidyabhushana, tried to prove.

Towards the end of his life, he is said to have become a devotee of Amitābha and to have written a work entitled *Aparimitāyus-Sūtropadeśa*, in which he gave expression to his longing for Sukhāvati[79].

In the 5th century A.D. there lived Sthiramati Dignāga, and somewhat younger Dharmapāla, teachers who arose from Vasubandhu's school.[80] Sthiramati was the great commentator on the Yogācāra works. He was the pupil of Vasubandhu and, Buston says, that he was "more learned (than Vasubandhu) in the Abhidharma." [81] He wrote brilliant commentaries on Vasubandhu's eight treatises on idealism, the most famous of which is the invaluable *Triṁśikāvijñaptibhāṣya*. The commentary on the *Madhyāntavibhaṅgasūtrabhāṣya* is also his. He wrote a commentary on the *Kāśyapaparivarta* or *Ratnakūṭa*. Buston says, "This teacher has composed the commentary on the *Abhidharmakośa* called the *Kārakāśani*, the commentary on the *Abhidharmasamuccaya*, the commentaries on the 8 treatises (of Vasubandhu) and numerous other works".[82] Excepting the first two, these are not available in Sanskrit. Dharmapāla wrote a commentary on the *Vijñaptimātratāsiddhi*, which forms the basis of Hsüan Tsang's translation.

With Sthiramati, the strictly idealistic phase of the Yogācāra system comes to an end. Thinkers were no longer interested in the constructive details of the idealistic metaphysics. The interest shifted from metaphysics to logic and epistemology. Idealism was maintained from the standpoint of ultimate reality; but, in order to supply a stable basis for the logic of empirical reality, the Sautrāntika conception of a thing-in-itself (svalakṣaṇa) was revived. This resulted in the formation of the hybrid school of the Sautrāntika-Yogācāra,[83] for which the name Vijñānavāda

78. IHQ, IV, 1929, p. 211 ff.

79. Cf. U. Woglhara in ERE, XII, p. 596.

80. "The question of the date of Sthiramati is very complicated and it is probable that there were more than one author of this name. One Sthiramati was pupil of Guṇamati, and lived before 435 A. D." HIL, p. 362.

81. HB, II, p. 147.

82. HB, II, p. 148.

83. *The Conception of Buddhist Nirvāṇa*, p. 30.

can be reserved. The most important names in this new school are those of Dignāga and Dharmakīrti. Their essential teaching was that of the Yogācāra as is evident from Dignāga's *Ālambanaparīkṣā* and Dharmakīrti's section on the *Vijñaptimātratā-cintā* in his *Pramāṇavārttika*. But their main interest being in logical elaborations, this aspect of their thought was allowed to remain uncultivated. The ultimate reality (paramārthasatya) was according to them consciousness alone ; but for logical purposes they accepted the svalakṣaṇa as empirically real (paramārthasat). This was the second phase in the development of Buddhist idealism. The first phase of pure idealism, represented by Maitreya, Asaṅga, Vasubandhu and Sthiramati, can be called the Yogācāra school; the second phase of idealism-cum-critical realism, represented by Dignāga and Dharmakīrti, can then be called the Vijñānavāda school, and the whole development, the Yogācāra-Vijñānavāda.

"The greatest and most independent thinker among the successors of Vasubandhu is Dignāga, the founder of Buddhist logic, and one of the foremost figures in the history of Indian philosophy."[84] According to Buston he belonged at first to the Vātīputrīya School[85] whch maintains that the ego is neither identical with the groups of elements, nor different from them, and that it has a quasi-permanent reality. But he was soon dissatisfied with this teaching and became a pupil of Vasubandhu. He is said to have written as many as 100 miscellaneous works,[86] including commentaries on the *Abhidharmakośa*, on the *Guṇaparyanta-stotra* and others. The *Ālambanaparīkṣā*[87] is a very small tract, consisting of only 8 verses with a short commentary, which examines the

---

84. Aecording to Tārānātha and Buston, Dignāga was a pupil of Vasubandhu. Randle, *Fragments from Dignāga*, p. 3, says, "All that can be said with certainty is that he lived somewhere between 350-500 A.D." Cf. Keith, *Buddhist Philosophy*, 305 ff. ; Stcherbatsky, *Buddhist Nirvāṇa*, p. 35.

85. HB, II, p. 149.

86. HB, II, p. 150.

87. The Sanskrit text with the commentary has been restored into Sanskrit by Aiyaswami Sastri, Adyar. He has also given the restorations of other commentaries, including that of Dharmapāla. Also S. Yamaguchi and H. Meyer, JAS, 1929, pp. 1-65 (in French). Cf. Also JAS, 1930 (oct.-Dec.).

object of cognition and refutes the reality of the external world from the Yogācāra standpoint. Dharmapāla has written a commentary on this. "But as these treatises were mere fragments (without any system) he resolved to compose the *Pramāṇasamuccaya*[88] in which (all the small treatises) would be united in one." He also wrote a commentary on this great work, which initiated a new era in the history of Buddhism. His other important smaller works are *Trikāla Parīkṣā*, *Hetucakra-nirṇaya*,[89] *Nyāyamukha*[90] and *Nyāyapraveśa*[91] (?).

The most famous of his successors is Dharmakīrti. His teacher was Iśvarasena, the pupil of Dignāga. His celebrated work is *Pramāṇa-vārttika*,[92] which is a sort of running commentary on the *Pramāṇasa-muccaya*. According to Buston he wrote seven logical treatises. "The seven treatises consist of three main works—and four supplementary. The first are the *Nyāyabindu*,[93] *Pramānaviniścaya*, and *Pramāṇavārttika*—(The subject of) inference is treated in detail by two works—the

---

88. Partially restored with vṛtti, ṭīkā and notes by H.R.R. Iyengar, Mysore, 1930.

89. Translated from Tibetan by Durgadas Chatterji, IHQ, IX, 1933, pp. 266-72 and 511-4.

90. Cf. G. Tucci, Hdbg., 1930, MZKB.

91. It is reconstructed in Sanskrit by N. D. Mironov, *T'ung-Pao*, XXVIII, 1931, pp. 1-25. The Tiberan text is edited by V. Bhatt-acharya, GOS, XXXIX, Baroda, 1927, and the Sanskrit text by A. B. Dhruva, GOS, Baroda. The Sanskrit fragments which are available in quotations have been collected and translated by H. N. Randle, *Fragments from Dignāga*, London, 1926.

Nyāyapraveśa, attributed to Dignāga, is really the work of Śaṅkara-svāmin. Cf. JRAS, 1927, p. 7; IHQ, IV, 1928, pp. 14-22 ; III, 1927, pp. 152-60.

92. It has been edited with the *Manorathanandinī* by Rāhul Sāṅkṛtyā-yana, JBORS, XXIV and XXV, Patna, 1938-39. He has also published parts available of Prajñākaragupta's *Pramāṇavārttkālaṅkāra* in the same journal, and Karṇagomin's commentary on the chapter on *Svārthānu-māna*, along with auto-commentary of Dharmakīrti, Allahabad, 1944.

93. The Sanskrit text has been edited by Peterson, *Bibliotheca Indica*, 1889-90 ; by Stcherbatsky, BB, VII, 1918 ; also published from Chowkhamba, Banaras. The Tibetan text is edited by Stcherbatsky,

Hetubindu[94] and the *Sambandhaparīkṣā*[95]....The syllogism is enlarged upon in the *Vādanyāya*[96]....The *Santānāntarasiddhi*[97] shows that, from the point of view of Empirical Reality, the inference of the existence of other minds on the basis of the existence of their words and actions does not conflict with Idealism."[98]

In Śāntarakṣita and Kamalaśīla we find another interesting development of the Mahāyāna philosophy. Śāntarakṣita attempted a synthesis of the Mādhyamika and the Yogācāra systems. Even previously some Madhyamika ācāryas might have had idealistic leanings,[99] but Śāntarakṣita is the first teacher to have consciously attempted at the formulation of a syncretic school.[100] His ultimate stand-point is essentially that of the Mādhyamika, but at places he shows his manifest inclination to idealism.[101] He devotes one entire section for the refutation of the external object. It appears that Śāntarakṣita has no repugnance to the Yogācāra from the empirical point of view, without giving up his ulti-

---

BB, VIII, 1904. It is translated into English by Stcherbatsky, *Buddhist Logic*, Vol. II, 1930, BB, pp. 1-253. The commentary is by Dharmottara.

94. It has been published in GOS, Baroda.

95. The entire work consisting of 22 verses is found in the *Prameyakamalamārtaṇḍa*, pp. 504-14.

96. The Sanskrit text is published by Rāhul Sānkṛtyāyana, JBORS, XXI.

97. The Tibetan text is edited by Stcherbatsky, BB.

98. HB, I, pp. 44-5.

99. Cf. "The latter (*Cittaviśuddiprakaraṇa* of Āryadeva) concludes that the mind, when without a touch of imagination, is the true reality, the apparent diversity which it exhibits being explained by the coloration of imagination, just as the limpid crystal is discoloured by the reflection of a coloured object, a doctrine which shows that Āryadeva was approximating to the views of Vijñānavāda." Keith, *Buddhist Philosophy*, p. 230.

100. Prof. V. Bhattacharya has made it seem extremely probable that the fourth part of Gauḍapāda's *Māṇḍūkyakārikās* is another such similar attempt, though on different lines. See his *The Āgamaśāstra af Gauḍapāda*, Calcutta, 1943.

101. See the Introduction to *Tattvasamgraha*, p. XXI ff.

mate standpoint of a Mādhyamika. "The teacher Śāntirakṣita composed the *Madhyamakālaṅkāra* and laid the foundaton to another school of the Mādhyamikas which denies the Empirical Reality of the External World, acknowledges the introspective perception (svasamvedana), but on the other hand does not consider consciousness to have an Ultimate Reality (differing in this from the Yogācāra-Vijñānavādins). The *Mādhyamikāloka* and the 3 *Bhāvanākramas* of Kamalaśīla, as well as the texts of Vimuktasena, Haribhadra, Buddhajñānapāda, Abhayākaragupta, etc., agree with Śāntirakṣita in the main stand-point (which is that of the Yogācāra-Mādhyamika-Svātantrika)".[102]

Śāntarakṣita[103] wrote a large philosophical work, *Tattvasaṅgraha*,[104] on which Kamalaśīla wrote the *Pañjikā*. Herein he refutes all the philosophical systems of his day, Buddhist as well as non-Buddhist. His other work is a short tract, the *Mādhyamikālankāra-kārikās* with the author's own commentary. This work has come down only in the Tibetan translation. Śāntarakṣita died in Tibet in 762 A.D.

After Śāntarakṣita there were no further doctrinal developments in the Yogācāra system. It was gradually superseded by the Nyāya-Vaiśeṣika and the Advaita Vedānta, and became extinct in India, but travelled to China and Japan.

---

102. Obermiller gives this quotation, HB, II, p. 136 n. ; and also p. 135. Cf. Obermiller, *The Sublime Science*, p. 83; *The Doctrine of Prajñāpāramitā*, p. 90 n.

103. He lived between 705-762 A.D. For a discussion of the dates and the life of this great teaeher see B. Bhattacharya's Foreword to *Tattvasangraha*.

104. The Sanskrit text is edited by Embar Krishnamacharya in GOS, Nos. XXX-XXXI, Baroda, 1926. Tbe entire work is translated into English by G. Jha, GOS, 1937-9. Cf. Satkari Mukherji, *Buddhist Philosophy of Universal Flux*, Calcutta, 1935.

Chapter III

REFUTATION OF REALISM

The Sahopalambhaniyama

The Yogācāra holds that consciousness is the sole reality. The empirical world reduces itself, according to him, to ideas[1] which are, so to speak, so many vibrations in consciousness. The independence of the external object confronting consciousness is only apparent.[2] The distinction naively made between the percept and its content is illusory. The blue and the consciousness of blue are identical (sahopalambhaniyamād abhedo nīla-taddhiyoḥ).[3]

Since the external object is invariably perceived along with the consciousness of it, its independence is not tenable. To establish the difference between two things it is necessary to perceive them apart. If two things are invariably found in conjunction they cannot even be enumerated as two. The relation of difference—granting that difference is a relation—presupposes the separateness of the relata; there must be found cases where one is present without the other. Otherwise their distinction remains chimerical. This principle is applied by the Yogācāra to prove the unsoundness of the realistic hypothesis.

Realists hold that the content perceived is independent of the act of perception.[4] Perception does not in any way alter the content perceived. It remains identical and emerges unaffected out of the process of perception. Perception can be compared to light; it does not make or unmake the things upon which it shines, but merely reveals or discovers what was before hidden in darkness. The change that occurs

1. MVSBT, p. 10 ; LAS, X, 687.

2. *Ālambana Parīkṣā*, 6.

3, Cf. also, sakṛd saṃvedyamānasya niyamena dhiyā saha. viṣyasya tato 'nyatvaṃ kenākāreṇa sidhyati. PV, II, 388 ; also II, 335.

4. Cf. *The New Realism*, pp. 126 ff. *Present Philosophical Tendencies* by Perry, p. 315.

to the content is only in this very respect; formerly it remained unperceived and now it is being perceived. The change pertains to our knowledge of objects and does not in any way touch the objects themselves. Perception is ontologically neutral. It reveals things as they are and does not construct, either wholly or in part. If perception in any way made the things perceived different from what they were before, we could never say that we perceive the same thing we perceived before; the two acts of perception being different, they would create different contents. If perception does not wholly create its content but only modifies it in part, then there would remain an unmodifiable core which is absolutely indifferent to its being perceived. If the being of this core again owed something to the fact of its being perceived, an infinite regress is at once started. Even this assertion that perception contributes only partly to the being of the content could not be made, since we have no means of evaluating and appreciating the two parts. The fundamental issue remains between rank realism and idealism of the Yogācāra type. The intermediary positions are unstable.

The content is only accidentally the object of perception. Perception reveals the object, but the object need not be revealed; there is nothing in its nature which forces it into the ken of perception. A content is a content in its own right and owes nothing to the adventitious fact of its being perceived, except this very fact of being perceived. The object which was previously unperceived enters into the knowledge-situation retaining its absolute identity[5] and without undergoing any other change than that of being perceived.

But the Yogācāra contends[6] that to trace this identity we must know the object in both the circumstances—before being perceived and during perception. We are thus led into a curious predicament. To assert that the object owes nothing to the fact of its being perceived, we must know what the object was before being perceived; that is to say, we must know without knowing. We can call a thing identical only when we find it in two or more sets of circumstances and recognise it as being the same. Here, from the very nature of the case, such a recognition cannot be had. All identity is relational—absolute identity, if there be such a thing at all, being necessarily non-conceptual,—but in the case

5. *The New Realism*, p. 35.
6. TS, I, 20, 30-31 ; TSP, I, p. 567-68.

of perception, one end of the relation is invariably lacking. We know the content only as it is perceived and cannot compare it with its unperceived state. To assert therefore the continued independence of the content the realist must set an impossible task beofre himself;[7] he must know the object when *ex-hypothesi* it is not known.[8]

The Yogācāra concludes that as the assertion that knowing makes no difference to what is known involves knowing what is defined as the unknown, the contention that the object is present in both the circumstances identically must be discarded. We can never transcend knowledge.[9] To say that perception only reveals objects already existent implies this transcendence. Consciousness is creative. The object has no separate existence of its own. Since it cannot be known to exist apart from the consciousness of it, the two are not distinct at all.[10] The

---

7. *Autobiography*, by R. G. Collingwood, p. 34.

8. The Advaita Vedānta is in a way realistic in its epistemology, as will be seen in the sequel (Chapt. 10). The Vedāntin performs the task of tracing the identity of the object in its two states, viz. when it is known and when it remains unknown. He cannot show this identity empirically, as in that case he would have to know the object without knowing; but he can prove this identity transcendentally, by an analysis of illusion. When the illusory snake is sublated, the underlying reality of the rope is discovered. The rope is then known to owe nothing to the fact of its being known ; it is also known to have existed in its own right, even when it was mistaken for a snake, The snake is illusory because it has no existence apart from its being known (pratibhāsa-mātra-śarīratva) i.e., it is not in space and time. Were the rope also in the same predicament, the very possibility of the mistake would be precluded. Granting even that the snake somehow appeared, there would be no ground for preferring the rope to the snake. The indifference of the rope therefore to its being known is a presupposition of the illusory appearance.

9. samvedanena bāhyatvam ato'rthasya na sidhyati samvedanād bahirbhāve sa eva na tu sidhyati, PVA, p. 32. Also VMS, p. 17.

10. TSP, I, 568. jñānajñeyayoḥ parasparam eka eva upālambho na pṛthag iti, ya eva hi jñānopalambhaḥ sa eva jñeyasya ya eva jñeyasya sa eva jñānasyeti yāvat. Also PV, II, 390-1.

blue is an abstraction ; what exists is only the consciousness of blue, i.e. consciousness having the form of the blue.[11] It cannot be said that in that case we shall not be justified in speaking of the consciousness *of* blue, but should speak only of a 'blue consciousness', as though the consciousness itself were coloured, since, the Yogācāra would argue, the sensa have no physical existence at all, and the question of a blue consciousness does not arise. There is no blue, but only the idea of blue. Nor should we be debarred from speaking "this is blue" and start speaking "I am blue"[12] instead, for that particular idea has this very form of "This is blue." Just as the blue has no independence of its own, so the "I" also has no separate existence apart from the discrete consciousness of "I" ; hence "this is blue " is not less justified than "I am blue."

It must be conceded, however, that the argument from "the egocentric predicament"[13] (the famous sahopalambhaniyama of the Yogācāra) does not prove the idealistic thesis. To say that the realists' contention is unwarranted is one thing; to conclude from that that idealism is therefore established is quite another thing. Though sahopalambhaniyama might seem a positive argument, in reality it is only an apagogic proof. The real sting of the argument lies in the fact that to assert the independence of the object we must find a way of knowing it when *ex-hypothesi* it is not known. How the Vedāntin does it has already been indicated. This is evidently a correct appraisement of the realists' position. But to infer from this that the object does not exist at all when not known is a false inference. The realists' retort that an epistemic predicament is being raised to an ontological status[14] holds good. It is like arguing that because we need microscopes to perceive bacteria, the bacteria cannot live without microscopes.[15] What is undoubtedly true of our knowledge of things is falsely held to be true of the things themselves. Be-

---

11. na hi keśoṇḍuka-jñānaviśeṣasya grāhakavad grāhyaḥ keśāvayavo' sti. kim tarhi keśābhāsaḥ prakāśa eva kevalaḥ. PV, p. 218.

12. SV (*Śūnyavāda*), 229 ; NM, p. 541 ; *Prameya Kamala Mārtaṇḍa*, p. 106.

13. The phrase coined by Perry.

14. *The New Realism*, pp. 11-12; Perry, *Present Philosophical Tendencies*, pp. 131-132.

15. *Idealism*, by A. C. Ewing, p. 31.

cause we can never see without light we cannot infer that light is a constituent of things seen. A person who wears red spectacles is certainly justified in saying that *he* can never see things which are not red; he cannot say that all *things* he sees are red. We cannot know without knowing—that is a tautology; things cannot exist without our knowing them—that is false. To be true, it must be supported on other grounds. It must be proved from the very nature of objects that they are essentially dependent upon the consciousness of them; the mere unavailability of them without consciousness holds good only for us. To say that things exist without our consciousness of them is a demand to know them as transcending knowledge; to say that they do not so exist is a similar demand. The predicament is the same in both cases. The same argument that invalidates realism refutes idealism as well. Idealism must be founded on some more positive grounds than the sahopalambhaniyama.

Realists hold that consciousness is different from the object conceived. The two have attributes contradictory to each other. Objects are characterised by physical qualities; they are great or small, are hard or soft; they are relatively nearer to or farther from each other. It is clearly absurd to call consciousness small or soft, or one consciousness being nearer to another in space. This, however, is a silly argument and is easily waived aside. The Yogācāra does not say that an idea itself has spatial attributes—some Western thinkers have gone even so far as that—but that it has a form manifesting those attributes. The attributes have no independent physical existence apart from their appearance before consciousness.

By the creativity of consciousness should not be understood the illusory notion that consciousness creates real physical objects. Its creativity consists in being diversified into so many modes[16] which, though having an apparent externality, are really but modes of consciousness. One idea generates another idea and not an external object. The idea itself masquerades as an external object. Objects are hypostatised ideas.

It is clear that by consciousness realists and the Yogācāra understand two entirely different things. Consciousness for one is a diapha-

---

16. na ca viṣayapratibhāsātmanā utpattim muktvā vijñānasyānyā kriyāsti, MVSBT, p. 21.

nous entity through whose transparence objects pass in and out without suffering the least modification. In itself consciousness is entirely formless, neutral. The forms we perceive are those of the objects, directly and immediately revealed by consciousness. Since the idealist has no other reality but consciousness, the forms perceived must pertain to consciousness alone, there being no external object[17]. Consciousness creates its own forms. The content of consciousness is not imported from outside, but is inherent in the states of consciousness themselves[18]. The issue between the idealist and the realist is whether consciousness is sākāra, i.e., has a prakāra (content) of its own or whether it is nirākāra, is contentless in itself.

The realist derives his strength from his criticism of the 'ego-centric predicament' which, however, proves nothing as seen just now. We need not also discuss the argument that the forms perceived cannot belong to the objects, since they are never perceived apart from consciousness, as this brings us back to the sahopalambhaniyama. And this moreover would land us in a form of agnosticism. What is required is that the idealist should put forward cases where the creativity of consciousness is definitely evident. Illusion and hallucination furnish such cases. Of other mental states memory may be discussed to show that consciousness is not entirely formless, does not merely reveal, but has an activity of its own, i.e., is sākāra.

Memory As Subjective

What is the content of memory ? What is the nature and status of that content ? The realistic hypothesis requires that it should be as external and independent as the content of perception. The object remembered should enjoy the same status as the object perceived. Recognition is another enigma to the realist. If consciousness were nothing but pure transparence what happens when we are said to recognise a thing, with the added consciousness of having cognised it before? The object certainly does not inform us of the fact of its having been

---

17. dhiyo nīlādirūpatve bāhyo'rthaḥ kim pramāṇakaḥ. dhiyo' nīlādirūpatve sa tasyānubhavaḥ katham. PV, II, 343.

18. svabījaparipākād rūpādyābhāsam vijñānam pravarttate na tu rūpādiko' rtho'sti. MVSBT, p. 20.

Cf. vaiśvarūpyād dhiyām eva bhāvānām viśvarūpatā. PV, II. 204 ; Cf. also 479.

cognised before; it has not acquired any extra characteristic[19] owing to our previous cognition of it. Nor can consciousness retain any memory of its previous cognitions, being a purely diaphanous entity. Hence either the hypothesis of an entirely formless (nirākāra) consciousnes has to be given up, or, over and above the nirākāra consciousness, a mind-stuff[20] has to be admitted which is transformed according to the various cognitions leaving their traces in it. But this unnecessary duplication of the subjective side only adds to, instead of solving, the difficulty. Alternatively, this subjective dualism itself can be retained and the reality of the object given up.

In memory, we may say, the actual presence of the object is not required to be cognised and hence this difficulty does not arise; but it does arise in a slightly different form. Being transparent (nirākāra), consciousness can have no memory; it can reveal the object only as actually manifested before it; it has no past or fututre. To admit, over and above pure consciousness, a mind which does acquire forms like wax impressions, is to raise several other problems as to the relationship between pure consciousness, mind and the object.

---

19. Here a curious doctrine of the Bhāṭṭas may be noted. The Bhāṭṭa is a frank realist. In connexion with the problem of knowability of knowledge, he holds an interesting doctrine. In being known the object acquires a familiar aspect, i.e., "knownness". This is a novel and peculiar quality called jñātatā or prākaṭya, and is the sole ground for an arthāpatti for the existence of knowledge. cf. *Nyāyakaṇikā*, p. 267.

20. The Sāṅkhya and the Advatia Vedānta accept the reality of pure consciousness and have consequently to admit a mind-stuff buddhi or citta) ; it is burdened with all the functions that cannot be attributed to pure consciousness. In the Advaita Vedānta, for example, the sākṣi-consciousness knows everything all at once. Change or succession plays no part in its knowledge. It is the pramātā or consciousness as limited by antaḥkaraṇa (an aspect of the mind-stuff) which can know succession and makes memory possible. But it is difficult to make the universal consciousness (sākṣi) relevant to the particular acts of knowledge (buddhi-vṛttis).

The more consistent realists have boldly declared the memory image to be as objective as the perceptual content. It is objectively given[21]. It is not a form of consciousness, as the latter is unmodifiable and merely reveals it. But how is the memory image to be conceived objectively ? Some hold that the same object which was previously perceived is the content of memory as well. Memory cognises the same object *as past*. This, however, makes no sense. How can the object which is past yet appear to a present consciousness ?[22] It might have been destroyed in the meanwhile, for aught we know. An image standing midway between the object and consciousness cannot be admitted, since it can be made of neither. The conclusion is that consciousness itself projects these images, and is therefore sākāra[23].

The Illusory as Subjective

Illusion is the mire in which all forms of realism flounder. Realism which is but self-conscious commonsense, holds that consciousness reveals the object literally as it is. It cannot distort or falsify; it can only discover. It is like light which does not add to or take anything away from the things it illumines. So long as the course of knowledge flows on smoothly without any hitch, this naive theory works out well. The immediate perceptibility of the content receives a rude shock when we consider that difference of perspective makes a considerable difference in the content perceived. There is a personal equation[24] in most perceptions, and how is this to be ever eliminated ? "A penny is a circular object; but what we directly perceive in the penny when we look at it from different positions is a series of ellipses of varying eccentricity, and it is impossible to deny this and also accept the facts of direct perception."[25] Which of these appearances should be accepted as truly revealing the object ? There is no ground for preferring any one to the others. The same object, when near, appears big, but upon walking away from it, it appears to diminish in its size. What then

21. Cf. *Concept of Consciousness*, by E. B. Holt. Also *A Study in Realism,* by Laird, p. 64.

22. PV, II, 375, nārthād bhāvastadābhāvāt; PVA, p. 112.

23. Imagination raises the same difficulties.

24. PV, II, 358 ; also 341.

25. *A Study in Realism*, p. 28 ; also Berkeley : *Three Dialogues*, pp. 213-14 (Everyman's Ed.).

is its real size ? The notion of oneness of the object precludes the hypothesis of its being merely a collocation of different sizes, or to put it in general terms, of different sensa. Again, no two percipients perceive any object in an identical manner. "How can the object be identical when the so-called revelations of it are mutually conflicting ?"[26] The realist might reply that though the perceptions are thus varying, the object remains identical because there is a common meaning and an identical reference in these perceptions[27]. But this identical reference itself is never perceived, and hence the alleged identity remains always problematical.

It may be said that these difficulties do not affect the fundamental contention that knowledge is discovery. The elliptical appearances of a round coin or the bent appearance in water of a straight stick are due merely to an optical predicament; these facts are not sufficient to establish the opposite theory, viz., knowledge is a construction. The appearances are not in any way mental; they are not imported into the perceived data by the mind. The elliptical coin is as objective as the circular coin.[28]

Though this is far from being a satisfactory reply, there yet remains the stubborn fact of the illusory content which refuses to fit in any realistic framework. The elliptical coin is not a mistake in the sense that it could not be perceived otherwise. Hence the activity of mind may not be directly evident here. But where there is a positive confusion, it cannot similarly be brushed aside. Were consciousness purely revelatory, the possibility of mistake, i.e., taking one thing for another, would be entirely precluded. We shall always see a rope as a rope and never as snake. But we do sometimes see a snake when there is none and this entirely upsets the commonsense theory.

An easy way out of this difficulty is to reject the transparence of consciousness and to hold that consciousness does not directly reveal the object but that it can perceive only its own 'ideas.' We have no longer a two-term theory of knowledge but replace it with a three-term theory. According to this hypothesis consciousness is mediated by its

---

26. VMS, p. 39 ; also PV, II, 400, 344 ; NM, p. 540.

27. *A Study in Realism*, p. 29.

28. This is known as the theory of subsistence, and this would be discussed later on.

own representations in its perception of objects. Here we have, not merely consciousness on the one hand and the object on the other, but in between these two we have a *tertium quid*—the images or 'ideas.' Objects are not immediately presented to consciousness but are represented indirectly through 'ideas' which are but signs of their presence and character. It is no longer "A perceives B", but now it is "A perceives C which stands for B." When C corresponds with B, we have right knowledge; if not, it is a case of illusion.

Once the immediacy of the perceived content is given up, the flood-gates of idealism are opened. If it be conceded that consciousness perceives only its own representations, the external objects dwindle into shadows and are perilously on their way to total discarding. If we can never perceive the objects, how can we even know that they exist ? There is no way to proceed from the images to the objects, if the latter are not independently known.

The representative theory of perception was put forward to explain cases of illusion where the theory of direct perception failed. When the image is referred to its correct original we have a case of veridical perception; but when it is supposed to refer to an object which is not its original, we have a case of mistaken perception or illusion. This is obviously a form of the 'Correspondence theory of truth' as formulated in the perceptual realm. The truth of a perception consists in its correct reference. But there we must distinguish. Truth may consist in this correspondence, which, to be truth, need not be known. But to *know* a perception as true is a different matter. In this case we must compare the image with its original[29] in order to know of their correspondence and yet, once the original is known, the knowledge of the correspondence seems futile.[30] If we are confined merely to perception of the images, we cannot recognise them as images and, even if we get somehow to know them as such, we can never compare them to the objects which, *ex-hypothesi*, lie beyond our konwledge. Representative theory of knowledge, to be true, presupposes a presentative theory of knowledge which, however, makes the former superfluous.

---

29. na hi dve nīle kadācit saṃvedyate, ekam jñānapratibimbakaṃ aparaṃ tadarpakam. TSP, I, 574.

30. Cf. *A Commentary to Kant's Critique of Pure Reason* by N. Kemp Smith, p. 587.

Lastly, it is not easy to explain how the reference is at one time correct and at other times becomes misleading. We are not asking for the genesis of illusion; that, as will be seen later on, cannot be explained. We merely ask that, granting illusion, all that is required to explain it must be posited. The representative theory fails in this respect.

But this theory has at least the merit of narrowing down the possible explanations. It demonstrates that no three-term theory is a consistent hypothesis and that, ultimately, either a self-conscious realism with a two-term theory, or full-fledged idealism, must be accepted.

Realists contend that though the identification of the rope with the snake may be false, yet neither of the two factors involved is individually false.[31] The snake and the rope are each separately real; illusion consists only in the wrong relation between the two unrelated reals. It is not that the snake is not; it is not a creation of the cognising consciousness. The snake is perfectly real in its own right. Its consciousness becomes false only when it perceives the snake where it is not.[32] Even then the illusory snake does not appear anywhere and everywhere.[33] An elephant is never mistaken for a snake. Some of the special features by which a snake is recognised are also present in the rope. Hence the perceiving consciousness does not create the snake from absolute nothing, nor does it project it anywhere it likes, but has to perceive it according to the rigid laws of objectivity.

But, the idealist objects, the sting of the illusory lies in its obstinate refusal to be appropriated by the empirical; the realist tries to find physical antecedents of the illusory. Once the illusory is found to be regulated by laws governing empirical experience,[34] an illusion becomes merely an optical predicament. The essential features of the snake cannot be the same as those of the rope; otherwise the snake would be identical with the rope. To conclude from some closely resembling feature of the snake to the being of the snake itself is the work of mind having no counterpart in the objective. The resemblance may be objective but there is always a gap left. If the rope were perceived in its entirety,

31. NB, V, 142-43.
32. This theory is the anyathākhyātivāda of the Nyāya.
33. MA, p. 42.
34. NB, V, 143.

the perception of it as snake would be impossible. Hence some filling in of the gap[35] is involved here, and this must be the work of the subjective. Were the nature of consciousness merely revelatory, a gap would always be perceived as gap. This transcendence of the given data indicates that mind can perceive only in fixed patterns, even if they are not to be found in the objective. It has a mechanism of its own.

A consistant realist therefore cannot accept even this much falsity of a wrong relation, since creativity in any form would undermine his fundamental contention. For a self-conscious realist aware of these pitfalls, illusion simply does not exist. His analysis of the so-called cases of illusion is very ingenious.

Apparently an illusion consists in perceiving a thing where it is not. A rope is mistaken for a snake. But the realist holds that the snake-consciousness is not a unitary consciousness at all.[36] According to his analysis, the consciousness of 'this is a snake' dissolves itself into those of the 'this' and the 'snake.' The 'this' is actually perceived and is real. The 'snake' however is not a percept at all. It is a memory image and its objective counterpart too is perfectly real. "Perception is in principle veridical."[37] What happens in the so-called perception of the rope-snake is this: the rope being imperfectly apprehended, only its this-ness is perceived, i.e., only its bare presence is noted. Its similarity with the snake evokes the memory of the latter, which is a perfectly real consciousness. These are two distinct states of consciousness having two distinct and real objective counterparts. But this distinction is not apprehended and, consequently, what are in reality two independent consciousnesses, having nothing to do with each other, are perceived as one unitary consciousness. Consciousness cannot perceive what is not given; it cannot import foreign matter to the given data. But it can perceive *less*. It cannot distort, but it can select. It is never the case that what appears in consciousness is not found in the objective. Confusion is not distortion, but merely non-apprehension of the distinction (vivekāgraha).

---

35. Cf. The Gestalt Theory of Perception.

36. This theory is the famous akhyāti-vāda of Prabhākara, who is in some respects even more consistent in his realism than the Nyāya. Cf. *Prakaraṇa-pañcikā*, p. 43 ff.

37. *A Theory of Direct Realism* by Turner, p. 9.

It is a very bold attempt by the self-conscious realist to explain the illusory away, but it is far from being convincing. Were the snake merely a memory-image the form of cancellation ought to be reinstating the snake as an image. But our sublating consciousness is not of the form that what is really an image was not distinguished from the consciousness of objectivity : it is rather that what appeared to confront us is absolutely nothing.[38] To equate the snake which appears here and now to some dubious creature seen we know not when is to assert something which by its very nature cannot be proved.[39] There is not simply non-apprehension of the distinction, but positive confusion. The realist is in fact aware of the distinction between the real and the illusory; otherwise how does he explain the latter in terms of the former ? And yet his attempt is to obliterate this very distinction. His whole analysis is therefore self-stultifying.[40]

One other attempt which is in a way realistic may be noted here. This is the theory of Essences.[41] It is a bold declaration that though the illusory content cannot be incorporated into the realm of existence, it is yet objectively real, belonging to another realm altogether. Ordinarily we do not distinguish between the character of a thing and its objective existence. In illusion the distinction between that which appears and that which exists must be made. Something appears and yet is not. It is a mere essence. An essence is what immediately and literally confronts consciousness, without having any existential implication. An object which is supposed to exist might later on turn out to be illusory. But the fact of its appearance cannot be denied. An essence is not at all affected by the vicissitudes of existence. It is something timeless. "An essence is what anything turns into in our eyes when we do not believe in it. We do not cease to conceive that which we explicitly deny,

---

38. Cf. anirvacanīya-rajatotpatti of the Vedānta.

39. The Nyāya attempts to evade this difficulty by boldly asserting that we are in direct contact with the real snake even here. The contact however is not an ordinary one ; it is jñāna-lakṣaṇā-pratyāsatti. The knowledge of the snake itself is the pratyāsatti here.

40. Cf. *Tattva Pradīpikā* (*Citsukhī*), p. 63.

41. or that of Subsistence which finds its best formuation in Santayana's *Scepticism and Animal Faith*.

and for us then this conceived but denied thing is an essence.... An essence is anything definite capable of appearing or being thought of; the existence of something possessing that essence is an ulterior question irrelevant to logic and to aesthetics."[42] An essence is neither true nor false. The essence perceived in the so-called illusory cognition is as much true as any other essence. It is not in space or time, is neither inside nor outside our consciousness, has no depth beyond what it seems, is in short just what appears. If we rigorously and consistently confine ourselves just to what is literally perceived we arrive at the realm of essence. The empirical objects as well as empirical concepts are so many constructions posited by our 'animal faith,' an irrational instinct. The essences are symbols or signs for the external world which is never really perceived but is always posited. What we do perceive are merely the essences, which constitute a pictorial alphabet as it were, with which we spell the dark world confronting us. This world is to be established not by an appeal to the testimony of our senses, but rather is to be taken for granted, as posited by the 'animal faith.' "Matter is in flux; spirit, while existentially carried along in that movement, arrests some datum, lending it an ideal unity, fixity, and moral colour such as neither the organ of sensation nor the stimulus can possess in themselves. We are, in the texture of our impressions, in the realm of essence; and it is only in the language of essence that spirit can describe its fortunes."[43] If the content of our sense-perception or conception is taken to be real objects and not pure essences, scepticism would dislove every shred of that objective world. Our perception invariably refers to what is not given, i.e., invariably involves a construction. What is actually given might be just a patch of blue, but we perceive a blue object in its stead. Scepticism would go so far as to assert that the patch of blue is not even sensed by the senses, since the mechanism of sensation itself has to be established first. The conclusion is that the essence is not even presented to the senses, but is somehow directly intuited by consciousness.

---

42. *Twentieth Century Philosophy*, p. 317 ; also *Essays in Critical Realism*, passim.

43. *Twentieth Century Philosophy*, p. 320.

It may be seen that this theory closely resembles that of representationism in many important respects. It rejects the naive realism and makes some third entity intervene between the consciousness and the object. But the resemblance stops here. The essence has no subjective associations like an idea or an image. It is not brought into existence by being perceived. It is not a mental fact at all. It is more like a Platonic Idea, eternal and self-subsistent, but has again no implication of universality and superiority over the sensed content like the latter. The theory is an attempt to combine apparently incongruous elements. An analysis quite in the Humean lines is made to yield a conclusion in the tradition of Platonic realism. And these complications merely add to the confusion.

The argument of this theory is rather curious. Criticism is exercised to destroy all evidence for the existence of the objective world, not excluding the spirit, and at the same time, to protect the same world, posited dogmatically by 'animal faith,' from the onslaught of scepticism. When the world is said to be posited by 'animal faith' it is not made clear whether that world exists only in thus being posited, or has a real though unknown existence. Criticism cannot accept the latter alternative, as that would land us in a vicious form of agnosticism. But according to the former alternative, the world would be a construction evoked by the mind because of the perception of the realm of essence. That would entail a full-fledged theory of Avidyā of the Sautrāntika or the Kantian pattern, with the important difference that the essences would not be the constituent data on which the transcendental construction is based, but would always form a separate world of its own. If animal faith be the last word of criticism, any dogmatism may crown the critical enquiry. Once the empirical categories are dissolved by scepticism, they can never be resuscitated by the magic of animal faith, since one dogmatism is as good as another. Moreover, if the whole of the empirical world be a mere construct—as it would be if animal faith were discarded—then there remain only the innumerable essences to be accounted for; and if there are only the simple essences, intuited immediately by the spirit, the illusory, to account for which the theory was propounded, remains as enigmatic as ever.

This brief analysis of the nature of illusion points to the conclusion that the creativity of consciousness must be accepted in one form or the other. But this is not enough to establish idealism, as it leaves a core of objectivity entirely unaffected. Granting that the snake is a subjective creation, it does not in any way tamper with the objectivity of the rope, whose reality in fact made it possible for the snake to appear. Hence the Yogācāra takes that class of illusion as his norm where the object is nothing; dreams supply this norm.

In dreams we get a perfect semblance to the real world which yet has no grounding in objectivity at all. That dreams are illusory there can be no doubt, since they are cancelled on waking.[44] And yet dreams present, not one appraently real event in a world of real events, as the perception of the rope-snake does, but a whole world, complete in itself, having events of its own and regulated by its own laws. When the rope-snake is cancelled, the world remains as it was; merely one element is detached which explodes into nothing; that is to say, it borrows the reality of the external world. But the dream-world is a unique achievement of the creativity of the subjective; it is a complete world in itself; it evinces its own certitude as long as it endures. Its apparent plausibility does not lie in the existence of the real object on which it is superimposed, as that of the snake depends on the existence of the rope, but its existence lies solely in its being projected. The idea of objectivity is certainly there but it is never more than an idea. The fundamental point in this analysis is that the apparent reality dreams possess is not derived from any concrete objective world but merely from the idea of objectivity.[45]

The realist would object that this idea, though efficient in creating the illusion of objectivity, is itself derived from our consciousness of an objective and real world. Even to mistake for the objective world, we must have come across the real objective world. Had we never experienced any real world, we could not have even the idea of objectivity. The Yogācāra answers that this idea is not empirical at all; its origin is sought in experience in vain.[46] The more pertinent objection is that though creativity in the sense of novel arrangement may be admitted, yet the content or the details of the dream-world are all supplied by our waking experience. The objectivity of the individual elements

44. Cf. PVA, p. 23.

45. na ca yad yasya kāraṇam tadabhāve tasyotpattir yujyate. tasmīn nirālambanam eva svapnādāvivānyatrāpi svabījaparipākād arthābhāsam vijñānam utpadyate ityeva jñeyam. MVSBT, p. 10.

46. See further Ch. 4.

of the dream-world is never cancelled.[47] No dream is fantastic enough to present an absolutely strange phenomenon;[48] what it can do is to loosen a thing from its familiar setting and present it in a new context.[49] Its laws are not, it is true, the physical laws of the objective world, yet are the psychological laws of association. The idealist contends that it must be conceded that the objects experienced in dreams lack any immediate objective basis, and the hypothesis of their being constituted by identically the same factors as constitute the waking experience is a possibility that has to be proved and not taken for granted. What the Yogācāra is immediately interested in is to show that a peculiar experience having a complete correspondence to the waking experience—so much so as even to be mistaken for the latter—is yet utterly destitute of any real perceptual basis. It might have a remote connection to the ordinary perception, but during its actual experience is merely a creation of subjectivity. The dream-snake, even if produced by a real snake, is immediately caused by the idea of snake. Dreams illustrate that consciousness can not only create the contents of perception but can even project them as objective, so that the experience of objectivity is no proof of their independence. Objectivity, rather objectification, is an act of consciousness, a transcendental function.

Sahopalambhaniyama demonstrated that the object can never be experienced apart from the consciousness of it. The analysis of dreams completes the argument by showing that consciousness can create and perceive even in the absence of real objects. It shows that consciousness is not transparent or nirākāra, but is creative.[50]

All this amounts, the realist urges, only to the admission that in some exceptional cases, consciousness may be creative in some of its aspects; the reality of the content in a veridical perception remains unchallenged. The idealist now engages himself to the task of demolishing the objective

47. NS, IV, 11-35.

48. Cf. MVSBT, p. 22.

49. The dream-objects must have been experienced before: NS, IV, 11, 34; also SV (*Nirālambanavāda*), 107. The dream-objects are contents of perception according to Gautama, of memory according to Kumārila.

50. MSA, pp. 60-61.

as such. The argument that the world is a dream[51] is, it might be said, an unwarrented universalization of what is applicable only in a limited sphere. Illusion is due to specific and determinate causes and cannot be universalised. Hence it must be shown by an analysis of the object itself that it is by its very nature untenable. Sahopalambhaniyama supplies an epistemological refutation of realism ; to show that the concept of the object is riddled with inherent contradictions, even apart from its relationship to the knowing consciousness being unintelligible, is to refute realism on metaphysical grounds. The question as to how the idealist becomes first aware of the fact of the whole of experience being of the nature of a dream is a different problem altogether and is to be tackled in a different context.[52]

The Category of the Object is Self-Contradictory

What is the content of perception ? What is it that we actually sense ? Obviously the everyday empirical objects, the realist answers. These objects exist independently of their own right, irrespective of their being perceived. The idealist urges that the notion of this object is not tenable. An object can be conceived either as a substance with its attributes or a whole of parts.[53] Mere sense-data are not sufficient to explain the notion of an object. In the perception of sugar, for instance. the senses convey the impressions of whiteness and sweetness. They are conveyed by different senses and yet the object perceived is identical. To connect these different sensations and to impart the sense of unity, the realist posits a substance over and above the attributes. The substance is not a construction but is actually perceived, and perceived by the same sense as conveys the corresponding impression of sense-data. A coloured object is perceived by the sense which perceives colour. But, the idealist asks, what is the substance apart from the various attributes which go to constitute the concept of an object ?[54] This concept is indeed not Lockian ; substance in the Lockian system is never perceived but is postulated. Realists hold that substance is perceived along with its attributes. It is not intelligible, however, how the senses can see an

---

51. tataḥ prabodhāvasthā yā na svapnād bhinnalakṣaṇā. PVA, pp. 28-29 ; also 44.

52. See Chapters 10 and 11.

53. TSP, I, p. 550-51 ; PV, II, 360, 410; also BSSB, II, 2, 28.

54. TS, I, 565, p. 190.

object. The eye can see a blue object, but never a blue and an object. Hence this distinction is not perceptual and it is not told how it has been acquired. It may be said[55] that the same object which is seen to be white, also tastes sweet and hence the distinction. But it is not easy to understand how one thing can be white as well as sweet—i.e., not white—at the same time. It is not that some part of it is white and the other sweet, but the same thing is both; and yet whiteness and sweetness are not identical and one must repel the other.

If substance were conceded to be a subjective fiction, all the difficulties are, it might be held, at an end. Along with substance go all other forms of unity, viz., extension, duration etc. The real splits itself into point-instants or unique particulars (svalakṣaṇas) on which is superimposed the substance-construction. This is a kind of atomism which we shall call the 'attributive atomism' to distinguish it from another kind of it to be mentioned hereafter. The substance is nothing and the attributes are atomised, or rather the attributes themselves are the substances, in the sense of self-existence.

Criticism, once started, cannot be stopped in the midway. What are these attributive atoms or point-instants or unique particulars? These are never encountered in our empirical perception. If the creativity of consciousness be granted to such an extent as to produce the ideas of thinghood, universality etc., it can as well produce those of particularity, uniqueness. If construction as well as objectivity be both admitted side by side[56], it cannot be explained why consciousness should group certain particulars alone and create the idea of a substance, to the exclusion of other particulars which have all ontologically the same claim. Such grouping cannot be governed by the laws of the particulars themselves, and yet, on the other hand, it cannot be arbitrary; hence, if the laws of the creativity of consciousness be admitted, they alone may be admitted and the doctrine of particulars be discarded as superfluous.

Nor can the object be held to be a whole of parts. If there be one universal whole of which the empirical objects are parts[57], then it must

---

55. TS, I, 560, p. 188.

56. This is done by Kant and the Sautrāntika, and, in a totally different manner, by the Advaita Vedānta.

57. This is the Sāṅkhya theory of production.

be asked whether the latter are identical with the whole or not. If not, they cannot be created out of the latter, being different from it; if identical with it their mutual difference cannot be maintained. If the object is a whole made up of its own parts[58], it must be asked what this whole (avayavī) is apart from its parts[59] (avayavas). Where is the cloth when the threads constituting it have been separated?[60] How is it related to the threads? Where does it exist? Does it exist wholly in each of its parts or only partially so? If the former, one part would be identical with the whole, and the rest superfluous. Then, is the whole identical with the parts or different from them? If identical, with which part? And moreover, if it is identical with its parts, it cannot be a separate existent apart from them. But if is something different from the parts, it cannot be related to them, like any other set of two differents. Again, some parts have some features while some have other contradictory ones. A part of the cloth is in the sun and the rest in the shade. Which should be supposed to pertain to the whole?[61] Both cannot pertain to the same whole at the same time, for how can that be one which has opposed characteristics?[62]

The wholes cannot be conceived as unique things[63], each existing in its own right irrespective of its parts, since in that case, they would lack a common measure, each being unique, and no two objects (wholes) can be compared to each other. Nor can the whole be a mere name (sanniveśa-parikalpa)[64] for the aggregate of the parts, since if the collocation does not add anything new to the parts, the very purpose of the collocation is defeated. If the cloth be nothing over and above the threads, nobody would care to make cloth. Moreover, the whole cannot simply be another name for the togetherness of the parts, since these parts again have further parts, and so on, so that each intermediary in the series would be a whole in its turn and so nothing apart from its own

---

58. This is the Nyāya theory of production.
59. TS, I, 579-83, p. 194.
60. VMS, p. 6.
61. PV, II, 200-1.
62. yo'sau viruddhadharmādhyāsavān nāsāvekaḥ.
This is the famous Occam's razor of Buddhism.
63. TS, I, 1998.
64. VMS, p. 8.

parts. Hence what will be left to be perceived will be only the ultimate parts, if any ; and yet what is actually perceived is a gross object.

Even the parts themselves cannot be admitted, since if they have further parts, or if they have no parts in their turn, in either case they cannot be brought to a common measure and yet if we stop anywhere in in the process of continued subdivision, it would be abrupt and arbitrary.

The Atomistic Hypothesis is Unintelligible

It might be held that some ultimate constituents must be accepted; otherwise a mountain would rival a mustard grain in size[65], each being composed of the same number of parts, viz., infinity. Hence we must stop somewhere ; we cannot stop with the least perceptible magnitude, since, being perceptible, it must have extension, and must be made of parts. Here again, we reach the concept of an atom which should be called "substantive atomism"; here a substance is not analysed away into its attributes, but rather is sub-divided into further parts, each of which in its own turn is a substance with its attributes. Each atom is therefore a complex of substance-attributes and is thus not atomic enough. The "attributive atom" or the point-instant is an atom in its true sense, but, to compensate for that, the "substantive atom" is more realistic, since the work of thought has been completely eliminated here.

Our empirical experience employs different kinds of categories; unity as well as diversity are both to be found there. One is not preferred to the other, or rather, sometimes one and sometimes the other is emphasised. The consistent emphasis on one at the cost of the other is the differentia of metaphysics. Even if all are retained, it is a conscious rejection of the negation of any one category, and as such is metaphysics. Categories are broadly of two orders—one which unifies, synthesises, connects and the other which makes for plurality, difference and diversity. The former functions according to the pattern of space and the latter to that of time. That philosophy which takes time as its norm of categories will necessarily be committed to a form of pluralism, and will accept the most unitary and simple as the ultimate real. Obviously only the point-instant (svalakṣaṇa) can be the real according to this philosophy and that realism which explains things from the standpoint of time will accept the "attributive atomism."

65. merusarṣapayoḥ sāmyaprasaṅgaḥ, NK, p. 31.

But the other philosophy which is modelled after the space-pattern will admit substance, the whole, the universal, etc., as the unifying categories. It can accept the attributes over and above the substance, or it may not. If it does, we shall have the "substantive atomism"[66]. But if it does not accept the attributes and has the substance as the sole reality we shall get one universal substrantum on which the plurality of atributes is super-imposed.[67] It will be a form of monism—as it is in the Sāṅkhya and the pre-Saṅkara Vedānta—and when rigorous, absolutism, as in Śaṅkara's system. It may be realistic, as the substance is conceived as something in itself, but is not realism ; the empirical plurality is done away with and yet pluralism is the very essence of realism. The unifying tendency is strong here and the danger always lurks of unifying the subject too with the object. Thus the only forms of realism are first, the rank realism, and secondly, the critical realism of the Sautrāntika type, each explaining phenomena from totally different points of view and each having its own atomism characteristic of its system. The monism[68] of the substance-metaphysics is also realistic, but cannot be called critical realism, since it excludes pluralism.

Hence all forms of realism are atomistic in their ontology, and this is because they are necessarily committed to some form of pluralism or other. This pluralism must be radical and ultimate and not to be accepted half-heartedly. The realistic formula for the deduction of ontological categories is that nothing is merely *in thought*. Every form of thought must have its corresponding form in reality as well[69]. Whatever appears in consciousness is also a factor governing reality. Nothing is merely epistemic. This transference of all thought-categories to the objective realm is the secret of realism. The analysis of thought-forms discloses all the categories : unity and diversity, identity and difference, the universal and the particular, the whole and the parts, are all given in

---

66. This, for instance, is the Nyāya theory of substance and attributes.

67. This pattern is illustrated in the systems of the Sāmkhya, pre-Sankarite Vedānta and Rāmānuja, Śaṅkara and Spinoza.

68. The Advaita Vedānta is the most consistent form of this metaphysics.

69. viṣayātiśaya-vyatirekeṇa pratyayātiśayānupapatteḥ, NM, p. 314.

thought and are therefore real and objective according to the realistic principle. If a plurality of real categories were not accepted, one or the other of these must be given up as merely subjective, as mere thought-construction, and this would be giving up realism altogether. Hence the necessity for a pluralistic metaphysics.

But there is a still deeper reason for the acceptance of pluralism by the realist. Pluralism is necessary for the discovery of the subject. Were the object absolutely one, the experience would be one of uniform monotonous going-on-ness, with no succession or change. In that case, it would be known not even as one ; in fact it would not be a case of knowledge at all.[70] The subject would not be dissociated from the object ; only when one experience ceases and another begins are we aware of a third factor whose continuity[71] is not affected by the change of content. Consciousness itself may not be admitted to be continuous, but its existence is evidenced only by a change in experience. When our experience is of the form 'I know A' and again 'I know B', only then are we aware of the 'I' which is distinct from both A and B.

The discovery of the subject is not the same as that of the subjective, since nothing is subjective for the realist. In fact, only when the subject has been extricated, can we speak of its work being strictly limited to revelation. The subject must first be discovered and analysed as such in order to be shorn of any trace of creativity.

The discovery of the subject is utilised for realistic purposes. The subject being denuded of all activity except that of bare revelation, it loses its place of supremacy and takes its rank as one more object in the democracy of objects. The spirit has nothing spiritual left in it; it is just like any other object. The subject of knowing and the content known both belong to the same category, viz., the objective. Everything is an object. The one does not enjoy any special privilege that the other does not have in the kingdom of things. The subject can even be made

---

70. Cf. *Theory of Mind as Pure Act*, by Gentile, p. 31.

71. We are not giving a particular theory of self ; we are only pointing out how we become aware of the subject as an entity of a different order. This entity, once discovered, would be interpreted differenty in different metaphysics.

the object of a subsequent knowledge; knowledge itself is known like any other object.[72]

The point of the realistic objectification of spirit lies in the fact that the subject being like any other object, its relation to the object is exactly the same as the relation of any one object to another. When a book lies on a table it is only accidentally related to the latter. The relation is temporary and is destroyed as soon as the terms are separated.[73] The book does not suffer any increase or decrease in its being because of its connection with or separation from the table. This doctrine of relations being accidental to the terms related is known as the 'theory of External Relations'. A relation is not intrinsic to the relata—intrinsic in the sense that the latter would not be what they are but for their relation. And since the subject is just another object, the relation of the object to the subject even is only external to the former. A book when known is just like the book on the table. It remains what it is in itself, unchanged before and after the process of being known, as it does in its relation to the table.

This theory of relations can be criticised on general grounds apart from its application to the knowledge-situation. If relation is so external and superficial as not even to touch the terms, it fails in its very purpose of relating. It is not quite intelligible how the relation, without entering into the texture of terms, or affecting their being in any way, can yet bind them together. If it is their nature to be together, they will always be so without the necessity of any *via media*; if it is against their nature,[74] no relation can make one relevant to the other. They cannot be completely indifferent to their being related, since relation does bring about a novelty, a situation which did not obtain before. A distinction must be made between mere A—B and A r B. One must bear upon the other and make its presence felt. Moreover, if relation is a third factor in between the terms it must itself be related to each of them and this leads to an infinite regress.[75] And relation, by its very nature, can never

72. Cf. The doctrine of anuvyavasāya in the Nyāya; also Perry, *Present Philosophical Tendencies*, p. 321.

73. *The New Realism*, p. 118 ff.

74. tasmāt prakṛti-bhinnānāṃ sambandho nāsti tatvataḥ. *Sambandha Parīkṣā*, 2, quoted in *Prameya Kamala Mārtaṇḍa*, p. 505.

75. *Sambandha-parīkṣā*, 4, ibid, p. 506.

be an independent *tertium quid* (pāratantryam hi sambandhaḥ)[76]. In the case of knowledge, were the object absolutely external to the former, it is not seen how the gulf can ever be bridged.[77] The unknown will always remain unknown.

It must not be thought however that because the idealist rejects the doctrine of external relations, he falls into the other error of accepting that of Internal Relations. Generally stated, the theory means that relation is an integral constituent of the terms. It enters into their very being and constitutes them, either partly or wholly. Being known is an essential ingredient of the things known. This might appear to be identical with the idealist's hypothesis, but is not so. If relation constitutes the terms wholly, there is nothing to relate; but if only partially, the term so constituted consists then of two heterogeneous parts, one that is precipitated by the relation and the other which is independent. But these two parts must themselves be related and the difficulty reappears in an aggravated form. In the knowledge-situation, if the object must be known, knowledge is not dependent on its knowing act.[78] In fact there are no two terms in idealism. Its logic is that one term, viz., the object, is wholly precipitated by the relation while the other, viz., the subject, remains entirely free. This conception of relation is neither external nor internal.

To return to atomism. This digression is to show that pluralism gives rise to atomism in some form or other and that realism is necessarily committed to pluralism, so that atomism is chronic in realistic theories. Now the atomistic hypothesis itself must be examined.

The concept of the atom is rather peculiar and realists differ in their accounts of it. The atom is nothing empirical and is never perceived. It is posited by a regressive cosmological analysis. It is a pattern of explanation or what Kant calls an Idea of Reason, postulated in quest of the Unconditioned in Cosmology. It is the Unconditioned, being the uncaused last link in the causal chain of conditions. It is arrived at by arthāpatti (postulation) or speculation and is therefore subject to all the vagaries of this pramāṇa whose employment is notorious in metaphysics. An atom has magnitude and yet is composed of no further parts. It

---

76. Ibid, 1.
77. TSP, I, p. 559 ; PVA, p. 6.
78. See Chapt. 7.

can be compared to the mathematical point[79] which has no extension and still occupies space.

It must never be lost sight of that the postulation of the atom is only the consequent of the pluralistic tendency and if the latter be discountenanced atomism is no longer inevitable. It is the necessary accompaniment of realism which has a predilection for difference rather than identity. Realism has been shown to be untenable on epistemological grounds. It remains to convict it or its atomistic implications of inherent contradictions.[80]

If the ultimate constituents of everything perceived be the atoms they should be perceived as such. Whatever is perceived is of a gross magnitude while the theory maintains that they are really atoms.[81] This disparity cannot be accounted for.[82] It cannot be held that what is perceived is the whole,[83] which, itself not being atomic, is yet made of atoms, since no whole can be admitted over and above the atoms or the ultimate parts.[84] So the dilemma is : the atom is not an object of perception,[85] yet the object of perception is nothing apart from the atoms.[86] Hence the conclusion that what appears in perception has no objective basis is inescapable.

The logic of atomism is that whatever is gross must have parts which have further parts and so on, till we reach the atom which is indivisible and is not of gross magnitude. It might be asked as to why one should stop with the atom. How is it to be certified that it is not constituted of further parts ? Why not continue the process of further sub-division *ad infinitum* ? The realist replies that in that case the biggest and the

---

79. Cf. *Hindu Realism*, by J. C. Chatterjee.

80. For the Mādhyamika criticism of atomism see *Catuḥśataka*, pp. 46-56. *Abhisamayālaṅkārāloka*, pp. 372-74.

81. sthūlākāragrāhakam vijñānam na hi ālambeta sūkṣmākāram viṣayam. anyālambanavijñānam anyālambanānupagrāhāt. VMS (JBORS), XIX, p. 24 ; VMS, p. 16 ; MVSBT, p. 21 ; *Ālambanaparīkṣā*, 1 ; PVA, p. 10.

82. PV, II, 321.

83, Cf. SB, II, 2, 28.

84. MVSBT, p. 21 ; VMS, p. 16.

85. TS, I, 1968-69.

86. VMS (JBORS), XIX, p. 24 ; *Ālambanaparīkṣā*, 2, 5.

smallest objects would be equal in magnitude. But if an object cannot have infinite parts and yet if the process of subdivision cannot be stopped unwarrantedly, it only shows that the hypothesis of ārambhavāda, of wholes being produced out of parts, is itself to be entirely rejected. The acceptance of atoms is only an evasion of the contradictions inherent in ārambhavāda. Once this order of creation is accepted, our stopping anywhere would be arbitrary to the extreme.

The acceptance of mere atoms cannot help the problem of perception, without the whole also being admitted. And yet atoms, even when combined, cannot give up their intrinsic nature (svabhāva).[87] How are the wholes created at all out of the atoms ? An effect cannot have characteristics not produced by any cause. The cause being atomic, wherefrom can the effect have acquired a totally different magnitude—that of grossness ? The parts of a gross object are themselves gross (sthūla) and so on ; then how does that entity which is supposed to stand lowest in the order of gross objects have parts of a different nature ? The hiatus cannot be explained and has to be dogmatically swallowed.

Some try to solve the difficulty by adopting the view that atoms have a dual aspect,[88] viz., individual and general. Only the latter is perceptible. The former can be perceived in Yogi-pratyakṣa. But this subterfuge hardly answers. How can one thing have a dual nature ?[89] In fact we would have, not a single object, but two distinct objects having disparate natures.

Dignāga urges[90] that all objects being atomic, they would give rise to identical perceptions. Diffrences in the perceived objects can be imported either by the number of atoms constituting them or by their size. But the latter alternative is ruled out as the atoms themselves do not have any size. And mere number of the constituent atoms cannot propuce objects of different natures, unless the atoms themselves are different in nature. But, as Śaṅkara argues[91], atoms can have different natures only because of their having different qualities. One atom is different from another because it has a lesser or a greater number of qualities than the other. This is not possible without the atoms varying in size as well, which is not accepted.

---

87. TS, I, 1970.
88. TS, I, 1980-83.
89. TS, I, 1984.
90. *Ālambanaparīkṣā*, 4.
91. BSSB, II, 2, 16.

Thus the crux of the problem is the way in which atoms combine. They must combine in order to produce the gross objects perceived, and yet their nature as something unitary and impartite precludes their combination. It is not easy to understand how one atom is to be conjoined to another[92] or how atoms come into contact with each other. All contact is of parts with parts.[93] An atom being absolutely partless cannot come into contact with another atom. An atom has either further parts or it does not have : if it has, it can no longer be called one and cannot really be an atom. It would become a whole. On the other hand, an absolutely unitary atom would always lead a solitary monadic life. To give rise to extension they must be arranged side by side. One side would be in contact witb one atom, another with another. And that which has sides must have parts.[94] Contact is either wholly or partially; if it is partial, an atom is not impartite and indivisible, i.e., it is not an atom.[95] But if one atom is wholly conjoined to another, the resultant too would be but atomic, as there would be no increase in size. If one atom touches another atom at the same point as a third one does, there would be no increase in size.[96]

In order to get rid of these difficulties the critical realist (the Sautrāntika) might contend that atoms are in reality ever discrete ; the whole is only a construction (vikalpa) superimposed upon these by constructive imagination (kalpanā). But this is a treacherous position to take, as it unwittingly leads to idealism. The construction of the whole is admittedly not due to any objective factor ; and if construction is granted to be purely subjective, the hypothesis of atoms is rendered superfluous, as the whole is all that is required for empirical purposes. Moreover if subjectivity is constructive enough to posit the whole, it can, with equal plausibility, posit the parts. If a basis for construction be required, consciousness itself would serve the purpose. It is thus seen that the concept of objectivity is a futile one and must be cancelled without compunction. It is consciousness alone that makes its own creation appear as though they were outside it (yadantarjñeyarūpam tu bahirvad avabhāsate).

---

92. Cf. *Theory of Mind at Pure Act,* p. 114, 169.

93. TSP, I, p. 556.

94. digbhāgabhedo yasyāsti tasyaikatvam na yujyate. VMS, p. 7.

95. TS, I, 1992.

96. TSP, p. 556.

Chapter IV

SOME OBJECTIONS ANSWERED

The argument of the previous chapter amounts to the refutation of realism, on epistemological as well as metaphysical grounds. But this is not enough to establish idealism. In metaphysics the Law of Excluded Middle cannot be applied in the form of an apagogic proof. Hence all systems of philosophy establish their own theories in two ways : (i) by employing the apagogic proof, and (ii) also by putting forward a claim to interpret experience consistently on its own principles. The first or the critical part of the Yogācāra Dialectic consists in refuting the hypothesis of objectivity—of an independent object existing outside consciousness and confronting it,— and to this extent it makes common cause with pure criticism (the Mādhyamika Dialectic). But being a speculative system it has to be on the defensive when it comes to the second part of its argument. Here, mainly the objections by the realist are to be considered.

The Empirical World is Regulated by Laws

The first question that arises is obvious enough. If the whole of our empirical experience be but a dream, what happens to the physical world, regulated by physical laws, strict and rigorous ? We cannot cause the falling of a single leaf from the tree, however hard we may think of it. If the object is only a creation of our mind, why can we not produce it at our sweet will ? No effort need ever be made[1] to bring anything about since all one has to do is to shut one's eyes and let loose unreal fancies. Mere ideas cannot feed and clothe; if they could all empirical intercourse would be at an end. Nobody has any relish for a Bermecide's feast. An idea has no efficiency.

The objection is based on a misunderstanding. If the nature of the dream-experience had been correctly understood the objection would not arise. It is accepted on all hands that dreams are sheer crea-

1. Cf. *Prameya Kamala Mārtaṇḍa*, p. 51.

tions of the subjective. Even then we cannot cause any particular event to happen in the dream-experience. Nobody likes to have bad dreams, yet bad dreams do happen. In fact dreams are governed by their own laws, different indeed from those which govern the so-called empirical world, but none the less exact for that. Our conscious or waking will has ordinarily no jurisdiction over the dream-experience. Seeds of the dream experienced at the present moment have possibly lain dormant for a considerable time till they were ripe enough to burst into efflorescence of the variegated dream. The cause of it lies deep in the innermost recesses of consciousness where ordinarily we cannot exercise our will and which is generated by our past experiences.

Now we can see why the empirical world, in spite of being a construction, can yet not be modified or affected by our empirical will. We cannot choose the objects of our experience. One can avert one's eyes, but if one sees at all, one cannot help seeing the empirical objects as they are. These latter indeed seem almost to force themselves upon our senses. That will in fact which constructs the empirical world is the Transcendental Will. No system of philosohpy can afford to tamper with the least factor of the empirical experience. To reduce the whole of experience to a subjective construction is indeed a radical departure in metaphysics, and yet it leaves all our empirical activities entirely unaffected[2]. The Yogācāra is an idealist only transcendentally; in empirical matters he has no quarrel with the realist. All philosophical issues lie between the conflicting interpretations of facts and not between the facts themselves. It is not the case therefore that idealism violates the empirical activities.

Efficiency is The Mark of The Real

Waiving these considerations aside, is it possible for a mere idea to do the work of the real objects ?[3] Can an idea be efficient ? Efficiency or arthakriyākāritva is the pragmatic test of reality.[4] Whatever has no efficiency can lay no claim to reality. It is obvious that ideas cannot have efficiency; ideas cannot feed and clothe us. Even if fantasies do seem to have some efficiency, in that they can elate or depress, no amount of

---

2. TSP, I, p. 553 ; PV, II, 394. sāpi tadrūpanirbhāsā tathā niyatasaṅgamāḥ. buddhirāśritya kalpyeta yadi kiṃ vā virudhyate.

3. *Prakaraṇa Pañcikā*, p. 58.

4. TSP, I, p. 553.

ideas can fill an empty stomach[5]. Moreover, even this limited efficiency is itself possible because of the existence of real, physical objects. An imaginary amour can entice one only so long as it is mistaken for reality. Were an idea to be steadily realised for what it is, it loses all power to fascinate us. Its apparent efficiency is a borrowed one.

An ideal feast would not be objected to if it were clearly distinguished from one enjoyed by the empirical imagination. The objection presupposes that the distinction between the imaginary and the real has been overlooked,[6] whereas the idealist is very much aware of the distinction. As has been said before, to reduce everything to ideality makes no empirical change.[7] That our experience is manifold and variegated cannot be gainsaid; the point is whether the content experienced is wholly within it, or enjoys an existence even when not experienced.[8] Even if it does not, experience as such remains what it would be were the content real. If the feast and the satisfaction therefrom were both ideal or real, it matters little; the incongruity will arise only if the feast were ideal and the satisfaction real, not otherwise.[9] Experience would remain the same. What is required is that this ideality should be sharply distinguished from the empirical one.

It is not true to say that an idea has no efficiency.[10] Who has not suffered from the horrors of nightmares ?—a suffering not a whit less poignant than the suffering engendered by real horrors. The fright of a rope-snake is not seldom potent enough to kill a man. Efficiency itself is a mere idea.[11] If it be said that here the apparent efficiency does not belong to the idea as such, but is acquired only when it is mistaken for reality, the idealist answers that this mistake is all that is required. He never maintains that an idea, even when realised as such, will still be efficient. An idea can bind, only when the illusion of objectivity is present. But it is never more than a mistake. Hence the ideal efficiency

5. Cf. Kant's Hundred Dollar Argument.

6. SV, *Nirālambanavāda*, 88-91 ; BSSB, II, 2, 28.

7. Cf. na jātu rūpasya abhāva (iti brūmaḥ), vijñānapariṇāmastu tad. VMS (JBORS), XIX, p. 22.

8. PV, II, 334.

9. PVA, p. 98.

10. TSP, I, p. 553.

11. Ibid, p. 553.

consists in this transcendental illusion of perceiving the ideal as something objective. This objectification is a transcendental category. An idea is itself generated only when impelled by this primordial Avidyā, so that its being and its efficiency are both due to the transcendental illusion. Real objectivity is superfluous; the illusion of one is sufficient.

Illusion is not Possible Without Reality

But is illusion possible without a real experience ? Even to be mistaken, that for which a thing is mistaken, must have been previously experienced.[12] A person who has had no real experience of a snake can have no illusory experience of it either.[13] Even dreams where the subjective is most at play do not present us with a totally novel experience. No dream is so strange but that its individual constituents can be traced to past experiences. Hence if we had not come across real objective things, the idea of objectivity could not have arisen and the transcendental illusion itself would not be possible.

The argument resolves itself into two totally different contentions. One is that the contents of an illusory experience can be traced back to real experience.[14] Since the illusory snake can be caused only by the idea of snake, which again is the impression of the experience of a real snake, so the latter is the indispensable antecedent to the experience of the rope-snake. But to insist too much on the supposed causal connection is to rob the illusory of its whole sting. The illusory snake would in that case be no more than the memory of a snake-experience. Granting even this, that an ideal snake has been objectified cannot be questioned, and so idealism is essentially established. The further question as to whether the idea itself is generated by a real experience is not so important after this concession. The idea has certainly a cause, but this cause itself may be ideal,[15] without any appeal to reality at all, and with no detriment to experience.[16] If all that is required for illusion is an idea, this may be supposed to be generated by another idea[17] and so on.

---

12. VMS, p. 17 ; VMS (JBORS), XIX, pp. 43-5 ; MVSBT, p. 15.

13. PV, II, 361-3 ; also Cf. MA, p. 54.

14. NB, IV, 2, 34; NM, p. 545 ; NK, p. 185 ; SV (*Nirālambana-vāda*), 108-11.

15. TSP, I, p. 582 ; PV, II, 323.

16. Ibid, p. 553.

17. *Ālambanaparīkṣā*, 6-7 ; PVA, p. 21.

The case with the idea of objectivity is different. There is no idea of objectivity in general. Particular things can be perceived as objective, but pure objectivity can never be perceived. In other words, objectivity is not a sensum; it is only a category, the most fundamental one for the idealist, which is diversified into all other categories. In fact this category itself projects the contents categoriesd (ātmadharmopacāra in vijñānapariṇāma), as if the form were to create its matter, It is the presupposition of all experience. So the realists' contention that were there no experience of real objective things the idea of objectivity could not arise, misses the point. Particular things can be experienced as objective and they can leave their impressions. Objectivity, not being a sensum at all, has no impression corresponding to it. Hence the idea of objectivity is strictly speaking not an idea at all, notwithstanding the fact that it governs all particular ideas constituting empirical experience. To perceive a thing and to perceive it as objective is one and the same function, since the form is only as it is manifested in its matter—a matter projected by the inherent creativity of form, according to the Yogācāra. There being no experience of objectivity as such, and yet all experience being as though of the objective, the idea of objectivity is nothing empirical. That is to say, it is not an abstraction from, but a presupposition of, experience. It is an *a priori* function —a transcendental category —the category of categories *par excellence.*

Since even an idea can serve as bondage, the objection that idealism cannot establish a discipline is futile. Suffering, it is said, is caused by the want of desirable things and by the contact with the undesirable ones. Somebody wants wealth but is prevented from acquiring it, and therefore suffers. Were there no real wealth, there would be no suffering. Spiritual discipline serves to create a feeling of indifference towards all worldly objects. It is not however true to say that the mere existence of objects creates suffering. So long as one does not hold them as *desirable* or *undesirable* they have no power to bind. Spiritual discipline causes no change in the status of objects. Only the wrong idea, that what is really dross is yet held desirable, is to be eradicated. Ultimately all discipline is to modify our idea of things, and not the things themselves. Not only is the idea a bondage, it is the sole bondage. This much granted, objects do not matter, since an idea can bind even in the absence of objects, as evinced by nightmares.

The Waking World cannot be Reduced to the Dream-World

Idealism holds that all over empirical experience is of the nature of a dream. Just as in the latter experience things appear as existing in space and time and yet have no existence apart from their being experienced, so in the case of our waking experience as well. Here, the realist objects, are not these two experiences utterly disparate and heterogeneous in nature so as to constitute two different realms altogether ? If there be no difference in their natures how is even a distinction made ? That there is a distinction is evident enough. Waking experience is never known to be sublated[18] and sublation constitutes the main criterion of the unreality of an experience. If the empirical experience be but a dream, why is it that a particular content is experienced only in a determinate space and time, as though it were governed by the laws of objectivity ? What is merely subjective need not be subject to any rigidity or determinateness. An ideal thing may happen at any time and anywhere[19] simply because it is not in space and time at all.

It cannot be questioned therefore that there does obtain a difference in nature between a dream and a waking experience. The ground of this difference must be closely enquired into. As has just been said, the criterion of unreality is sublation. One experience is sublated by another when that latter itself commands our conviction ; otherwise it would not cancel the former at all. Dreams are realised to be subjective only on waking. An illusion can be cancelled only by perceiving the real. So, the reality of the waking experience must be granted since there is no other way of sublating the dream-experience. We are aware of the subjectivity of the latter because it is purely ideal, not based on reality. The difference can be maintained when the dream is held to be ideal while waking experience is supposed to be rooted in reality.

Once this difference is obtained, the whole thing is set upside down, the realist urges, by the idealist. Experience in general is taken to be unreal, just like a dream. The argument cannot be enforced, since the example itself cannot be established. We are thus led into a curious predicament. The reality of the waking experience is the presupposi-

---

18. BSSB, II, 2, 28 ; *Śavarabhāṣya*, 1, 1, 5 ; SV, p. 237.

19. NK, p. 130 ; MA, VI, 55. Another point of distinction is also made that dreams are not subject to the moral law, while the other is. VMS, p. 9 ; Cf. NV, IV, 3, 34.

tion of the sublation of dreams, and yet the former itself is sought to be proved unreal on the strength of the latter[20]. Were the waking experience unreal, we lack the only means for realizing the unreality of dreams, and this therefore cannot serve as an index of the unreality of the former.

The Yogācāra contends that these considerations do not affect his idealism. As to the argument that since the waking experience is never sublated[21] it cannot be unreal, he replies that the unreality of an experience cannot be realised so long as the experience is actually enjoyed. The common folk who are under the sway of the Cosmic Illusion are not expected to find the empirical world illusory. Only the elect who, after practising a strenuous discipline, literally sees everything as subjective, can realise the illusoriness of the empirical experience and to him alone is the world but a dream.[22] In fact, were the world real no discipline would ever be needed.

Because it is ideal it does not mean that the empirical world is subject to no laws.[23] Ideality should not be construed as chance or lawlessness. Dream-objects are admittedly ideal, yet they are governed by their own laws. That an empirical object is determined by a fixed space and time is no proof of its reality, since even a dream-event does not happen anywhere and at any time. As said before, creativity belongs, not to our empirical imagination, but to the transcendental will. Past ideas and experiences leave their impressions in the Âlaya-Vijñāna, which are the seeds ripening into the present ideal experiences. Simply because all efficiency (arthakriyākāritva) is transferred to the ideal realm, it does not detract one whit from their rigour and precision.

That there does obtain a difference between the dream and the waking experience, it is not in the interest of the idealist to deny. He does make a distinction between them though he may assert their natures to be identical. The sublation of dreams by waking experience means, not that the latter must be accepted as real, but that respective subjectivities of the two experiences are of different orders. Dreams are relatively more unreal than the other; their ideality is more easily recognised.

---

20. Cf. *Prameya Kamala Mārtaṇḍa*, p. 50.
21. Ibid, p. 78.
22. VMS, p. 9 ; PVA, p. 59.
23. PV, II, 336.

It is as though there are dream-episodes in one universal drama of dream, and the former may serve as index of the subjectivity of the latter. The sublation of dreams is still within the background of a cosmic subjectivity. The difference is one of degree, not of kind. Dreams are of short duration, i.e., are less coherent than the other; the sublation of the latter is not of anything in particular, but of the objectivity itself. There is no incongurity in both of them being essentially the same, and yet one maintaining a sort of a relative distinction from the other. The world perceived by the waking experience may be taken as real for all empirical purposes; it is ideal only transcendentally.

The Empirical World is Intra-Subjective

Another objection which is really fatal to some kinds of idealism is made much of by the realists. The object is nothing apart from the experience of it. In dreams things appear to exist outside consciousness but are merely subjective projections. This is to be applied to the waking-experience as well. This overlooks a fundamental difference between dreams and the waking experience. A dream is peculiar to that person alone who is actually experiencing it. Other minds have no inkling even of it. Such is not the case with the waking experience.[24] It is not the exclusive privilege of any one individual to perceive it. Whosoever has the capacity of experiencing can perceive it irrespective of his individual mental make-up. It is not a private world, as the dream-world is; it is *the* world. This intra-subjective nature of the empirical world would not be possible were it identical with the experience of it, since in that case there would be as many worlds as there are persons experiencing. No two persons can communicate with each other, having no common platform to stand on.

The Yogācāra agrees that what we call the common world does not really exist. The so-called intra-subjective world is only another name for the harmony between the experiences of the various streams of consciousness (cittasantāna). Each subject creates his own world[25] which exists solely in his experience of it. The creation of one coincides, not

24. bahu-cittālambanībhūtam ekam vastusādhāraṇam, tat khalu naikacittaparikalpitam....kintu svapratiṣṭham. *Yogasūtrabhāṣya*, IV, 15.

25. MVSBT, pp. 16-17.

indeed in all respects, but in some important respects, with that of another ; this produces the semblance of *the* world. What obtains in reality is an infinite plurality of worlds,[26] i.e., of experiences, each experience being objectified into a world ; the objective world is not a reality. The partial coincidence of the various experiences results in a harmony ; and since one cannot jump out of one's skin and see the other people's worlds, the slight differences in the various worlds remain unnoticed, there being no way of comparison. It is as though two persons were to suffer from the same or similar hallucination.[27] The experience of each is peculiar to him and yet their similarity seems to be a corroboration of the objectivity of the contents projected by the hallucinations.

This is not all, the realist urges. The existence of other minds is itself not compatible with the idealists' doctrine of sahopalambhaniyama. The same consideration which does away with the objective world makes short work of other minds as well. If whatever is experienced has no existence apart from the experience of it, other minds also must be reduced to so many ideas in *my* mind—other minds returning the compliment to me. There is no justification in distinguishing between the objective world and other minds; both are in the same predicament. This doctrine entails therefore the absurdity that 'I' am the sole existing being, everything else, including other minds, being just so many creations of my own ideas. The logical conclusion of idealism is a solipsism of an extreme type, and the idealist wanders about, poor and solitary, with nothing more substantial than his ghostly phantasmagoria. As to who this privileged 'I' is to be, the minds, if any, may quarrel with one another ; each 'I' will think this quarrel itself as purely ideal.

---

26. This bears a close resemblance to Leibnitz' Doctrine of Pre-established Harmony. Monads are 'windowless' ; they cannot interact. Each is governed by laws intrinsic to itself. Its entire experience is merely the budding forth of its own latent seeds. But because of a partial identity, confusedly apprehended, there arises the illusion of interaction and the intra-subjective world. Cf. *The Philosophy of Leibnitz* by Bertrand Russell, pp.43-48 ; 137-38.

27. VMS, p. 9; MVSBT, pp. 16-17 ; *Buddhist Logic* by Stcherbatsky, I, p. 523.

Here we shall make two points ; first that solipsism is not as contemptible a doctrine as realists try to make it ; and secondly, that the Yogācāra is not a solipsist.

As to the first contention. Since the subject evaporates along with the object, it is wrong to urge that the subject or the ego alone remains. The 'I', if not as unreal, is as unstable as the object. The experience of the seemingly independent object can alone sustain the subject-object relation. Hence even solipsism might serve as one of the approaches to the Absolute[28]. Nor is any of the empirical activities violated by solipsism. If we can dispense with the intra-subjective world, the other minds can as well be dispensed with. Whether the whole of the empirical experience be real or ideal, the facts themselves are not changed. Only their metaphysical status is affected and that too fundamentally. Hence no empirical activity nor any discipline need be any the worse for solipsism.

Granting even that solipsism as a metaphysical doctrine is seriously inadequate, it is no charge against the Yogācāra, since his idealism does not entail solipsism. To be involved in the subject-object relation presupposes a lapse on the part of pure Will, which lapse cannot be further explained; it has to be taken for granted. Once this is clearly grasped, the question whether the number of the subjects should be one or many would seem a fruitless one. The subject is a subject only so long as the false duality of the subject and object (grāhadvaya) is superimposed upon pure Will, i.e., so long as it suffers under an illusion. There can be no necessity in Cosmic Illusion. The very essence of illusion is that it is something arbitrary, a freak out of nothing as it were. Just as there is no justification for the undivided consciousness even to assume the role of a solitary subject, so it may as well become many, due to the same transcendental lapse.[29] So the plurality of subjects may not be established on epistemological grounds and may yet be granted on metaphysical considerations. Taking this ultimate arbitrariness into consideration, the Yogācāra is not repugnant to the existence of other minds.

---

28. Cf. The doctrine of ekajīvavāda in the Vedānta. *Siddhānta-Leśa-Samgraha*, pp. 20-21 ; Cf. *Citsukhī*, p. 383.

29. Cf. Bradley, *Appearance and Reality*, p. 226.

Svasamvedena is Unintelligible

A very fundamental objection is raised by the realist against the Yogācāra. Knowledge by its very nature is knowledge *of* something outside knowledge. The 'of'-relation is a real relation. Were consciousness the sole reality, knowledge cannot even arise. If the idea of blue be the only reality, and the blue be identical with it, then the idea has to perform two functions at once:[30] it has to project the blue appearing as its form or prakāra and at the same time to know it as blue. It has to be both the subject and the object and these two are incompatible with each other.[31] An idea cannot turn upon itself and view itself as the other. How can one thing become the knower and the known at the same time ? It is as plausible as an axe cutting itself. That which operates and that which is operated upon are two totally different, if not opposed, things and cannot be reconciled in the bosom of the same entity. Were knowledge to know itself, its mode would be 'I know knowledge' and not 'I know blue.' This latter is possible when the blue is something distinct from the experience of it.

The Yogācāra answers that the content-knowledge arises because knowledge has that peculiar form. Knowledge as such cannot be known and this precludes the possibility of the mode, 'I know knowledge.' A knowledge is a particular idea which has its specific content projected by itself. As to the same thing performing two functions at once, his contention is not only that it is possible for consciousness to know itself, but that it is even necessary for any knowledge to occur. Strictly speaking, it is not only two, but even three functions performed at once. An idea is objectified, and has to know this objectified self ; this awareness itself must be immediately known. Consciousness is bifurcated into subject and object, and the subject knowing the object must be aware of its knowledge. And yet these three are not different parts or aspects of a single thing. To be objectified and to be aware of this object is one and the same function. All consciousness is self-consciousness, not indeed in the sense that the knowledge 'there is a blue' is identical with 'I know blue', but in the sense that the knowledge of blue is not to be evidenced by another knowledge. Each knowledge

---

30. MA, p. 59 ; BCA, p. 392-9.
31. TS, I, 2063 ; SV (*Śūnyavāda*), 64.

stands self-revealed.[32] Were it the case that knowledge did not know itself, it would have to depend upon another to be made known, and this would lead to an infinite regress.[33] Moreover, if one moment of consciousness is to be cognised by another, the former can no longer be said to be consciousness ; it becomes for all intents and purposes an object. In fact, the subsequent moment cannot know the previous moment at all, since the latter is dead by the time the former arises[34]. The knower has to know and cannot therefore be in the necessity of being known. It is because knowledge is self-evident, that it can make other things evident.[35] If knowledge were not self-revealed, it would be on a par with the object.[36] Light reveals objects, but if it had itself to be revealed by another factor, there would be no end to the process, with the result that nothing would be revealed after all.[37] That which does not know itself, cannot know anything else.[38] Even if, *per impossible*, it does know other things, it would not be aware of its knowledge, and that is the same thing as not knowing it at all. To know is at the same time to be conscious of knowing; unconscious knowledge is a contradiction in terms. It is not that the subject is explicitly referred to in each case of knowledge ; the subject stands self-revealed.

Realists cannot accept this. Once it is admitted that objects depend upon another to be evidenced while consciousness is self-evident, the latter must necessarily be put in a higher category than the object, and the main plank of realism, viz., everything is an object, is demolished. The place knowledge occupies in the kingdom of things becomes unique and the relation to knowledge becomes a necessity for all objects, thus losing their independence. Realists therefore reduce knowledge just to one object among other objects. Knowledge itself is known, like any other object, by a further knowledge (Nyāya) ; or, awareness of knowledge is deemed impossible (Bhāṭṭa). In either case knowledge

---

32. PV, II, 326-27.

33. TS, I, 2025.

34. PV, II, 427.

35. apratyakṣopalambhasya nārthadṛṣṭiḥ prasajyate, TS, I, 2074; also 2021.

36. PV, II, 480.

37. PVA, p, 73.

38. PV, II, 444.

is not possible. In the Vedānta, consciousness itself is never known[39]; but it is the presupposition of all particular knowledge. The Yogācāra does not accept pure consciousness in empirical knowledge ; for him all knowledge is sākāra ; hence its form and the awareness of that form are identical. Therefore the phala of perception is said to be, not content-knowledge, but only self-knowledge.[40] It perceives its own form, i.e., itself.

It may be asked : how is inference to be distinguished from perception ? Inference is understood as mediate knowledge, i.e., where the object is not actually perceived, but is accepted to be present because of some mark or sign. But since nothing exists apart from the knowledge of it, the distinction between mediacy and immediacy cannot be maintained. The fire perceived and the fire inferred are alike in both being non-different from their respective knowledges, and hence the question does not arise whether the fire is immediately present or not. The distinction between the perceptual and the inferential knowledge is that in both cases the object remains identical while our mode of knowing it differs. But since each knowledge creates its own object, the object of perception would be different from that of inference, the knowledges being different. And without the identity of the object the distinction between the pramāṇas cannot be maintained.

As has been repeatedly urged, idealism has nothing to do with experience as it obtains empirically. All distinctions are scrupulously retained ; only they are enveloped by one sweeping experience. Granting that the objects are different with difference in knowledge and their identity is not factual, an idea yet arises having that very form of identity. Real identity is not required, the semblance of one being sufficient.

The same consideration is applicable to the case of memory also. In memory, the object perceived and the object remembered are different[41], since the knowledges are different. Yet the semblance of identity is itself just an idea, which refers indeed to the previous idea

39. avedyatve sati aparokṣavyavahārayogyatvam. *Advaita Siddhi*, pp. 768 ff.

40. PV, II, 332, 339 and 350.

41. *Śāstra Dīpikā*, p. 156.

having the form of perceptual content. The knowledge of a recalled object is rather a very complex idea, but a mere idea nevertheless.

Some realists contend that the idealists' assertion that an idea is produced *as though* like an external object is very queer. A thing can be like another when the latter itself is real. Nothing can be compared to a barren woman's son or a square-circle. Were objectivity as fictitious as these, it cannot be said that an idea is projected like an external object. The idealist is in fact aware of the distinction between an internal idea and an external object,[42] and still his whole task is to obliterate this very distinction. The objection is only a new guise of a previous one that there can be no illusion without a real objective basis. Objectivity is a transcendental category which is not reducible to any further extent. An idea is projected having the form of objectivity[43] and there the matter ends.

These and similar objections[44] can be infinitely multiplied, but can be met if the fundamental pattern of idealism be kept in mind. The Yogācāra concludes that objectivity is an illusion; experience suffers no loss, loses none of its richness and variety, if an unintelligible hypothesis is discarded.

---

42. BSSB, II, 2, 28 ; Also *Prameya Kamala Mārtaṇḍa*, pp. 50-51.

43. MVSBT, p. 15 ; PVA, p. 95.

44. Objections against the momentariness of consciousness, raised in very many places in Brāhmanical texts, are not considered here, as kṣaṇikavijñānavāda is not the ultimate position of the Yogācāra. Cf. Chapter 7.

CHAPTER V

THE THREE VIJÑĀNAS

In the last chapter the Yogācāra maintained that there is no unsurmountable difficulty in accepting idealism, that no empirical distinction is ever done away with, whatever metaphysics be embraced. But establishing idealism merely on these general grounds is not enough. The claim that all phenomena are explicable on its own principles must be substantiated. Vijñāna which is the sole reality, yet diversifies itself into the complex of terms and relation, and every step of this process must be shown in detail. Here we come to the system proper, i.e. the constructive aspect of the Yogācāra metaphysics for which the last two chapters have paved the way.

The only existent is Vijñāna, and yet what we perceive is an infinite plurality. This plurality must be reflected in Vijñāna itself. Kinds of Vijñāna therefore must be accepted to account for the empirical distinctions. The Yogācāra accepts three kinds of Vijñānas, viz., 1. Ālayavijñāna, 2. Manovijñāna, and 3. Pravṛtti-vijñānas. The evolutes of Vijñāna are infinite, and yet these are the three stages of its evolution.

These three are not to be construed as distinct and static categories, but rather as so many phases of the cosmic evolution of Vijñāna. Vijñāna diversifies itself and gives rise to the whole panorama of empirical existence, and these three Vijñānas represent different stages of this diversifying process. The difference is only that of the degree of self-determination. Again, just as none of the evolutes has an absolute existence of its own so here none of these three is ultimate. The evolution itself is not ultimate, though it is a real process; it is caused solely by an illusory idea. Once this idea of objectivity is eradicated, all the three Vijñānas revert to the pristine purity of Vijñaptimātratā. Nevertheless each of them is a Vijñāna, being essentially creative. The essence of Vijñāna is creativity, since the whole being of the content consists only in its being projected by the knowing consciousness ; and this activity is exercised by all the three.

Ālaya-Vijñāna

The first and most fundamental of these three is the Ālaya-Vijñāna. It is the first phase in the process of differentiation of pure Vijñāna. It is called Ālaya,[1] as it is the place or the receptum in which are contained the seeds or impressions (vāsanā) of any karma whatsoever, good, bad or indifferent. All dharmas ensue from it as its effects or evolutes.[2] It is called therefore 'sarva-bījaka,' being the cause of everything empirical. It is vipāka because any kind of karma, done by the individual in any sphere of existence, leaves its trace in the Ālaya.

Thus the Ālaya serves two functions in the cosmic process. It is the receptum of the impressions of past vijñānas, while in its own turn it gives rise to further vijñānas by maturing those impressions.[3] The whole order is cyclic. The cosmic evolution has therefore two aspects : first, the replenishment of vāsanās in the Ālaya, and secondly, the fructification of these into further vijñānas, which again lay their own seeds in the Ālaya and so on.

The accumulation of seeds of vijñāna in Ālaya is called the hetu-pariṇāma, while their actualisation, the phala-pariṇāma.[4] Both are pariṇāma, since the Ālaya incessantly undergoes change; it is momentary. Hetu-pariṇāma is the development and maturity of vāsanās in the Ālaya, and phala-pariṇāma is the emerging into existence of their respective effects. Vāsanā is to be understood as the motive force[5] governing the evolutionary process. It is of two kinds.[6] : 1. Vipāka-vāsanā

---

1. VMS (JBORS), p. 49 ff. ; MVSBT, pp. 27-28; Cf. *Note sur l' Ālaya-vijñāna* by Poussin, MCB, II, 1934-5, pp. 148-168 ; also G. Lamotte, MCB, III, pp. 169-255.

2. sarvadharmā hi ālīnā vijñāne teṣu tat tathā. anyonyaphalabhāvena hetubhāvena sarvadā. *Abhidharmasūtra* quoted in MVSBT, p. 28.

3. dharmāḥ ālaya-vijñāne dharmeṣu ca vijñānam tathā phalasvabhāvaśca anyonyam hetusvabhāva api sadā. *Mahāyāna-Abhidharma-Sūtra* quoted in VMS (JBORS), p.53. Cf. also *Mahāyāna-saṃgraha* quoted in the same page. Also, MVSBT, p. 28.

4. VMS (JBORS), p. 46-47 ; VMS, p. 18.

5. iṣyate vāsanāvidbhiḥ śaktirūpā hi vāsanā. PVA, p. 22. Cf. jñānasyaiva śaktimātram vāsanā. *Nyāyaratnākara* on SV, *Śūnyavāda*, 17, p. 273.

6. VMS, p. 18 ; MVSBT, p. 28.

and 2. Niḥṣyanda-vāsanā. Vipāka-vāsanā is more ultimate, being that which keeps going the stream of mental process, i.e., the continuity of the individual through the successive births. When the repercussions of previous karmas come to an end and death intervenes, the activity of vipāka-vāsanā forces the Ālaya-vijñāna into a new stream, beginning from the next birth of the individual. Niḥṣyandavāsanā is the fructification of the present experiences ; due to the maturity of this, the other vijñānas—kliṣṭa manas and the various pravṛttivijñānas—evolve out of the Ālaya. Vipākavāsanā maintains the cycle of births ; niḥṣyandavāsanā supplies the content of each birth. Pravṛttivijñānas alone, being conscious experience proper, can lay both sorts of vāsanās in the Ālaya ; only a conscious experience can be good or bad and can supply the seeds of future experiences. Manovijñāna is more or less a function; it supplies only the niḥṣyanda-vāsanā, the force which impels the present experiences.

It has been seen before that vijñāna is essentially creative. A transparent and diaphanous consciousness cannot be admitted. It must by its very nature have a content, a content projected by itself.[7] The Ālaya therefore must have a content. Its content cannot be any empirical one, since it is itself nothing empirical. Its content is an objectivity not differentiated into specific forms. It is an indeterminate content,[8] a bare otherness confronting the Ālaya. The object is so pure that it is not even felt as an 'other.'[9] Since the object is absolutely indeterminate, the subject is totally engrossed in a colourless contemplation of it with no idea of its own dissociation. It is not knowledge in the ordinary sense of the term. The subject is not even a subject in the sense of a self-conscious knower. The knowledge here is a mere 'going-on-ness,' a perpetual monotony.

This bare objectivity is the first precipitation of the transcendental illusion, the primal projection by pure consciousness. The Ālaya is not therefore pure : it already contains the seed of self-disruption in the form of this implicit duality. The process of bifurcation of consciousness has started. Hence it is said that the Ālaya functions in two

7. Why the Absolute Consciousness does not have a content with be discussed in the seventh chapter.

8. VMS, p. 19.

9. Ibid, p. 19.

ways : (1) internally, i.e., consciousness appearing as the constituents of an individual, and (2) externally as consciousness of the undifferentiated objectivity[10] (aparicchinnākārabhājana).

This bifurcation is very essential for the Ālaya to give rise to further determinations. Were an entity integrally one and wholly of one piece, nothing can disturb its eternal quiescence. It will be just like space whose unitary nature precludes the possibility of its ever being unbalanced. Hence an initial lack of harmony must be posited to account for the cosmic evolution. It must be internally unstable. The idea of pure objectivity or of bare otherness, confronting the Ālaya, cannot let it rest in peace; as soon as the externality is consciously realised, its indeterminateness dissolves itself into an infinite plurality of empirical determinations, since it has been shown above that there can be no conscious awareness of bare objectivity. To realise anything as objective, it must be known as dissociated from the subjective, and this is possible only when the objective is a plurality. Consciousness as ridden by the idea of indeterminate objectivity is the Ālaya. But both the terms of this opposition are still pure, i.e., are not at an empirical level.

As has been noted, the root of all projections is their respective vāsanās—the vāsanā of an individual ego and that of the objective elements of existence; it is because of the presence of these that the illusion of an ego and of a world is created. But the presence of these vāsansās in the Ālaya cannot be noted by any consciousness.[11] Vāsanā is not an object of knowledge but its presupposition. It is the tendency or the propensity on the part of consciousness to create an 'other' and to project it as distinct from itself. This tendency itself, not being a thing or an entity, cannot be known as such. So also, the objectivity that confronts the Ālaya is said to be unknown[12]; to know a thing is to make it definite, to fix its place in the order of things, by differentiating it from all the rest of the objective. The knowledge of a thing is possible as much because of its identity as because of its difference from all other

---

10. These two are known as darśanabhāga and nimittabhāga respectively. Cf. also VMS (JBORS), p. 61.

dvisvabhāvam sattvacittam bāhyābhyantarabhāgataḥ.

11. VMS, p. 19 ; asamviditakopādisthānavijñaptikam (ca yat). Also VMS (JBORS), p. 60.

12. Ibid, p. 19.

things. In the case of the indeterminate objectivity this is not available, and hence, though consciousness has started in the way to self-differentiation, the 'other' which it has projected out of itself is not known as an 'other.' The idea of the 'other' will indeed not let it rest in peace ; it must be known and as soon as it is known as an 'other,' it is known as a determinate other. The Ālaya-situation is inherently unstable ; and yet the consciousness of a determinate other leaves its impression in the Ālaya as a vāsanā, which makes it impossible for the Ālaya to be wholly determined; as one moment of the Ālaya gets differentiated, another moment of indeterminateness takes its place to be further differentiated, so that though the Ālaya is unstable, it can never be exhausted[13] till the idea of objectivity itself is eradicated.

The Ālaya stands therefore on a transcendental level. The determinate knowledge represents the last stage in the process of categorisation of consciousness. The Ālaya marks just the dawn of this process of determination, and is itself still indeterminate. It is the receptum of the forces of categorisation, the hot-bed of unrest as it were. It is only in its function and never as what it is in itself, being the very seat of the *a priori*.

Ālaya and Prakṛti

The concept of Ālaya-vijñāna bears a certain amount of similarity to that of Prakṛti in the Sāṅkhya system.[14] Both the systems accept the doctrine of evolution, one from a realistic standpoint, the other from an idealistic one. Prakṛti also is sarvabījaka, since everything objective, i.e., whatever appears before consciousness, is traced back to Prakṛti as its ultimate source. Prakṛti is the cause of all, every other thing being just a mode or determination of Prakṛti. It is the indeterminate or the undifferentiated whole. Then again, like the Ālaya, it undergoes incessant change. It is not a dead or inert mass, but is dynamic to the core.

The principle that unless a thing is inherently unstable, it cannot give rise to further differentiation is applicable to Prakṛti also. Were it all of one piece, with no seed of disruption in its texture, nothing can disturb its eternal quiescence. Prakṛti is necessarily accepted to be of a composite nature as constituted by the three guṇas. The problem in

13. na caikajñānanāśena vinaṣṭāḥ sarvavāsanāḥ, PVA, p. 21.
14. Cf. Stcherbatsky, *Nirvāṇa*, p. 32.

the Sāṅkhya is to reconcile the unity of Prakṛti with the plurality of its composition. The three guṇas cannot be separated in it, each being Prakṛti itself, and yet the mystery is that one is not the other. Though each of them is continually evolving, the evolution is only of its own kind. When the impact of puruṣa disturbs their equilibrium so that one is mixed up with the other, the creation of the world begins.

The differences between the concepts of Prakṛti and Ālaya are still more fundamental and are characteristic of the two systems. The Sāṅkhya system is realistic though it is not realism, and hence its conception of evolution is bound to differ from that of the idealist. For the Sāṅkhya, whatever changes is not consciousness and consciousness does not change. Consciousness therefore is pure or contentless and cannot give rise to evolution. The evolution is that of the objective alone. But the idealist accepts no other reality than consciousness, and all contents are projections of consciousness. The initial impulse that gives rise to the process of evolution is in both the systems an illusory idea, but the evolution itself is not illusory in either. For the Sāṅkhya, evolution pertains to what appears before the changeless consciousness while the idealist maintains that consciousness or the subjective alone can evolve.

Prakṛti is the last result obtained by the regressive analysis of the empirical determinations. It is the Unconditioned ; but the Ālaya is consciousness as has already been conditioned by the idea of objectivity. It is subject to two kinds of conditions, viz., the hetu-pariṇāma and the phala-pariṇāma. The Ālaya is not therefore ultimate. Though to all intents and purposes it may be taken as the starting-point of evolution, it is itself the first precipitation of the transcendental illusion. The Yogācāra is not only an idealist; he is an absolutist *par excellence.* No absolutism can stop with a duality, implicit or explicit. The weakness of the Sāṅkhya is that it wants to make the plurality of the three guṇas ultimate and make Prakṛti the Unconditioned. The reason for this is obvious; if we go still further back we may arrive at an integral unity; but from this nothing more can be extracted, and the creation of the world, to account for which such a unity was posited, would remain an enigma. The evolution can, to be sure, be imposed upon it, but that undermines the whole theory of this process being real. The only other alternative is the Yogācāra absolute of pure Will, which reconciles the apparently conflicting doctrines of an absolutism and a real evolution. This point will subsequently be dealt with in detail.

Prakṛti, being the Unconditioned, has no limits. No amount of evolution can exhaust it; i.e. the whole of Prakṛti can never be determined. The Ālaya, however, being conditioned, must be continually replenished by fresh vāsanās, or it will revert to pure consciousness. So also, Prakṛti can never come to an end; all determinations may lapse back to it, but Prakṛti itself continues to exist eternally, evolution or no evolution. The Ālaya is on a different footing ; not being ultimate, it can function only so long as the primal illusion remains potent. In the final state, the Arhat obtains the two knowledges of having exhausted all his previous vāsanās and of having eradicated the force impelling further differentiation of consciousness. In that state all the impediments obstructing the purity of consciousness are completely annihilated from the Ālaya, with the result that the Ālaya itself comes to a stop.[15]

Apart from these the logics of the two conceptions of evolution are fundamentally different. The Sāṅkhya pattern is identity-in-difference, identity being basic. In each of the evolutes Prakṛti remains identical, because of its underlying unity permeating the modal differences on the surface. The identity is that of substance, the difference being of modes only. In the Yogācāra school, the situation is peculiar. All the three vijñānas are momentary. The Ālaya is not one unchanging consciousness that persists throughout the duration of the evolutionary process ; it is a stream of discrete moments that flows on like the current of a river[16] with a perpetual succession of vāsānas of the different karmas and the further effects of them. Everything being momentary, causality should be understood as one moment of consciousness emerging on the death of the preceding one. The latter is annihilated totally without any residue. This being the case, when a pravṛtti-vijñāna is said to evolve out of the Ālaya, it is not meant that the former is a manifestation of the latter. That ālaya-moment is in fact dead which gave birth to the present pravṛtti-vijñāna. The Ālaya is more ultimate because it works at a transcendental level and not because it is more solid or enduring than the moments of empirical consciousness. The moments of the Ālaya and those of empirical consciousness may be similar in their

15. VMS, p. 22.
16. VMS, p. 22.

evanescent nature, but the content projected by one is the presupposition of that of the other. The Ālaya does not pervade or underlie its evolutes.

If the Ālaya is not an underlying identity binding the several pravṛtti-vijñānas, can pure Consciousness, which is the most ultimate, not serve this purpose ? This can be taken as the basic unity binding all the discrete moments of consciousness, from the Ālaya to the pravṛtti-vijñānas. The nature of the Yogācāra Absolute will be discussed in a subsequent Chapter ; here the answer may but be broadly indicated. When the Absolute rests in its pristine purity, the question of its underlying the discrete moments does not arise; the latter do not exist. But when the process of self-differentiation has started, consciousness begins to project contents. The fact that consciousness is here understood as will must never be lost sight of. The willing consciousness of a particular content is exhausted in the realisation of that content, and cannot be carried over to the willing of another content. The underlying identity is available in the Advaita Vedānta because there the Absolute retains its absoluteness even in spite of the appearance of the modes. But here bifurcation is a real process and the fact of the momentariness of will has to be accepted. Each willing is a separate individual act. The pure Will itself is differentiated into the Ālaya, and cannot therefore serve as the underlying unity. When the Ālaya starts functioning, there is no Absolute, since the Ālaya itself is the Absolute defiled.

The fact that the pattern of evolution is pure difference in this system can be illustrated in another way. It has been said that the Ālaya is a series of moments. The question arises as to the relation obtaining between these moments and Time. Though the Ālaya is a momentary stream, it is yet not in Time. Time is understood in all Buddhism as the moments themselves. The absolute Time, as the receptum of all change and duration, a doctrine countenanced by the Nyāya, is not accepted as a reality. Change is the changing elements themselves ; there is no Time over and above this. The Buddhist conception of Time, as indeed of thinghood in general, is closely modelled after the Sāṅkhya pattern. Prakṛti is not in time, but Time itself. It is a space-time-stuff. In Buddhism this is dissolved into atoms, so that the dharma as svalakṣaṇa is a space-time-point entity. The Yogācāra repudiated the spatial function as well, as pertaining to the dharmas. Space is intrinsically an objective characteristic ; ideas, far from being in space, cannot combine to produce even the semblance of it. A moment of consciousness is a time-point merely.

Here the doctrine of Prakṛti presents a difficulty. Prakṛti is not in time, the latter not being available apart from it. The very essence of Time is succession, perishing. Pure Time is a chimera ; it can only be the succession of events. There is a perpetual succession going on in Prakṛti ; so far the assertion that it is Time itself is clear enough. The difficulty begins with the consideration that Prakṛti is not mere succession. The modes change, but the substantial background remains identical. It persists through all change and succession. Hence Prakṛti is Time, and yet is something over and above it which is not time, and these two should neutralize each other. The contradiction is due to the fact that the Sāṅkhya system is based on the Space-pattern ; change is a superimposition on it which does not fit in well with it.[17]

It can now be perceived that a Time-pattern of pure succession precludes all continuity and all identity. It is absolute difference, and not the modal difference of the surface alone, as it is in the case of Prakṛti. All the moments of Ālaya are utterly discrete, as indeed all dharmas are in Buddhism. If the Time-pattern be undermined, the whole structure of evolution must be abolished.

The fact that the Ālaya is momentary raises another important issue. It has been shown that the Ālaya is the primal subject. It is the most fundamental term in the initial opposition of the subject-object duality. The question arises as to what the nature of this subject is. There are many gradations in the subjective side corresponding to the nature of the objective content projected. To what level does the Ālaya belong ?

The Ālaya is not the ego. The ego is the most empirical of the subjective order. By ego is not meant the Unity of Apperception which is the very presupposition of experience ; it should rather be understood as the "I" which is explicitly referred to in any case of knowledge, when such reference is made at all. This "I" is not a presupposition, since in that case it can never be referred to, but is a reflex. It is that which appropriates all knowledge as its own. The sense of "I" arises only as a reflex, i.e., only when a conscious dissociation from the object takes place. That, as shown before, is possible when the objective is a plurality. In the case of the Ālaya, the content being an indeterminate

17. Cf. CPB, p. 62.

objectivity, such dissociation is not available and this reflex or turning back upon itself cannot be had.

Ālaya and Sākṣi

Nor is the Ālaya to be confused with the Ātman as propounded in the Brāhmanical systems. It is the most ultimate category on the subjective side in these systems, as the Ālaya is in idealism. However variously it may be conceived, its real significance can be understood if the essential function it serves in the Ātma-epistemology be analysed.

The very essence of Ātman is changelessness or persistence through time. This is true even where no distinction is made between the Ātman and the ego, as the sense of "I" endures throughout one's life. The acceptance is necessitated for supplying the unity which binds together the discrete acts of knowledge. It must always be borne in mind that the epistemology of the whole Ātma-tradition is based on the nature of consciousness as knowledge. Ātman is invariably understood as a passive spectator of the temporal series of knowledge. The will-function of the subjective, if accepted at all, is an element foreign to the nature of the Ātman. To supply the stability of the perspective, the changelessness of the Ātman is necessary.

In the Yogācāra, the nature of consciousness is understood in an entirely new light. The subjective is not a passive spectator of what goes on before it, but is the dynamic will which creates its contents. It must change therefore with the least change in the content, which change cannot otherwise be accounted for. The Ālaya therefore is said to be momentary. Even the unity binding all knowledge, which entails the acceptance of Ātman in the Brāhmanical systems, is itself a projection. If the objectivity of the dharmas is an illusion, the unruffled continuity of a changeless Ātman is no less an illusion. Both are equally projections created by the willing consciousness, apart from which neither has any reality.

The Ātman is not therefore a reality. It was discarded by other systems of Buddhism, and the Ālaya, which apparently is the Ātman appearing in a Buddhist guise,[18] is something fundamentally different, the entire metaphysical pattern having changed. The Yogācāra offers

18. Cf. MA, p. 59.

some arguments[19] against the reality of Ātman. It can be conceived either as identical with the mental states or as different from them, or lastly as both identical with and different from them. If it is identical with the states its separate existence is superfluous; nor can it act as the unifying link. But if it is different from them, they can have no relation whatsoever, and its acceptance is again futile, it not being affected by the change in the states. The third alternative is unstable, and must be dissolved into either of the former two. Again if the Ātman be of an eternal ubiquitous nature like space, it is hard to distinguish its individuality, and yet without this distinction all empirical intercourse would come to an end. It is difficult to connect an all-pervasive Ātman to a specific body ; on the other hand, it cannot be limited by the body, since the body being of a variable magnitude, it would militate against the changelessness of the Ātman. The fundamental contradiction in the Ātman is that it must enter into the various mental states, and retain its identity inspite of them, and these two functions cannot be reconciled.

The Ālaya therefore represents a stage where the sense of ego has not yet arisen. The closest parallel to this conception in the Brāhmanical systems is that of the Sākṣī in Advaita Vedānta. The Sākṣī is pure consciousness as covered by indeterminate ignorance (avidyāvacchinna) and is sharply distinguished from the empirical subject (pramātā). Consciousness has not yet been individualised by mind (antaḥkaraṇa). Ignorance here performs only its obscuring function (āvaraṇa). It is just undifferentiated darkness. The similarity in nature between this indeterminate veil and the indeterminate objectivity confronting the Ālaya should be noticed. The veil is still a "whole," and has not started importing difference to the Pure Being. Both the Ālaya and the Sākṣī are the first phenomenalisation of the Absolute. The defilement determining the Absolute is in both cases still pure, i.e., not empirical. The duality of the Sākṣī is not known as such, and that for the same reason that the bare objectivity confronting the Ālaya is not known as an other. It is pure contemplation. The nature and function of the Sākṣī is discovered by a regressive analysis of the state of consciousness in deep

---

19. MSA, p. 154-160 ; VMS, pp. 7-13 (JBORS), Vol. XIX.

7

sleep. It is characteristic of speculative metaphysics that the same state of deep sleep is described as evincing the working of the Ālaya. Further, though the Sākṣī itself is not sarvabījaka, the ignorance belonging to it may be taken as the material stuff, out of which the empirical determinations emerge and return to it again. Avidyā is Prakṛti rendered epistemic. Again, in both the Ālaya and the Sākṣī, the terms of the duality belong to different orders altogether. Ignorance and consciousness do not lie side by side in the Sākṣī ; one is *of* the other. So also, the other posited by the Ālaya is not another co-ordinate reality; there is no real objectivity, but only the idea of one. The duality is within the Ālaya itself. The difference between the evolutionary process in the Sākṣī and the cyclic development of the Ālaya is that all determinations return to Avidyā in a very subtle form, while in the Yogācāra they themselves perish and leave only their seeds in the Ālaya. It is like a lotus alternately unfolding and shutting itself up in the case of Sākṣī, while in that of the Ālaya it is like one wave giving rise to another.

The difference between the doctrines of the Sākṣī and the Ālaya ensues out of their different standpoints. The Sākṣī consciousness is a contentless and changeless transparency, while the Ālaya is a momentary series, each moment creating its own content. This is so because the defilement of the Sākṣī is a superimposition which leaves the purity of consciousness unaffected, while in the Ālaya consciousness has undergone a real transformation. The difference between these two patterns will be dealt with in the seventh Chapter.

The Ālaya is that consciousness where individuality has not yet arisen, it being the most basic substratum of all empirical consciousness. It is something more fundamental than the ego. The question arises therefore whether the Ālaya, being the store-house of the seeds which constitute egohood, is one universal receptum on which the plurality of egos is based, or whether it is peculiar to each ego, in which case it will itself be a plurality. Here again the conception of the Sākṣī offers an illustration of the same problem. The Sākṣī is more fundamental than the pramātā ; it represents a stage where egoity has not arisen. It might be held[20] therefore that it is one universal consciousness, covered

20. Cf. *Siddhānta leśasaṅgraha*, pp. 31-34.

by bare ignorance, but not individualised into a plurality of subjects. The other theory is that individuality is inherent in ignorance. It is the very nature of ignorance to make pure consciousness a centre of experiences. Hence even in the Sākṣī, though individuality is not explicit, nor is it known as an "I", yet it is present in an indeterminate manner. Were individuality not present in the Sākṣī, a person might wake up from a deep sleep as somebody else, since the Sākṣī consciousness is itself contentless, and its ignorance has absorbed all empirical determinations of individuality. Were the Sākṣī universal, the genesis of individuality is inexplicable. The orthodox tradition however favours the former view of the Sākṣī as one universal consciousness. Its individuality can be due either to the fact that ignorance is a plurality, or that ignorance, though indeterminate, cannot swallow individuality. The latter alternative is unsound since intellect (antaḥkaraṇa) itself, the root of egoity, returns to its primary cause, ignorance, as a mere potency. The plurality of ignorance cannot be maintained ; the only ignorance is that of oneself and self is the Absolute ; ignorance is therefore one. It provides individuality by a mere freak as it were, in spite of its being one. Individuality has to be taken for granted and cannot be explained further. The predicament of somebody waking up as somebody else is precluded by the consideration that the one indeterminate ignorance contains nevertheless the germs of an infinite plurality of egos in a subtle and implicit form.

The same considerations are applicable to the concept of Ālaya also. It may be taken as one universal under-current of the Unconscious in which every ego stores its individual share of karmic seeds ; or, the conception may be interpreted as an infinite plurality of store-house, a separate receptum for each ego.

The latter alternative is apparently more plausible than the other. There are reasons for believing that the Yogācāra is not a solipsist, that he accepts a plurality of empirical subjects. This being so, there would be parallel streams of karmas which cannot give rise to an identical series of seeds. The Ālaya is not a repositary in the sense of a hold-all in which all kinds of things are put. It is a dynamic series each moment of which is conditioned by an empirical consciousness. Each Ālaya moment is simple and unitary ; it is not engendered by a plural series of karmas. It may be said that there is a kind of spread-outness in the Ālaya ; different egos may have their individual cycles in different centres of one Ālaya—like waves in one sea. This is possible only by conceding a substantial identity of Ālaya which is incompatible with its nature as an incessant total substitution. If parallel series in the Ālaya be accepted, it would amount to a plurality of self-sufficient series. There cannot be only one series, since different orders of vāsanās cannot be reconciled in it. Conversely, one identical Ālaya-moment cannot sprout into moments of empirical consciousness pertaining to different egos. If different trees cannot give rise to an identical seed, one seed cannot produce and nourish different trees. The case with the Sākṣī is different. Ignorance, the material stuff of the plurality of egos, is one. But here there can be no question of a universal upādāna The very conception of universality is repugnant to Buddhism.

The unity and universality of the Ālaya is not so plausible, but can be argued. The unity of the Ālaya can certainly not mean the continuity of a single series ; that, as we have seen, is not defensible. The unity can only be the harmony obtaining between the moments belonging to different series, as between moments of a single series. It must be understood horizontally as well as vertically. Causality is interpreted as substitution. One moment is succeeded by a similar moment, bearing no real relation to it, and yet, the latter occurs only on the occurrence of the former. This is the unity of the temporal succession. There can be a similar unity of simultaneous occurrence. The different series have no connection with each other, and yet one somehow bears upon the other. In connection with the doctrine of the intra-subjective world, it was seen how the different worlds, though utterly distinct from each other, do yet evince a marked resemblance. The same is the case here. The parallel series are all cooperating and interacting with each other, retaining nevertheless their individuality and uniqueness. The unity of the Ālaya can be construed only as this coordination. The difficulties in this hypothesis are similar to those confronting the doctrine of the unity of the temporal or vertical series. Each moment is unique, and yet one happens because of the other.

This is, however, more a plea for realising the instability of the doctrine of non-relational coordination than a defence of the unity of the Ālaya, horizontal as well as vertical. Reciprocity is as unintelligible as causality. Lacking any textual support, we refrain from coming to a conclusion, but this much is clear ; the Ālaya as a constructive hypothesis must be accepted either as one or as many ; in neither case is it free from difficulties. This indicates only that it is not ultimate, that we cannot stop with the Ālaya, but must go further back.

Kliṣṭa Mano-Vijñāna

So much about the Ālaya, the first of the three stages in the evolution of consciousness, enumerated above. We come to the second, the mano-vijñāna. The function of this consciousness in the evolutionary process is rather obscure, and the text is not very illuminating.

Why is this consciousness accepted at all ? What is its significance and importance ? The pravṛtti-vijñānas present no problem because, according to the idealistic principle, they are the universe itself as identical with the knowing consciousness. And without a repositary in which the latent forces lie dormant, the flow of phenomenal existence would come to a stop. Consciousness is momentary, and unless its seeds are stored in the Ālaya, its further continuity will of its own accord come to an end.[21] Further, in certain states like deep sleep and trance, the empirical consciousness does not exist at all. Here the unbroken sequence of the Ālaya must be posited to account for the resuscitation of the waking life. The Ālaya must therefore be accepted over and above the various pravṛtti-vijñānas.

If these two strata of consciousness suffice to explain phenomena, the manas need not be accepted as a distinct consciousness. It cannot however be dispensed with, because it mediates between these two consciousnesses. Whenever two terms are posited, the intervention of a third entity as a connecting link becomes necessary. If two unrelated reals are accepted, they cannot even be known as two. In the case of manas the mediation is all the more necessary since the empirical consciousness arises wholly out of the Ālaya; the question of unrelated reals does not arise. On the one hand there is the Ālaya with an indeterminate content; there are the pravṛtti-vijñānas with wholly determinate contents on the other : in between these is the process of determination. This transitional function is served by the manas. It makes possible the emergence of the object-consciousness out of the Ālaya, and at the same time maintains the distinction between the two. It may be said that if a *tertium quid* is required to establish the separation and at the same time to mediate the relation between two terms, by parity of reasoning

21. Cf. LAS, p. 38.

another entity must be posited between one of the original terms and this *tertium quid*, and this clearly leads to an infinite regress. This only means that ultimately two distinct terms cannot be accepted as separately real. The consideration here is that the acceptance of two entails that of a third as well, and for empirical purposes this complex must be granted. Theoretically any duality requires the intervention of a third entity, including the duality between a term and this third entity itself; practically, the acceptance of three serves all purposes, but three at least must be accepted. Hence the necessity for manas.

Manas is so-called because the process of intellection (manana)[22] is always going on in it. The content of Ālaya is indeterminate objectivity. As soon as this content is known as an other, its indeterminateness gives place to empirical determinations. And known it must be; pure contemplation of the other cannot last for ever. The transition from the act of willing of this fundamental content to those of the determinate contents is the work of manas. It breaks up the monotony of the indeterminate objectivity by projecting the latter through categories; its essence is categorisation. The bare otherness is indeed itself a category, the most fundamental one; but it has not been differentiated into categories of empirical knowledge. It is only in the case of a self-conscious awareness of objectivity, that these categories are brought into play. The pure objectivity is not categorised, except by itself. This work of determinate categorisation is done by the manas. It actualises the empirical contents which are implicitly contained in the pure objective. Manas is not the consciousness of these contents but is the function of this actualisation itself. The 'other' can be realised only as a determinate other and the splitting up of the pure form into determinate forms resulting in the precipitation of matter or content is intellection. The bare 'other' is certainly itself matter, but is so only in relation to the transcendental consciousness of the Ālaya ; in relation to empirical objects it is their form. It is so bare that it cannot be distinguished from its form, i.e., from its awareness. Only after consciousness is determinately categorised, does the awareness of the distinction between form and matter, or consciousness and its content, characteristic of empirical knowledge, arise. Manas is not the result of this process, which are the several object-know-

22. VMS, p. 22.

ledges, but is the process itself. It is the fructification of the seeds lying dormant in the Ālaya into the content-consciousness. It is the ripening of the fruit, not the ripe fruit itself.

An apparently different account of manas is given in the text. It is invariably referred to as defiled (kliṣṭa) because it is surcharged with a particular class of "Mentals"[23] (caittas), i.e., the four nivṛtāvyākṛta kleśas. As long as manas functions, it must be accompanied by these four,[24] viz.,

1. The false notion of an ego (ātmadṛṣṭi) ;
2. ignorance about ego (ātmamoha) ;
3. elation over it (ātmamāna) and
4. attachment to it (ātmaprema).

The imposition of the false notion of an ego upon the constituents of an individual (upādāna-skandhas) is the ātmadṛṣṭi, also known as satkāya-dṛṣṭi. In reality there is no "I" but only the momentary constituents (skandhas). This notion of the "I" arises out of ignorance about the real nature of the Ālaya. As soon as the sense of ego arises, one gloats over it, proudly proclaims its existence, with the result that one gets attached to this false notion.

It is clear that the manas is understood more as concerned with the projection of the ego, than that of the objective, and this seems not to be in accordance with the mediational function just now attributed to it. A deeper probing into the problem will however reveal that these two accounts are not so disconnected as might appear. Manas represents the stage of categorisation of the objective. The knowledge of the objective is connected with the sense of "I" in two ways. First, "I know" is the invariable condition for any knowledge to occur. This alone imparts the unity required in the synthesis of knowledge. Without this, the manifold would not be appropriated, and consequently there would be no synthesis. It is however only a presupposition; there is no self-consciousness in the sense of the consciousness of the self. The form of ordinary knowledge is 'there is a tree', though the other form, viz., 'I know the tree', is always there in the background. The explicit reference to the knowing subject takes place when the content-knowledge has thrown

---

23. An explanation of these will be given in the next chapter.
24. VMS, p. 23.

the subject back upon itself, i.e., when the subject is consciously dissociated from the content. Here the knower turns back upon himself; the former 'I' is a presupposition while the latter a reflex. The two forms of the "I" are radically different, but may be comprised in a common concept of ego. The notion of ego is thus the alpha and omega of all empirical knowledge in a literal sense. The dawn of ego-consciousness indicates that the process of categorisation of the objective has started, since an uncategorised objective would be indeterminate which cannot yield any reference to the ego. The twin processes of the categorisation of knowledge and the dawning of the notion of ego are very vitally connected with each other and are rather two ways of looking at the same function of manas.

The ego is real neither in this system nor in the Advaita Vedānta. In both, it is a construction; yet a construction in fundamentally different senses. In the Yogācāra, it is a construction superimposed upon the incessantly fleeting states of Ālaya-moments, while the Vedāntin thinks it to be ascribed to the unchanging pure Sākṣī consciousness. Though the ego is unreal according to both the systems, it is so for opposite reasons. In Vedānta it is unreal, because it veils the universality and the ubiquity of consciousness; it is unreal because it imports change into the unchanging real. In the Yogācāra the reason for its unreality is precisely antipodal to this. The ego masquerades as something permanent and stable, while in reality the Ālaya is a continuous series. It is unreal because it imports permanence to the changing series. Experience requires both analysis and synthesis. Metaphysics picks up one pattern and universalises it to such an extent as to explain the other away. The function of manas is more synthesis. It binds together the different states under the common concept of the ego. It supplies the requisite element of stability which makes discursive knowledge possible. In common with the whole Buddhist tradition, the Yogācāra is initially prejudiced in favour of impermanence. The other aspect of knowledge is explained away as an illusory construction. The pramātā, on the other hand, makes room for analysis, i.e., change and succession, which the Real, as unchanging consciousness, cannot render explicable, and which is yet required to make experience possible.

The activity of manas is directed towards the actualisation of the potential forces stored in the Ālaya; it is the Ālaya therefore which supplies the data on which manas operates. Manas is not an independent consciousness; its status is somewhat different from that of the Ālaya as well as the object-consciousness. It is more or less a relational function, and requires a base of operation. Its locus[25] (āśraya) is the Ālaya. Categories cannot float in vacuum ; they require a *locus standi* which is to be categorised. The category of the 'other' in the Ālaya is indeterminate and manas determines it empirically.

It has been said above that no contentless consciousness can be admitted. If the manas is to be accredited as one, it must have its own content. Peculiarly enough, its content[26] also is said to be the Ālaya. That is to say, it projects no new content ; its function is exhausted in categorising the indeterminate objective created by the Ālaya. It projects the same content through many more lenses added, as it were. This again shows that manas enjoys no independent status of its own. Just as a relation is exhausted in relating its terms, but is not a term in itself, so the manas is not a consciousness co-ordinate with the Ālaya or the pravṛtti-vijñānas. The activity of the Ālaya itself, as its content gets differentiated into this and that, is the manas. It is the function of incessant unrest in the Ālaya.

By certain meditations and practices this process of intellection can be stopped[27]; the categorisation of the determinate content over which our will has ordinarily no jurisdiction, can be affected by intense meditation. In the state of Arhat who has destroyed all the defilements without any residue, the kliṣṭa manas does not function; the flow of the Ālaya itself ceases there and hence the manas is stopped automatically. So also in certain transic states the manas does not exist,[28] and after the trance is over, it arises again out of the Ālaya. During the trance, the Ālaya revolves round itself, with no categorisation, like the sajātīya pariṇāma of prakṛti. Manas is said to be absent in no less than five states.[29] This again shows the close parallel existing between the concepts of the Ālaya and the Sākṣī. In the state of nirvikalpa samādhi, the pramātā or the empirical subject evaporates, but arises again out of the Sākṣī at its termination.

---

25. VMS, p. 22.
26. Ibid, p. 22.
27. Ibid, p. 24
28. Ibid, p. 24.
29. Ibid, p. 34-35.

Pravṛtti-Vijñānas

The third stage of the evolution of consciousness is the determinate awareness of the object. This is the only consciousness which matters in empirical discourse. This alone is empirically known ; the former two form its submerged base as it were. For all practical purposes this constitutes our universe, since it includes everything whatsoever as can be presented before the empirical consciousness. This consciousness is not a unity but a class, comprising six kinds of consciousness, all of which are grouped together because of their common empirical nature. These six kinds of consciousness can be classified into : (1) External; (2) Internal. The former includes the five consciousnesses corresponding to the five sense-organs which give us all the information we have about the so-called external world. The five senses make possible the awareness of matter (rūpa), sound (śadba), smell (gandha), taste (rasa) and the tactual data (spraṣṭavya). The sixth or the internal consciousness is manovijñāna, the knowledge of ideas (dharmas). Though these ideas are 'internal' they are as much objects of consciousness as rūpa etc are. Dharma is a miscellaneous category which includes whatever confronts consciousness, except in the objective way. This manovijñāna is not to be confused with the kliṣṭa manas; the latter is a transcendental function, while the former is merely the knowledge of empirical ideas.

There is one point about the five sensual consciousnesses that needs clarification. The senses give us, the Yogācāra holds in accordance with the Buddhist tradition, merely the sense-data, and the resultant consciousness also is of this alone. Colour is a sense-datum; the coloured object is not. The consciousness also is of colour alone. Then how is it that one has the knowledge of a coloured object at all ? If consciousness is identical wih the object known, consciounsess itself should be of a coloured object, and not of a bare colour. It has been said before that though the object known is identical with the knowledge of it, yet, owing to the cosmic Illusion, it appears as independent and as objectively present. So, though in reality there is merely the consciousness of colour, that colour, when objectified, is known only as a coloured object. The concept of substance is a category through which the form of knowledge, when objectified, must be cognised. We cannot perceive an objectivity which is bare colour; it would invariably be an object merely by the fact of its being objectified. To invest the sense-data with this object-hood is the work of manas. The sense-data are certainly not objectively real; but consciousness has that form alone. Of the object-hood there can be no consciousness ; it is the form of projection ; to be projected is to be projected as an object.

All these six viṣaya-vijñānas arise out of the Ālaya due to their respective seeds; they can arise either singly or simultaneously.[30] To create the illusion of a full-fledged object, many sense-data must combine which is possible if their consciousnesses arise simultaneously. This conception can be compared to the emergence of waves in an ocean : the number of the waves is not fixed, but depends upon the wind passing over the ocean. So also the empirical consciousnesses arise out of the Ālaya, due to the presence of ālambana-pratyayas (object-conditions), one or many. By the ocean should not be meant an identical and substantial substratum ; the whole ocean must change every moment, to be comparable to the Ālaya.

None of the three or rather eight vijñānas is ultimate. Consciousness is disturbed owing to the impact of a wrong idea, and once this idea is eradicated or realised to be illusory, the agitated commotion of consciousness is calmed down, and it regains its eternal quiescence.

This progression of the evolution of consciousness must be understood merely in a logical sense and not as a historical process. Because it is said that the object-consciousness arises out of the Ālaya, mediated by the manas, it must not be imagined that at first there was only the Ālaya, and that in course of time the other vijñānas emerge. Pure consciousness has no tendency to get defiled; it must be posited as already defiled. So also the cycle of the karmic forces and their actualisation is an infinite one,[31] like the trite cycle of the tree and its seed. The dependence is reciprocal; one cannot be had without the other. The pravṛtti-vijñānas arise because of the seeds latent in the Ālaya, while the Ālaya itself is further replenished by the former,[32] but for which it would come to a stop. The priority is merely logical, and not factual. The Ālaya with all its parapharnalia must be accepted as beginningless and it lasts upto the cessation of the phenomenal existence itself. The other vijñānas have gaps in between them, but the Ālaya suffers no break whatsoever in its continuous flow.

---

30. VMS, p. 33
31. *Ālambana Parīkṣā*, 8.
32. vāsanātaśca tajjñānam bhavet tebhyaśca vāsanā; PVA, p. 22.

CHAPTER VI

DHARMA THEORY IN THE YOGĀCĀRA

We have seen in the first Chapter that the Yogācāra accepted the phenomenology of the early realistic Buddhism, and yet radically modified it so as to incorporate it within the folds of idealism. Being a constructive system, it does speculate about the dharma-theory—their number and the nature of each—but never forgets their merely phenomenal reality. From the transcendental point of view, consciousness alone exists ; the rest is appearance.

The problem arises as to the relation idealism bears to the dharma-theory. Only consciousness is real, objectivity is an appearance. Objective dharmas are therefore in the same predicament as all things objective are ; their independence is illusory. But the diversification of consciousness itself is because of the illusion—because something, as though external, confronts it as an other to it. The natural state of consciousness is a 'pure Act' unchecked by any content. Dharmas are not real then even as pertaining to consciousness. Pure consciousness harbours no dharmas. And granting even that consciousness does get diversified, it is bifurcated into the subject-object duality : where do the dharmas come in then ?

Since objectivity is an illusion there can be no objective dharmas. If there is no substance apart from the consciousness of it, nor can the external modes be accepted as real. Hence if the dharmas are admitted at all, they can be accepted only as qualifying the subjective, as sustaining its internal diversity.[1] The transcendental Will as pure Act has no dharmas. They enjoy therefore only a phenomenal reality ; they pertain to the Will-Consciousness when it is no longer a pure Act, but is actually creative. When consciousness gets phenomenalised by being infected with the idea of objectivity, it acquires various forms or modes. It then becomes particular and discrete; its universality is broken up into

---

1. MVSBT, pp. 26-7.

infinite "moments" of consciousness. One moment of consciousness can be individualised only by being qualified by some factor which colours it in various ways. This extraneous factor cannot be intrinsic to consciousness, since in that case the moments will be stabilised, and this, as will be seen in the next Chapter, must be rejected as contrary to Absolutism. But nor can it be an extraneous factor, as there can be nothing which is other than consciousness ; this otherness is an illusion. When consciousness is diversified, its moments are qualified by so many overtones as it were; these do not form an integral part of consciousness, but nor can they be granted an independent status. It must be clearly understood that they pertain to consciousness only in its infected or bifurcated aspect; they are evolved only in its phenomenalised state. These are the dharmas in the Yogācāra system. Though the dharma-phenomenology is accepted, yet its entire significance has been radically altered. Formerly they were accepted as ultimate elements of existence. Now their ultimacy is rejected altogether ; they belong only to the empirical realm. They are yet real as pertaining to consciousness; consciousness never loses its reality in whatever form it may be. Consciousness infected by the subject-object duality is consciousness still, and as such is perfectly real. And if the phenomenal forms of consciousness are real, so are their various modes of existence. The importance of the dharmas lies in this very fact, since their function is to keep these forms individual and discrete. The particularity of consciousness is real, and yet not ultimate (Ch. 7), and so are the dharmas ; they qualify consciousness only in its phenomenal state, and not in its absolute aspect. That does not make them unreal, but only takes away their ultimacy.

Consciousness *qua* consciousness is invariably the same. Yet we have to distinguish one moment of consciousness from another. This distinction is not possible if regarded from the standpoint of the object, since the individuality of consciousness lies, not so much in the object cognised, but rather in the attitude consciousness takes towards it. The same object may give pleasure to one person and offence to another. Moreover, since the object itself is nothing but a mode of existence of consciousness, the reason for the individuality or particularity of the latter must be sought in itself. Dharmas perform this function, being the marginal fringes as it were of the central focus of consciousness, and serve to set each moment into sharp relief against all others. Moreover, the whole of the objective world is reduced to consciousness, in the sense that the object is a form of appearance of the latter. Hence the objective distinctions between the various sense-data, between visual sense-data and sound for instance, must be incorporated as the distinctions between different moments of consciousness. Consciousness itself appears in these forms and therefore the respective moments are distinguished only by these. Here these forms, i.e., rūpa etc., are the dharmas. That is to say, though the whole of objective reality is reduced to consciousness, the objective distinctions between rūpa etc., can yet be accepted as so many dharmas qualifying the respective moments of consciousness. It is now clear how rūpa etc., inspite of appearing as something objective and external, are in reality dharmas qualifying consciousness.

Each moment of consciousness is thus a complex constituted by ever so many dharmas which nevertheless are not distinct and independent realities. The several dharmas can only be distinguished as so many tonal aspects whch lend the distinctive colour to the complex. The dharmas are not to be had by themselves, nor can they be separated, or the unity of the complex would be lost. All empirical distinctions are retained in the shape of the distinctions between the various dharmas, and yet the fundamental logic of idealism is unaffected, since all these distinctions are fused into the central unity of consciousness. Nor does it militate against the supremacy of consciousness for two reasons: first, because the dharmas are not independent, and secondly, they are not ultimate, and these two circumstances are closely related. The speculation about the dharmas supply the data for constructing a cosmic phenomenology within the framework of idealism.

In the Yogācāra cosmology[2] as many as one hundred dharmas are

---

2. The table of elements according to Sarvāstivāda is given in the *Central Conception of Buddhism,* APP. II, pp. 95-107. The Theravāda list is discussed in *Abhidhammatthasangaho*. The supposed Sautrāntika list is collected from Tamil sources and given, also as an Appendix (D), in the Adyar Edition of *Ālambana Parīkṣā*, ed. by Pt. Aiyaswami. In the third Appendix to the same work, the editor gives a restoration of Vasubandhu's *Mahāyana Śatadharma Vidyā-*

accepted. They are classified under five heads[3]: (1) The citta-dharmas, (2) the cetasikas or caittas, (3) rūpa-dharmas, (4) citta-viprayukta-saṁskāra-dharmas, and lastly (5) the Asaṁskṛta-dharmas. From this classification it is clear that dharmas are divided first into the Asaṁskṛta and the saṁskṛta, the noumenal and the phenomenal. Phenomena are comprised by the first four. The saṁskṛta dharmas themselves may be divided into two broad classes; first, those which are closely connected with consciousness in some way or other, and secondly, those dharmas which have nothing distinctive about them in their relation to consciousness. Related to consciousness they must be, as apart from the latter they are nothing. Yet their peculiarity does not obviously lie in this relation. Dharmas whose bearing to consciousness is more directly apparent are further sub-divided into those which are material or objective and those which are not. The latter finally consist of mind and the mentals, i.e., consciousness proper and its satellites, as explained above. The classification is strictly dichotomous and can be tabulated thus:

Dharmas (elements of existence)

- saṁskṛta (phenomenal)
  - cittasamprayukta (related to consciousness)
    - arūpa
      - citta
      - caittas
    - rūpa (objective)
  - cittaviprayukta
- asaṁskṛta

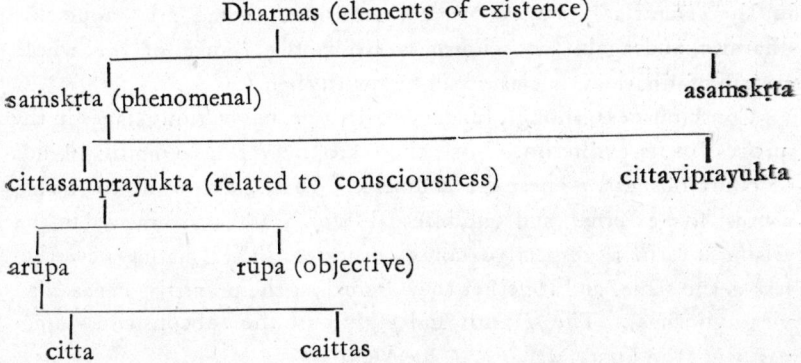

I. The first class of dharmas is constituted by *consciousness* itself. It is rather intriguing that consciousness is classified as one of the ulti-

---

mukham, which is a list of the 100 dharmas accepted by the Yogācāra. The list is in perfect agreement with that given in VMS, pp. 25-33. The 100 dharmas are discussed, with comparative details on every point, in Mcgovern's *A Manual of Buddhist Philosophy*, Vol. I. They are also enumerated in Sogen's *Systems of Buddhist Thought*, pp. 219-230.

3. Cf. MSA, XI, 37.

mate factors of existence. We have just seen that consciousness is not one of the reals but is reality itself. It is the only reality. The other dharmas are not coordinate to it. They can be real only as being the tonal aspects qualifying consciousness. Why consciousness and the other satellites are both indifferently classed as dharmas, as though both enjoy the same ontological status, is apparently perplexing. That it has no such implication will be clear if we pay attention to the structure of the dharma-phenomenology. The earlier doctrine of the dharmas being the ultimate existents is not discarded, but is, on the other hand, radically modified. The entire dharma-theory is based on a pragmatic standpoint and has nothing to do with metaphysical considerations. All kinds of categories are classed together as dharmas, irrespective of their various ontological status. Even the Absolute, as will presently be seen, is enumerated as a dharma. The broad denotation of the dharmas is thus everything which is accepted in this system ; whether this is in the ultimate sense or not is beyond the scope of the dharma-theory. Some dharmas are accepted only in the empirical stages of consciousness, some are noumenal dharmas, and again consciousness itself, the centre of the whole system of dharmas, is classed along with them.

Consciousness, though fundamentally one, has various stages in the process of its evolution. First, there are the various empirical kinds of consciousness. These are enumerated as six, according to the six senses, five external and one internal, which are instrumental in the arising of their respective consciousnesses. Their nature nevertheless is the same, and together they are called the pravṛttivijñānas (also viṣayavijñānas). The seventh and eighth are the subconsicous vijñānas, viz., the kliṣṭa Manas and the Ālaya.

Early Buddhism admitted only the first six ; moreover, consciousness in early Buddhism was accepted as pure or contentless, hence it was counted as one single dharma. The differences were imported in it by extraneous factors, and it became six. The last two were added by the Yogācāra and this addition completely changed the significance of the dharma-phenomenology, and indeed the ultimate metaphysical pattern itself. An explanation of these vijñānas has already been given in the previous Chapter.

II. Next in importance are the "*mentals*" (the cetasikas or, more briefly, the caittas). Strictly speaking, only these should be classed as dharmas, and Vasubandhu takes cognizance of these alone. The various vijñānas are reality itself, and not merely dharmas. Or rather, if the denotation of dharmas includes them, then the cetasikas are certainly not dharmas. Since everything however is indifferently classed as a dharma, the cetasikas take their places along with the vijñānas.

In early Buddhism, these were really distinct realities, besides the one contentless citta. They were ultimate existents, independent and absolute. Here, on the other hand, they are merely the phases in which the complexity of consciousness is exhibited. They are so many hues as it were, radiated by the prismatic consciousness. Consciousness in its pristine purity is absolutely indeterminate, nnd no caittas can pertain to it in that state. They are not independent as in early Buddhism but ensue out of the conmplexity of consciousness itself. In early Buddhism, one moment of consciousness is constituted by the moments of citta *and* the appropriate caittas : in the Yogācāra, it is merely one unitary moment in which different aspects however can be distinguished.

Cetasikas are 51 in number, as against 46 accepted in the Sarvāstivāda and as many as 52 in Theravāda. These are further divided into 6 subclasses : (1) universal cetasikas-5; (2) determinate cetasikas-5; (3) meritorious cetasikas-11; (4) defilements-6; (5) minor defilements-20; and lastly (6) indeterminate cetasikas-4, making up a total of 51.

(1) *The sarvatraga dharmas*[4] are those universal features which are invariably present whatever the type of consciousness may be. No consciousness can be without them. These alone are present in the Ālaya. Wherever there is the cognitive distinction between the knower and the known, the sarvatraga dharmas accompany the mental state. The Ālaya is no exception though the distinction is still on a transcendental level. It is however difficult to see how they can pertain to the Ālaya. Take saṁjñā for instance. This is the relating activity of the mind—apperceptive synthesis, in Kantian terminology: this can be present only when there are distinctions in the objective. But the object of Ālaya is indeterminate and there is nothing to synthesize or relate. Perhaps the doctrine of sarvatraga dharmas was taken over from the Sarvāstivāda, and the modifications required in idealism

4. VMS, pp. 20-1 ; VMS (JBORS), p. 69 ff.

were not made. They are five in number, viz., sparśa, manaskāra, vedanā, samjñā and cetanā.

(a) *Sparśa* is defined as trikasannipāta. In every case of knowledge there are three factors present—the content cognised, the instrument of cognition, and the cognising consciousness. These three must flash simultaneously in a causal relation. Consequently the instrument or the sense-organ is excited in a certain way and gets a particular form (vikāra), evoking a feeling, pleasant or unpleasant as the case may be. The content is accordingly determined by consciousness, and this definite awareness of the object, which touches as it were the sense-organ, but in reality is a determination of the object, is sparśa. Its action is to excite feelings.

(b) *Manaskāra* is that by which citta is attracted towards the object (cetasa ābhoga).[5] It is attention, which holds citta towards the object. This last clause in the definition is necessary because manaskāra or attention functions, not in a single moment of consciousness, but in the series. One moment of citta does certainly go to some object or other, and there would be no case of inattention. Attention means, not the attention of a single moment which is exhausted in that very moment, but the directing of the citta again and again, to the same object.

(c) *Vedanā* is affection or reaction of consciousness (anubhava-svabhāva) towards its contents. It can be of three kinds according as the reaction is pleasant, painful, or merely indifferent. The object however being in reality non-existent, these different feelings are due to one's past karma, good or bad. Pleasant feeling means having pleasure in coming in contact with the object and pain in being separated from it. So painful feeling is pain in contact with, and pleasure in separation from, the object.

(d) *Saṁjñā* is specifying or defining the object by its characteristic marks (nimittodgrahaṇa). It is of the form, "this is blue, not yellow." It is the conceptualising activity of the mind—marking and defining the object by means of a concept. In Buddhism, things are discrete and particular, and therefore unrelated. Knowledge however cannot even begin without judgment, i. e., without relating things by naming them. This function is served by samjñā, which thus accompanies

---

5. *The Yogasūtrabhāṣya* also uses this term "ābhoga," p. 21.

all knowledge. How this can be present even in the indeterminate knowledge of the Ālaya is not made clear.

(e) *Cetanā* is volition, that by which citta is impelled towards the content as iron is towards magnet (cittābhisaṁskāro manasaśceṣṭā). It is more active than attention.

(2) *The Viniyata caittas*[6] also are five in number: (a) chanda, (b) adhimokṣa, (c) smṛti, (d) samādhi and (e) dhī. They are not so universal in scope as the sarvatraga class, but are peculiar to some kinds of consciousness.

(a) *Chanda* is wish for a desired object (abhiprete vastuni abhilāṣaḥ). It is not a universal caitta; its essence is desire so that without it there can be no chanda, and desire is not universal. Desire is the urge to make the object a content of the senses. To wish for the sight, and hearing, etc. of the object is chanda. It gives rise to effort (vīrya).

(b) *Adhimokṣa* is determinate judgment about an object made definite (niścite vastuni tatraiva avadhāraṇam). The object is defined either by reasoning or by testimony, and to determine it as it really is is adhimokṣa; it is a judgment of consciousness (cetasa abhiniveśaḥ). One who has adhimukti or firm belief cannot swerve from one's own doctrines.

(c) *Smṛti* is memory (saṁstute vastuni asampramoṣaś cetaso abhilapanatā)[7]. When an object experienced before is made the object of consciousness again, so that citta remembers it repeatedly as its former object, this steady activity of the mind is smṛti.

(d) *Samādhi* is concentration of mind on the object which latter is exmined either on its merits (guṇato) or its demerits (doṣato) (upaparīkṣye vastuni cittasya ekāgratā). This gives rise to correct knowledge, since the concentrated mind knows a thing as it is.

(e) *Dhī* is prajñā or insight into the nature of things. It is metaphysical insight as to whether the object is apprehended rationally or fallaciously, i.e. right knowledge regarding the validity or otherwise of the svalakṣaṇa and the sāmānyalakṣaṇa. Rational apprehension can be either by pratyakṣa, or anumāna, or āptopadeśa. The correct ascertainment of an object is of three kinds, or rather stages, viz. śrutamaya,

---

6. VMS, pp. 25-26.

7. Cf. The *Yoga Sūtra* definition of smṛti : anubhūtaviṣayasya asampramoṣaḥ smṛtiḥ ; I, 11.

cintāmaya and bhāvanāmaya.[8] First, there arises a verbal knowledge through āptavacana. This is deepened by pondering over it through reason. Then it is realised in samādhi. Empirical knowledge (laukika vyavahāra) is neither yogavihita (valid through reason) nor ayogavihita (fallacious). Dhī or prajñā removes false doubts by correctly ascertaining the nature of things.

These five viniyata cetasikas do not necessarily arise together; where one is present, the rest may or may not be present.

The distinction betmeen the sarvatraga and the viniyata dharmas is not recognised in the Sarvāstivāda. In the latter, all the ten are cittamahābhūmika, present in every moment of consciousness, while in the Yogācāra there are only five sarvatraga (universal) dharmas.

(3) Then come the *kuśala* (meritorious) *caittas*[9]. They are eleven in number, viz. (a) śraddhā, (b) hrī, (c) apatrapā, (d) alobha, (e) adveṣa, (f) amoha, (g) vīrya, (h) praśrabdhi, (i) apramāda, (j) upekṣā and (k) ahiṁsā. Vasubandhu mentions only 10 by name and omits upekṣā. Sthiramati however thinks that it is also included by implication. Sarvāstivāda has only 10 kuśalamahābhūmika dharmas, and omits amoha a which, according to it, is already subsumed under prajñā or mati, a universal dharma, but for which no knowledge would occur. There it connotes merely discrimination between one dharma and another, so that there is nothing especially meritorious about it. In the Yogācāra, not only prajñā or dhī is not a universal factor—it is one of the viniyata dharmas explained above—but amoha is distinguished as a kuśala dharma.

(a) *Śraddhā* is faith in the Noble Truth of Karmaphala and the consequent equanimity (prasāda) or purity of citta. Being the contrary of mental impurity (cittakāluṣya) it removes all kleśas and upakleśas. It is the incentive to chanda (desire).

(b) *Hrī* is shame (lajjā) due to the idea of sin committed, either because of one's conscience or because of religious injunctions (ātmānam dharmam vā adhipatim kṛtvā avadyena lajjā). The sin may or may not be actually committed. It prevents evil conduct (duścarita-samyama) but does not rule out the desire for such conduct.

---

8. The corresponds to the śravaṇa, manana and nididhyāsana of the Vedānta.

9. VMS, pp. 26-8.

(c) *Apatrapā* is also shame, but it is distinguished from the former in that this shame is because of social disapproval or fear of public censure. This serves the same purpose as hrī.

(d) *Alobha* is the contrary to lobha. Lobha is attachment to and desire for the world (bhava) and its luxuries. It takes away the incentive to evil conduct (duścarita-pravṛtti.). It is distinguished from hrī in that here even the desire for evil conduct is eradicated.

(e) *Adveṣa* is benevolence (maitrī). It is contrary to dveṣa, which is a pursuit leading to pain to the people. Adveṣa also leads to the absence of desire for bad conduct.

(f) *Amoha*[10] is the opposite of perverse knowledge, which latter is the knowledge of things as they are not and ignorance of the Noble Truth of Karmaphala. Amoha is the knowledge of things as they are, and serves the same function as alobha and adveṣa.

(g) *Vīrya* is enthusiasm for the good (kuśale cetaso abhyutsāhaḥ). It is the opposite of kauśīdya which is enthusiasm for the bad (kliṣṭa). Vīrya lends support to the side of the good.

(h) *Praśrabdhi* is the opposite of dauṣṭhulya. Dauṣṭhulya is the dullness or inertia (akarmaṇyatā) of body and mind, and is the root of all bad dharmas. The opposite of this is the activity of body (kāya-karmaṇyatā), i.e., the application of it to its object with ease, and the activity of mind (citta-karmaṇyatā) which arouses proper attention, delight and ease in it, making the mind flow towards its object. This makes possible the withdrawal of the phenomenal activity of vijñāna (i.e. āśraya-parāvṛtti) and the consequent destruction of all kleśas (aśeṣa-kleśāvaraṇa-niṣkarṣaṇa). It is only because mind remains petrified and passive before the object (cittasya akarmaṇyatā) that the object seems to be independent of it, and this leads to all kinds of defilements. When the mind becomes active, it absorbs the object in itself, and then the Ālaya ceases functioning.

(i) *Apramāda* is the opposite of pramāda. Owing to apramāda, the activity of alobha etc., is directed towards the avoiding of the akuśala dharmas and the concentration on the kuśala dharmas.

---

10. Linguistically these terms, "alobha" etc., appear to be negative but they are really positive. Thus amoha is not merely the absence of false knowledge ; it is rather the positive presence of right knowledge.

These alobha etc., are apramāda. Its function is the accumulation of benefits in this world and in the world to come (laukika-lokattara-sampatti-paripūraṇa-karmakaḥ).

(j) *Upekṣā* has three stages : (i) citta-samatā ; (ii) citta-praśaṭhatā ; (iii) citta-anābhogatā.

(i) *Citta-samatā* is equanimity of mind, its balance and poise, and absence of waywardness (auddhatya).

(ii) *Citta-praśaṭhatā* : Then the mind becomes steady (samāhita), and its poise (sama) is applied to empirical activities without the least effort. That is to say, it is only an application of cittasamatā.

(iii) *Anābhogatā* : mind reaches then such a height of meditation (bhāvanā-prakarṣa) that the waywardness of mind cannot even arise. It has been completely destroyed. Mind has no longer the need to concentrate on the opposite of waywardness : the state becomes natural to it.

Upekṣā precludes the possibility of the arising of all kleśas and upakleśas (sarva-kleśopakleśa-anavakāśa).

(k) *Avihiṁsā* is the contrary to cruelty. It is compassion for beings (sattveṣu karuṇā), being grieved at the grief of others, and the desire to relieve them from death and bondage.

(4) *Akuśala caittas*[11] are classified into the (A) 6 kleśas and (B) 20 upakleśas[12], making up a total of 26 dharmas. The 6 kleśas are (a) rāga, (b) pratigha, (c) moha, (d) māna, (e) dṛṣṭi, and (f) vicikitsā. The 20 upakleśas are (a) krodha, (b) upanāha, (c) mrakṣa, (d) pradāśa, (e) īrṣyā, (f) mātsarya, (g) māyā, (h) śāṭhya, (i) mada, (j) vihiṁsā, (k) āhrīkya, (l) anapatrāpya, (m) styāna, (n) auddhatya, (o) āśraddhya, (p) kauśīdya, (q) pramāda, (r) muṣitā smṛti, (s) vikṣepa, and (t) asamprajanya.

In the Sarvāstivāda, the kleśas and the upakleśas are not subclasses of the akuśala dharmas but are coordinate with it, so that the vicious caittas are divided into three classes, and not two as here, viz., (A)

---

11. VMS, pp. 28-32.

12. The basis of this distinction is never discussed. The kleśas perhaps are understood as basic and primary, while the upakleśas are their derivatives. In this connection, the admirable account given by Spinoza in his *Ethics*, Pt. IV, '*Of Human Bondage*,' may be profitably consulted.

the kleśa-mahābhūmika dharmas, (B) the akuśala-mahābhūmika dharmas, and (C) the upakleśa-mahābhūmika-dharmas. Kleśas are of the same number as those in the Yogācāra, viz., 6, but the two sets do not correspond to each other. The Sarvāstivāda list of the kleśas is (a) moha, (b) pramāda, (c) kauśīdya, (d) aśraddhā, (e) styāna, and (f) auddhatya. Of these only moha is classed as a kleśa in the Yogācāra ; the other five are only upakleśas here. The akuśala-mahābhūmika dharmas are two, viz., āhrīkya and anapatrāpya, both of them upakleśas in the Yogācāra. The upakleśa-mahābhūmika dharmas are 10, viz., (a) krodha, (b) mrakṣa, (c) mātsarya, (d) īrṣyā, (e) pradāśa, (f) vihiṁsā, (g) upanāha, (h) māyā, (i) śāṭhya, and (j) mada. The Yogācāra list of upakleśas includes all these 10, as also the 2 akuśala-mahābūmikas, along with 5 kleśa-mahābhūmikas ; the last three upakleśas do not figure at all in the Sarvāstivāda classification of the 18 vicious dharmas. Of the 6 kleśas in the Yogācāra list, moha is a kleśa in the Sarvāstivāda as well, while four of the rest, excluding dṛṣṭi, are included in the list of aniyata-bhūmi dharmas in the latter, and dṛk or asamyagdṛṣṭi is merely the negative of mati.

(4) *The kleśas* are, as enumerated above, 6 in number : (a) *Rāga* is attachment to phenomenal existence and desire for objects of enjoyment (bhavabhogayor adhyavasānam prārthanā ca). It gives rise to pain, i. e., the upādāna-skandhas. That is to say, rāga keeps the cycle of existence going, and this is pain.

(b) *Pratigha* is animosity and bitterness towards beings (satveṣu āghātaḥ rukṣacittatā) because of which one thinks of their death and bondage. It gives rise to uneasiness of mind and evil conduct.[13]

(c) *Moha* is ignorance[14] about the good, the Lord Buddha, and lastly, nirvāṇa and the means to it along with their mutual necessary relationship. It gives rise to three kinds of evils, viz., kleśas (bad mentals), further accumulation of karma, and consequently the continuance of the cycle of births.

(d) *Māna* is satkāyadṛṣṭi, false construction of an ego, because of which the mind gets elated. By the imposition of the concepts of 'I' and 'mine' on the constituent skandhas, one thinks specially of oneself,[15] and distinguishes it from the rest of existence. This elation of

13. Cf. Spinoza, *Ethics*, Pt. IV, Prop. XIV.
14. Ibid, Prop. XXIII.
15. Ibid, Prop. XLVIII-XLX.

the mind (cittasya unnati), though intrinsically one, can be described in 7 stages : (i) māna, (ii) atimāna, (iii) mānātimāna, (iv) asmimāna, (v) abhimāna, (vi) ūnamāna, and lastly (vii) mithyāmāna.

(e) *Dṛk*, or more correctly dṛṣṭi, comprises the 5 false constructions. Their difference is only as regards the constructs projected, and not the construction itself. These constructs are :

(i) *satkāyadṛṣṭi*—the construction of an ego ;

(ii) *antagrāhadṛṣṭi*—to take this ego either as eternal śāśvata) or as perishing (uccheda);

(iii) *mithyādṛṣṭi*—denial of the causal relation, or of a real existent. The last two are *dṛṣṭiparāmarśa* and *śīlavrataparāmarśa*.

(f) *Vicikitsā* is the wrong interpretation of the Noble Truth of Karmaphala, and the doubt regarding its existence.

(5) The *upakleśas*[16] are as many as 20. These are not so fundamental as the kleśas ; they are subsidiary evils.

(a) *Krodha* has for its object the present injury to somebody. It is not intrinsically different from the kleśa of pratigha, and is only a phase of the latter. Pratigha connotes injury in general, whereas krodha only present injury.

(b) *Upanāha* is the sentiment of enmity. Even after anger has subsided, one keeps on thinking "He has done me this harm" ; it follows anger as its aftermath. It gives rise to akṣānti, the desire to retaliate. This also is only a phase of pratigha.

(c) *Mrakṣa* is deceitfully hiding one's faults. It is an aspect of moha and gives rise to repentance (kaukṛtya) and uneasiness (asparśa).

(d) *Pradāśa* is the state of mind when uttering harsh and stinging words. It is a result of anger (krodha and upanāha), and is not therefore essentially different from pratigha. It gives rise to abusive language and also uneasiness of mind (asparśa).

(e) *Irṣyā* is anger at others' prosperity or any other superior trait in them (profit, respect, high birth, nobility of character, learning etc.). This also is a phase of pratigha or dveṣa and gives rise to asparśa-vihāra (uneasiness of mind).

(f) *Mātsarya* is the opposite of charity—the desire not to part with what one has (aparityāgecchā). It is a phase of rāga or lobha.

---

16. VMS, pp. 29-32.

(g) *Māyā* is to interpret, with a view to deceive others, the meaning of śīla etc., in a way inconsistent with their real meaning (paravañcanā yā abhūtārtha-sandarśanatā). It leads to false living (mithyājīva).

(h) *Śāṭhya* is crookedness of mind consequent on the attempt to hide one's faults by misleading others. This misleading is only imperfect here, whereas the deceit is complete in mrakṣa. It distracts mind's attention (yoniśo manaskāra).

(i) *Mada* is conceit, born of one's attachment to wealth, high birth, sound health and virility, strength or good looks, or intelligence etc. Mada is a kind of delight mind takes in these, because of which it loses its power of judgment. This gives rise to all the kleśas and upakleśas.

(j) *Vihiṁsā* is causing harm to beings by death, bondage, injury, menace etc., because of which they get harm and worry. It is a phase of pratigha. Vihiṁsā is, in short, harshness to beings.

(k) *Āhrīkya* is shamelessness of one's bad qualities, in spite of realising one's worthlessness.

(l) *Anapatrāpya* is indifference to others' condemnation, even knowing that the act committed is revolting to moral conscience or social judgment. Āhrīkya and anapatrāpya help to nourish all kleśas and upakleśas.

(m) *Styāna* is lethargy of mind, its inactivity or dullness. The mind is not active towards its object. It is an aspect of moha and helps to nourish all kleśas and upakleśas.

(n) *Auddhatya* is the opposite of a Stoic calm—taking delight in the memory of pleasures and sports and furthering the kleśas and upakleśas.

(o) *Āśraddhya* is lack of conviction in the Noble Truth of Karmaphala. It is contrary to faith in the existence of this Truth, its moral nature and its rigorous inevitability. It gives rise to kauśīdya which comes next.

(p) *Kauśīdya* is lack of interest in the meritorious dharmas. It is the opposite of vīrya (enthusiasm for such dharmas), and is therefore detrimental to the side of the good. One feels no enthusiasm in the good activities of body, mind and speech, because of an animal torpor. It is a phase of moha.

(q) *Pramāda* is the absence of any attempt to protect the mind from the kleśas of rāga, dveṣa, moha and kauśīdya, nor any meditation or concentration on their opposites. These lobha, dveṣa, etc., are known as pramāda, and result in the increase of vice.

(r) *Muṣitā* (*kliṣṭā*) *smṛti* is defiled memory and gives rise to distraction.

(s) *Vikṣepa* is the tossing of mind hither and thither. It is an aspect of rāga, dveṣa and moha. Because of the presence of these, mind is distracted from the object of samādhi towards external things. It obstructs vairāgya (detachment).

(t) *Asamprajanya* is defiled understanding. Owing to this, the discipline of body, speech and mind is not known aright, and duties are understood as not to be duties. It leads to harm (āpatti).

(6) The last class of cetasikas comprises the *aniyata dharmas*.[17] They are four in number, viz., (a) kaukṛtya, (b) middha, (c) vitarka, and (d) vicāra. These 4 dharmas are called aniyata since they can be bad (kliṣṭa) as well as akliṣṭa. When they are kliṣṭa, they are counted as so many more upakleśas. In the Sarvāstivāda, the number of aniyata-bhūmi-dharmas is increased to 8. To the four in the Yogācāra list are added rāga, dveṣa, māna and vicikitsā ; all of them are elevated to the rank of kleśas in the Yogācāra. In the Sarvāstivāda, they are held to be kleśas, but since these four cannot combine with each other, they are put as aniyata dharmas.

(a) *Kaukṛtya* is repenting of an action done. This repentance can be a meritorious as well as a vicious dharma. When a good action not done, or a bad one done, is repented of, it is an akliṣṭa dharma in that case. But when a bad action not done, or a good action done, gives cause for repentance, it is defiled kaukṛtya, and must be classed as an upakleśa.

(b) *Middha* is torpor of mind, the contraction of its freedom towards its object, the inability to fix its attention to the body or mind. All the senses are deadened by it. It is an aspect of moha.

(c) *Vitarka* is "an indistinct murmur of the mind" (Stcherbatsky)—manojalpa[18]—as to the determination of an object. It is an aspect of cetanā (volition—the "fluttering of consciousness") and prajñā (discriminating as good or bad). It is a subconscious operation of the mind.

---

17. VMS, pp. 32-33.
18. VMS, p. 32.

(d) *Vicāra* also is a particular phase of cetanā and prajñā. But here there is "an attempt to fix the object" (Stcherbatsky)—pratyavekṣaka. It is of the form "This is that," while that of vitarka is "What is this ?". While the latter is grosser, more indefinite (audārikatā) vicāra is more refined, more definite (sūkṣmatā). Vitarka and vicāra produce sparśa as well as asparśa, as the occasion may be. These two caittas are not forms of cognition, but of volition rather. Vitarka is "should it be done ?" while vicāra is "it should be done."

The sarvatraga dharmas are the universal factors invariably present in all moments of consciousness. The Ālaya-vijñāna has these five caittas alone. The Kliṣṭa Manas has these five and four nivṛtāvyākṛta kleśas as distinguished from the two akuśala kleśas. The various pravṛtti-vijñānas have all the caittas as far as possible. All of them need not be, and cannot be, simultaneously present in a single moment of a pravṛtti-vijñāna. But it is this kind of vijñāna alone which is capable of having them, some in one moment and some in another.

Vedanā is, as has been said before, of three kinds, viz., pleasant, painful and indifferent. The vedanā (feeling) in the Ālaya[19] is only the last. Pain and pleasure pertain only in relation to determinate objects and the consciousness of them. The ālambana of the Ālaya being indeterminate, the feeling there can only be neutral or upekṣā. The feeling in the Kliṣṭa Manas also is upekṣā, but it is anivṛta and avyākṛta in the Ālaya, as are all the dharmas there, while in the Manas it is nivṛta and avyākṛta, and so are other dharmas as well found in it. The feeling in the pravṛtti-vijñānas can be of all the three kinds. A pleasant feeling is associated with alobha, adveṣa and amoha, a painful feeling with lobha, dveṣa and moha, while an indifferent feeling with neither.

III. The third class of dharmas is constituted by the *rūpas* out of which the objective world is made. This world having no real existence, the rūpas must be held to be forms of consciousness, supplying the contents of it. It is consciousness itself which creates and projects these rūpas, making them seem as though external and independent. The rūpa-dharmas and the cetasikas are both real only as pertaining to or qualifying consciousness ; their difference lies

19. VMS, p. 21, 33.

in the fact that when consciousness is diversified into the subject-object duality, the cetasikas inhere in the so-called subjective side, while the rūpa-dharmas constitute the so-called objective side. In reality, they are both adjectival in nature, qualifying and distinguishing the moments of consciousness, from different points of view.

Rūpas are of two kinds, viz., the mahābhūtas (ultimate constituents of matter, four in number), and secondly, the bhautika rūpas, the derivatives, which are actually experienced. For some unknown reason the mahābhūtas are not considered separately ; the reason probably is that matter as such being the product of mind, the problem of the ultimate units of the objective material universe is not a relevant one, and the classification of the rūpas is confined to the gross things actually apparent before consciousness.

Rūpas are eleven in number, viz., the five senses, their five respective sense-data, and the 11th rūpa is that included under dharmāyatana or dharmadhātu. It is significant that only sense-data are enumerated here ; realists would necessarily admit a substance over and above these, which would impart unity and thinghood to them. This conception of a substance is repugnant to the whole tenor of Buddhism, a tradition accepted by the Yogācāra only empirically; really speaking sense-data are equally projections of the knowing consciousness.

The 11th rūpa in the Sarvāstivāda is the avijñaptirūpa. The conceptions of this rūpa in the two systems are however poles asunder. Avijñapti-rūpa is the general character of a man—"the vehicle of moral qualities" (Stcherbatsky)—which is, peculiarly enough, held to be material in the Sarvāstivāda. The rūpa included in the dharmadhātu is, according to the Yogācāra, matter not sensuously known, e. g., atoms etc. It includes matter objectively existent (empirically speaking), or only imagined to exist. It is thus a miscellaneous category including, among other things, avijñapti-rūpa as well.

IV. *Citta-viprayukta-saṁskāra-dharmas* are the next class of dharmas. They are so called because there is nothing distinctively conscious about them. Though they must ultimately pertain to consciousnes in order to attain reality, their relation to consciousness is not very apparent. They are really 'forces' or functions which are neither specifically material nor mental ; they can belong to either indifferently. It is a miscellaneous class including all kinds of categories, like space and time, number and order, conjunction and separation, subsistence and impermanence, significance of words, etc., all more or less abstract, and as such the principal point of attack by the Sautrāntika. They are 24 in number, viz., (a) prāpti, (b) jīvita (-indriya), (c) nikāyasabhāgatā, (d) pṛthagjāti (aprāpti), (e) asañjñi-samāpatti, (f) nirodha-samāpatti (these two are included here as, in these two stages of samādhi, consciousness becomes so subtle as practically to cease), (g) asañjñivipāka, (h) nāmakāya, (i) padakāya, (j) vyañjanakāya, (k) jāti, (l) jarā, (m) sthiti, (n) anityatā, (o) pravṛtti (srotaḥ santati), (p) evam bhāgīya (samādhyantara), (q) pratibandha, (r) javanya, (s) krama, (t) deśa (dik), (u) kāla, (v) saṅkyhā, (w) sāmagrī (samyoga), and lastly (x) bheda (viyoga) . In the Sarvāstivāda, only the first 14 are accepted as rūpa-citta-vipraryukta-saṅskāras.

V. The *Asaṁskṛta dharmas* are not subject to causes and conditions ; they are the "immutable dharmas." Nor are they governed by the law of impermanence since they are not phenomenal at all. That does not make all of them noumenal however.

In the Sarvāstivāda, three asaṁskṛta dharmas are accepted. The Sautrāntika rejected the class altogether. Even nirvāṇa was merely of a negative import ; it was the total extinction of all dharmas. The Yogācāra, as an absolutist, had to reinstate the asaṁskṛta dharmas, and indeed increased their number to six, viz., (a) ākāśa, (b) pratisaṅkhyā-nirodha, (c) apratisaṅkhyā-nirodha (these three are common to Sarvāstivāda as well), (d) acalanirodha, (e) saṁjñā-vedayitṛ-nirodha, and lastly (f) Tathatā.[20] This last is the ultimate essence of everything (bhūta-tathatā), the Absolute itself. Really speaking, this is the only asaṁskṛta ; there can be but one Unconditioned. That Tathatā also is enumerated as one of the dharmas leaves no room for doubt that the dharma-phenomenology is entirely unaffected by any metaphysical considerations. Whatever is accepted, whether in the ultimate sense or merely for empirical purposes, is counted as a dharma.

20. The introduction of this as a dharma made a complete revolution in the theory of dharmas. Instead of being eternally distinct they became but modes of the Absolute.

Chapter VII

THE YOGĀCĀRA CONCEPTION OF THE ABSOLUTE

From Idealism to Absolutism

Idealism as a constructive pattern for explaining phenomena has been established. It is proved that the object is nothing apart from the consciousness of it. The subjective alone is real. The blue is a form of consciousness, and as such is real. Its externality is only the mode of its appearance. It appears to be 'out there', possessing independence and self-existence ; that however is only the way in which consciousness projects its contents. The subjective is governed by its own laws ; it is independent of the object. One state of consciousness gives rise to another owing to its inherent dynamism. The causal law operates between moments of consciousness and not between consciousness and the object.

Is this position ultimate ? Can the object be negated and yet its form in consciousness reinstated and retained ? Consciousness is momentary when ridden by the false idea of objectivity ; when this idea is realised to be false, will consciousness still go on perishing every moment ? The issue needs clarification, if only to realise its implications.

Negation must be total and absolute. The content negated must be rejected totally. A half-hearted negation is no negation. Even if negation is partial, that part which is negated is absolutely rejected.[1] If the part again is only partially negated, it clearly leads to an infinite regress, with the result that nothing is negated at all. If objectivity is to be negated, its sublation must be rigorous and consistent. The objective does not merely mean externality to consciousness. Any content which is an 'other' to consciousness is its object. Ideas which

---

1. Cf. the doctrine of Aristotelian logic that even an O Proposition distributes its predicate.

are the contents of manovijñāna, the sixth pravṛtti-vijñāna, are objects of the latter in the same sense as the so-called external objects are. Negation of the object means an absolute denial of the 'other' in any form. If it is surreptitiously introduced in the subjective order, consciousness is still confronted with an 'other', so that nothing has been negated after all. The assertion that consciousness is the sole reality is belied by the continued existence of the 'other'. The negation of the object is only half-hearted.

Why is the object rejected? What constitutes its unreality? The object is rejected as false because it has no independent existence, it cannot be had apart from the consciousness of it. All negation implies an evaluation. Consciousness is real because it is something *sui generis.* It enjoys an absolute self-existence and, to be manifested, does not depend upon the 'other'. This preference in favour of consciousness can hold good only when consciousness can be shown to exist in its own right. The object is rejected because it is not independent. It must necessarily be revealed by consciousness. This dependence is one-sided ; if it is reciprocal there can be no ground for preferring one to other. If the 'other', whether external or not, is an intrinsic form of consciousness, we walk into the realists' parlour. The object must then be granted a co-ordinate status with consciousness. Or, if it is rejected because it is dependent upon consciousness, the latter also, being in the same predicament, must be deemed unreal.[2] The sole reality of consciousness requires that it should be free from any trace of objectivity, that it should be capable of existing without any other to it.

This is the great advance that the Yogācāra makes over Hegel. For Hegel idealism does not mean the rejection of the object. Its externality and independence is denied, but that does not make it a creation of the subjective. Both the terms are related to each other ; their falsity consists in their being viewed in isolation. Abstraction is the only thing that is condemned by Hegel ; otherwise the concept of unreality finds no place in him, there being no ground for evaluation. Of the subject-object opposition, each of the terms requires the other for its own realisation, and one therefore cannot be preferred to the other. Both of them are indeed included in a higher unity—

2. This is the Mādhyamika view.

that of Reason ; but Reason again is itself bifurcated into this opposition, because of its inherent necessity. The 'other' can never be dispensed with ; hence the assertion that the 'other' is a projection remains dogmatic. The counter-asseertion that the subject itself is a projection of the 'other' would in that case be equally justified. To substantiate the former statement what is required is that the subject should be shown as existing without projecting the 'other'. Only then can it be known as the basic reality, and the 'other' as a mere creation.

To envelop the whole of phenomena in an all-comprehensive Reason leaves the relation between the subject and object entirely unaffected. The subject does not create the object, but rather both are creations of the universal Reason. They are related through a third entity—Reason ; in themselves they should have nothing to do with each other. Curiously enough, this position is little different from that of the rank realist. He also maintains that both are ultimate, and that the object cannot be dispensed with. The Hegelian position is certainly not realism, since here the object has no independence ; it is essentially related to the subject. Nor is it pure idealism, since the subject is not primal and the object is not its own creation. Hegel stops short with relativity ; his system may be described as Rational Idealism, since both the terms are projections of Reason ; it is not, however, Epistemological Idealism which makes consciousness the sole reality. The Hegelian Absolute is also consciousness, but it has no absoluteness in it ; it is a mere system of determinate relations.

The Yogācāra is wise enough to perceive that if the object is to be rejected, it cannot be retained even as a form of consciousness. If consciousness is invariably confronted by an 'other', be it by its own form, the sublation of the object is meaningless. Knowledge is the only index for us of phenomenal existence, and if the object persistently raises its head in knowledge, it matters little whether it does not objectively exist. No change has been effected in our knowledge by the negation of the object.

Is it possible for consciousness to be aware of an 'other' which is not external to itself ? In reality, externality is an illusion ; what exist are only the forms of consciousness. But can these forms be known as the 'other' even when their objective projection is lacking ? If the object is not an other to consciousness, it is not an object at all. Consciousness is a consciousness *of* something : that 'of'-relation may be an illusory one ; it is required nevertheless to sustain the knowledge of objectivity. Consciousness is essentially the subject ; it projects the form of objectivity owing to the primary illusion; of itself it is never objectified. When the illusory form of objectivity falls away from it, its subject-function also lapses automatically.[3] The subject acquires all its significance and meaning because of its relation to the object ; without the latter it is nothing. If one of the terms of a dualism is rejected as false, the other also cannot be maintained.

In order to sustain the internal diversity of consciousness, the existence of the 'other' is required. That 'other' may be in itself illusory ; nevertheless, if consciousness is diversified at all, it is diversified only as the 'other' confronting it. When the 'other' is negated, the duality is made internal, it might be held. Here there are three alternatives to be considered. First, though there is no real objectivity, the idea of objectivity is present ; and this is all that is required for the bifurcation of consciousness. This position however just misses the point. The object is nothing in itself, and cannot therefore be sublated. When the object is said to be negated, it is meant that its false idea should be eradicated. To reject the object is therefore to annihilate the idea of an object.

Secondly, the object may not be objectively known, but may be present as a mode of consciousness. Even the idea of objectivity is lacking here. The consciousness of blue does not project the 'blue' as an external other. Still there arises the consciousness of blue owing to its own inner conditions. This hypothesis is hardly plausible. What is this consciousness of blue ? It is not a unitary entity but must be split into its various elements. First, there is the '*blue*'. It may not be an 'other', but only a form of consciousness, but still, so far as it is a 'blue', it is a form appearing in consciousness, and not consciousness itself. Secondly, there is the *awareness* of blue.[4] The mere factual occurrence of 'blue', whether in or outside consciousness, has no meaning. It must be *known*. Hence though it is a mode of consciousness, yet its function of awareness must be carefully distinguished from this mode. This does not entail the accep-

3. grāhyābhāve tadagrahāt; VMS, p. 43 ; also tatra ekasyāpyabhāvena dvayamapy avahīyate tasmāt tadeva tasyāpi tattvam yā dvayaśūnyatā; PV, II, 213.

4. PV, II, 337 ; also p. 235.

tance of a transparent awareness, because the distinction is not of distinct factors, but of aspects merely. Thirdly, the consciousness of blue must stand *self-revealed*; it must not be in necessity of being known by a separate act of knowledge.[5] This function of self-awareness must again be distinguished from the consciousness of blue. There are thus three functions in consciousness : (1) the appearance of blue (nīla), (2) the consciousness of blue (nīlavijñāna), and (3) the self-awareness of this consciousness (svasaṃvedana). These three are by no means so many separate factors in each case of knowledge, but are rather the distinguishable aspects of a unitary consciousness. It is one and the same consciousness that has these three functions. Still this concept is hardly intelligible. How can these three aspects be distinguished,[6] and yet the whole—strictly speaking no whole, since there are no parts—the whole remains a unity, is an unsolved enigma. Moreover, there is another fundamental difficulty in accepting this position. Consciousness is the one unitary whole which may be differentiated into the three aspects ; it is however also the second of the three aspects differentiated above. It is therefore in a peculiar position : it must occupy two positions at once; it is one of the aspects, and also that of which it is an aspect, and these two militate against each other. One thing cannot be both at once. However strongly we may defend the unity and partlessness of consciousness, so long as it has different aspects, it must act in this double role, and this is theoretically indefensible. And aspects it must have; otherwise, there would remain only the bare consciousness, and the distinction between blue and yellow cannot be maintained.

There is still a third posibility to be explored. The consciousness of blue is not a whole which can be differentiated into separate aspects, but a unitary surd not to be further explained. Each consciousness is what it is. The consciousness of blue is not consciousness *and* blue, but is a brute unity. This theory however is still more fantastic than the previous one. If there are no aspects in that unitary consciousness one might as well call it the object as the consciousness of it. The

5. svarūpavedanāya anyad vedakam na vyapekṣate na ca aviditam asti idam ityartho' yan svasamvidaḥ. TS, I, 2012.

6. kriyākārakabhedena na svasamvittirasya tu, ekasya anaṁśarūpasya traividhyānupapattitaḥ. TS, 1, 2001.

subject is known only as contrasted with the object; here this distinction is lacking, and it is indifferent to the surd, whether it is an object or not. Again, consciousness of blue is not blue consciousness, since consciousness cannot be burdened with physical attributes. Therefore the 'of' here is a real 'of'; blue is merely a form which can be maintained only by being projected as the 'other'. The subject knows the object; brushing the question aside whether this object is a form of consciousness or an external reality, if the distinction itself is done away with, it must know itself to be entitled consciousness. Even the distinction of aspects is repudiated here; the same thing is both subject and object at once. But this is an impossible feat: even the most expert acrobat cannot climb his own shoulders. The same finger cannot touch itself, nor can an axe cut its own self. A thing can turn back upon itself only when it is arrested in its forward movement; the subject is aware of its own function by realising the otherness of the object. Here this reflex is an impossibility; but still it has to know itself, since there is nothing else to be known.

Moreover, without making a distinction of aspects how is the consciousness of blue to be distinguished from that of yellow? Each is a surd and is what it is; then why are both called consciousness? What is the common ground underlying both, which prevents each being merely a blue or a yellow, but makes both of them consciousness? These questions cannot be met if forms of consciousness, which are yet not 'other' to it, are accepted.

Idealism must therefore find a consciousness which is absolutely free from any trace of objectivity. Merely making it internal is not sufficient to establish idealism. It is indeed the first step, but a further step must be taken. The object is so identical with consciousness, that it cannot be distinguished even as its form. It loses its individuality entirely and without any residue. The forms of consciousness are there merely because of the illusory reflection of the unreal object. With the sublation of the external object, the forms are automatically merged in consciousness. This does not mean, however, that an identical or continuous pure consciousness underlies the various forms of blue and yellow[7]. Consciousness itself is diversified into these forms and when identity is established between the object and its consciousness, the

7. MSA, p. 61.

forms are completely lost in it. We may not call this consciounsess pure, in the sense of transparence, but it is pure in the sense that the forms cannot be distinguished in it.

These considerations apply with equal force to the doctrine of momentariness of consciousness as well. When the specific forms are lost in consciousness, even the different moments cannot be distinguished. This does not make consciousness identical; it means only that difference is no longer perceptible. The same argument which establishes identity between blue and its consciousness, makes away with the distinction between consciousness of blue and that of yellow. Each is so completely identical with consciousness that neither can be maintained apart from it, and hence their mutual distinctions also lapse. Moments are distinguishable so long as difference of content holds ; a pure difference is no difference, there being no novel emergence.

We arrive therefore at the conception of a consciousness which is not diversified into the empirical forms[8], and of which momentarines cannot be predicated. Consciousness acquires these forms because of an illusory 'other'. When the blue is sublated, even the consciousnes of blue must go.[9] It might be urged that even after the cancellation of the illusory snake, the snake-consciousness, which is real by itself, remains. Hence it is possible that when the objective world as a whole is negated, its consciousness might still persist. This possibility is ruled out because there is a difference between the negation of the snake and that of the world. When the snake is negated, the world as such suffers no loss. The idea of objectivity reigns unchallenged. The forms of subjectivity, which are sustained and nourished by their projections, are still there. When objectivity as such is negated, there being nothing to confront consciousness, it cannot serve even as the subject.[10] Even to know a form as subjective, it must be distinguished from the objective, which indicates that the negation of the latter has been merely verbal. The consciousness of there being nothing objective entails the entertaining of this objectivity[11] before consciousness. It has not been reduced to mere naught.

8. MSA, VI, 1. 9. MSA, VI, 7-8 ; PV, II, 330-1.

10. MSA, XI, 48 ; also PV, II, 332.

11. na upalambhopalambhaprayogataś ca dvayānupalambhanā dvayopalambhāt; MSA, p. 191.

Consciousness therefore is diversified into the various forms because of the illusory idea of the 'other'. These forms are sustained by being projected as objective. With the sublation of objectivity, there remains nothing to confront consciousness, and hence these forms, which are so many reflections of the objective, dissolve themselves into consciousness again. Consciousness is intrinsically free from the duality of subject and object.[12] Nor does succession inherently belong to it. It is the Absolute.

The Conception of the Absolute

Absolutism is the logical culmination of idealism. Consciousness is the subject so long as it is opposed by an other. Negation of the latter entails the disappearance of the former. When there is nothing to know, the knowing function also ceases.[13]

The Absolute is a non-dual consciousness. The duality of the subject and object does not pertain to it.[14] It is said to be void (śūnya), devoid of duality ; in itself it is perfectly real, in fact the only reality. It is śūnya, because it cannot be characterised by any of the empirical predicates, of which the subject-object relativity is the most fundamental. It is nothing empirical, being free from all determinations.[15] A thing can be characterised only by its relation to other things, i.e., by being determined by its relations. The subject-object relation is the matrix of all relations,[16] and when this itself falls away, there remains nothing to determine the Absolute, and as such it is śūnya. It is eternal, as it is beyond Time ; Time is, as we have seen, nothing else than the succession of forms of consciousness. When these latter have subsided, all change in consciousness lapses.[17] It is transcendent to Reason or discursive thought. Thought works within the framework of the 'other'; relation and distinction are the very essence of thought. Though the

---

12. PV, II, 354.

13. grāhyābhāve tadagrahāt ; VMS, p. 43 ; MVSBT, p. 10, 14, 22-23 ; PV, II, 213 ; LAS, X, 563 ; TSN, 36.

14. tatra dvayena grāhyagrāhakabhāvena nirūpayitum aśakyatvāt ; MSA, p. 191.

15. MSA, XI, 41.

16. PV, II, 215.

17. VMS, p. 41-42 ; sarvakālam tathābhāvāt.

Absolute is arrived at by an analysis of the nature of consciousness as evinced by empirical knowledge, it is yet something beyond it. There is no consciousness *of* the Absolute ; Consciousness is the Absolute. It is intuited by the Intellectual Intuition, the culmination of the Transcendental Wisdom.[18]

The Absolute is not however a mere bundle of negatives.[19] It is indescribable in terms of empirical discourse ; in itself it is very positive. The negatives are required to show its transcendent nature. It is characterised as what cannot be characterised. It is contentless consciousness, Will as pure Act, unlike the passive Being of the Advaita Vedānta. The latter seems only a dead inertia to the idealist, for whom consciousness, divested of its creativity, is nothing.

The Absolute as Pure Will

The form being identical in all absolutistic systems, no distinction can be made in the Absolute itself. Only different approaches to it indicate the different metaphysical standpoints. The idealist will not however admit the possibility of an alternative approach, being himself the champion of a speculative system.

The Yogācāra approach is the conception of consciousness as pure Will. Consciousness denotes a determinate relation between the subject and object. This relation will differ fundamentally according to the emphasis placed upon either of the two terms. It may be understood as mere revelation of the object which exists in its own right. Or, the object may be construed as being nothing apart from its consciousness. The latter is the idealistic approach, as exemplified in the Will consciousness. The willed content owes whatever reality it possesses to the fact of its being willed. If exists solely in and through the willing of it. In itself it is nothing. Consciousness however is not so dependent upon the content, since in that case it would have to depend upon a thing which is itself not established. The subject is the primary reality ; the content is real only as its form.

In realism and realistic systems the relationship is put on an entirely different footing. The object is the only reality ; whatever is found in consciousness is traceable in the objective ; consciousness of the object

18. VMS, p. 43 ; jñānam lokattaram ca tat.
19. Cf. MSA, VI, 1; IX, 24.

is itself *one more object*. It has no unique position of its own. Consciousness is helpless before the object which is absolutely indifferent to the former. Knowing is the knowing of something objectively given. The subject has nothing which it can call its own, i.e., which is not given to it by the object. It is pure awareness. Hence when the subject is nothing, consciousness is understood as knowledge, whereas when the object is nothing, it is will.

It is a paradox that the willed content is the negation of that will. When a content is will*ed*, it becomes an accomplished fact and consciousness loses all hold over it. It becomes in fact a content *known*, though by its origin it is a willed content. When I will to do a particular deed, my consciousness remains will, only so long as it is not realised. As soon as the action is done, no amount of will can undo it again. It can only be *known*, as it has already taken its place in the comity of things. The will is repelled by the actualised willed content which constitutes a limitation or negation of it.[20]

Action is generally taken to be the jurisdiction of the will consciousness. Our information about the so-called external world is supposed to be received by our knowing consciousness. Metaphysics is interested in abolishing this dual conception of consciousness. If action, which *is* accepted as the realisation of will, yet constitutes a negation of it, consciousness of the external world is a far greater negation of it ; here there is not even the faintest consciousness of willing. The will has been completely paralysed here.

The paradox is that consciousness can be termed will only when it wills contents, but the latter negate it at the same time. That very characteristic by which will is recognised constitutes its negation. The reason is that no empirical consciousness can be obtained in its absolute purity. Every empirical case of will is subdued by the knowing function of consciousness which is its negation. Even in the highest flight of productive imagination where will as the subjeetive reigns supreme, there is yet an alien element of knowledge. When I imagine that I go to a dream-land and do all kinds of fantastic things, I am conscious of the fact that this is all within my mind, without the least vestige of objective truth, and to this extent it is a case of will. I am not taken in by it, and the corrective self-consciousness is there all along. But still

20. Cf. *Mind as Pure Act,* p. 261.

it is not free from the knowing function, and is not therefore a case of pure will. Can anybody imagine anything whatsoever which is not imagined objectively, i.e., as occurring in space and time ? One may certainly be aware that this is all subjective, but so long as one imagines at all, one does it only *as though* the content were objective. That is to say, there is no case of will which is not still-born, not waylaid by knowledge.

The same is the case with knowledge as well. By definition the knowing consciousness is one where the subject is nothing apart from the revealed object. It must not oppose itself to the object. But in any case of knowledge, however transparent consciousness might be, it will yet be an other to the object ; it will contemplate the object only from outside, and not reveal the inner nature or essence of it. Strictly speaking, knowing an object must be being[21] it; there is no other way of knowing it. However negligible the subject might be, it will yet constitute an opposition or dualism, and as such negation of the object.

Consciousness can will a content, only by ceasing to be will; hence, paradoxically again, the pure will wills nothing.[22] As soon as it wills a particular content, the latter is instantaneously precipitated into a known content. In all empirical consciousness there is this perverse confusion of the subjective functions, so that one annuls the other. To reach the purity of the will we must go beyond phenomenal consciousness. Pure Will is the Absolute, where all dualism[23] of the will and the willed content is done away with. The Absolute is the pure activity of Will, unobstructed by the willing of any content.

No empirical will is pure. Its will aspect, if made pure, will become the Absolute. This aspect is the only reality. The other aspect, which is invariably associated with it and makes for its defilement, is the knowing aspect ; this is unreal. Knowledge makes its object independent of the act of knowing ; hence this idea of an independent 'other', or of objectivity in general, is the falsification of will. Objectivity is the transcendental illusion, and is the work of Avidyā. What is really

---

21. Cf. brahma veda brahmaiva bhavati.

22. Citta is thus really acitta. VMS, p. 43.

23. na hi abhūtaparikalpaḥ kasyacid grāhako nāpi kenacid gṛhyate kim tarhi grāhya-grāhakatva-rahitam vastumātram ; MVSBT, 10.

willed is taken to be *known*, because of this. The content is real as a form of consciousness. Its appearance as external, as an other to consciousness, is false.

Avidyā is therefore the objectification of consciousness. The Absolute consciousness is non-dual, but when infected by the illusory idea of the 'other', it is diversified into the subject and object.[24] The function of Avidyā is the creation of this fundamental duality. Pure Will, as we have seen, ceases to be will, i.e., it wills no contents. It is like an ocean, unruffled by any hostile element. The idea of an 'other' acts like the wind which disturbs its calm, compelling the insurgence of waves.[25] These waves are as it were the particular moments of consciousness, whose contents are projected as though objective. This creates the duality of the subject and object, which in reality does not belong to consciousness. The subject is certainly not unreal as the object is, but consciousness assumes the function of a subject as soon as it is confronted by an 'other. It does not inherently belong to it, as that would mean the perpetuation of the object. With the negation of the object, the subject also lapses.

Advaita Vedānta arrives at a form of the Absolute by an analysis of the knowledge function of the subject. The object is indifferent to the knowing of it. Its being is not relative to its being known. It may be known, but it need not. Whether the rope is perceived as a snake or as a rope, it remains entirely unaffected.

We have said that no empirical consciousness is pure. It is neither pure will nor pure knowledge, but is invariably a confusion of these two. Our experience is constituted by both the factors; but their different origin is lost sight of, since one is superimposed upon the other. What is the contribution of the subjective is taken to be objective and this is the nature of the Cosmic Illusion in both the forms of absolutism. They depart from each other in their evaluation of these two factors of experience.[26] For the Vedāntin, the real is the pure object, as unrelated to the knowing act ; subjectivity constitutes its negation. The Yogācāra makes subjectivity itself the only reality ;

---

24. avibhāgo'pi buddhyātmā viparyāsitadarśanaiḥ grāyhagrāhakasamvittibhedavān iva lakṣyate ; PV, II, 354.

25. Cf. MA, VI, 46 ; LAS, X, 56-7.

26. CPB, p. 320.

the independence of the object is its negation. The illusion of the rope-snake occurs because the snake which is subjective in its nature is yet projected as though objective. For the Vedāntin the function of Avidyā consists in covering up the real which is the unrelated object, the rope, and showing in its place, the snake ; the snake is false *because it is subjective* which has being only as it is related with consciousness (prātibhāsika). The Yogācāra holds that the function of Avidyā is just the reverse ; the snake is perfectly real as the form of the subjective ; its illusoriness consists in its objectification ; the snake is false *because it is objective.*[27]

The acceptance of subjectivity as real is connected with another important issue. The illusory appearance of the object may be condemned, but the fact of its appearance cannot be denied. Vedānta is interested in denying even the fact of the appearance. The real is the rope, and from its point of view, the appearance of the snake is not a fact. The rope as the unrelated was never involved in it.[28] The snake is a freak of the subjective, and the subjective does not exist, in the sense that the rope does. The fact of the illusoriness is itself illusory; or at no time was the snake real; it never existed. But the Yogācāra makes this unrelatedness of the object false. The snake is real only as a subjective fact. The snake-illusion may be cancelled, but that it did appear, and did create a problem, cannot be in dispute. The subjective being real, the fact of the appearance, which is a subjective creation, is also real. Hence for the Yogācāra the Real does get involved in the transcendental Illusion ; it cannot remain neutral (kūṭastha) in the presence of the illusory. It can certainly regain its purity on negating the object ; but the subjective does change and get modified according to the false appearance. Vivarttavāda cannot be maintained by the Yogācāra.

The Real is the Will. Will must get involved in the projection of contents. It will be modified according to the forms which it creates and objectifies as the 'other'. Were it unaffected by the change of contents, it will no longer be will ; it will degenerate into a mere passive spectator of the change presented before it. It will be reduced to

27. Cf. *Bhāmatī*, p. 26.

28. pratipannopādhau traikālikaniṣedha-pratiyogitvam vā mithyātvam ; *Advaitasiddhi*, p. 94.

knowledge, and will lose its creativity. Since the forms are identical with the creating will, the latter cannot be a dead inert Being, but must evolve into the diversity of forms. Avidyā defiles the Real ; this defilement itself is unreal in Vedānta, whereas, according to the Yogācāra, the Real is really entangled, though that can be helped.

Pure will gets defiled when it falsely takes what is its own form as something objective. The transcendental Illusion consists in confusion between the subjective and the objective, and its cancellation is the analysis or distinction between these two. But the question arises : why can we not stop with this distinction ? Only the ascription of the objective on the subjective is false. For the correction of this illusion all that is required is the denial of this ascription or false relation between the two. The negation of objectivity as such seems unwarranted. Both may be real in their own places ; their confusion gives rise to all the trouble, and only this much need be condemned. The two terms are individually real ; only their relation is false.[29]

This contention is based upon a wrong understanding regarding the nature of negation. The negation of the illusory will itself show that the two terms are not on a par. With the problem of the negation, that of reality also is intrinsically connected. When the illusory is negated, the real is perceived in its true form. The issue is therefore as to which of the terms is taken as basic, and the other the falsification of it. The 'other' may be real in its own right, but that which appeared here in place of the real is totally negated. That it is real somewhere else has nothing to do with its appearance here. All negation involves an evaluation ; one is preferred to the other. The negation cannot be false without one of the terms being false.[30] When the appearance of the snake is sublated, the sublating consciousness is that the objective snake is absolutely nothing ; it never existed. That the snake is somewhere else objectively real is irrelevant to the present appearance. Its objectivity is cancelled once for all. It cannot be urged "should we evaluate at all ?", since evaluation is the very form of

29. This is a variation of the anyathā-khyātivāda.

30. This logic applies to the Advaita Vedānta also. For the Mādhyamika, both the terms, i.e., the entire relational complex, are false. Cf. CPB, Ch. 13, passim.

negation. When the snake is negated we realise that its objectivity has no self-existence. It is nourished only as a projection of will-consciousness. In Advaita Vedānta, when the snake is negated, it is not reinstated as a subjective fact. The subjective in fact can function only through a mistake, only by falsifying the objectively real. In itself the subjective is nothing. There cannot be a consciousness of snake which does not appear as an objective snake. The subjective is only the way of distorting the real. The distortion itself is not a fact; it is only distortion *of* a fact. And when the Yogācāra takes the dream-consciousness as illusory, he is aware that the apparent objectivity in dreams can never be an individual fact by itself. All the contents of the dream are in reality only subjective facts : when these are subtracted, there remains nothing which can be said to belong to the objective realm. There cannot be a contentless bare objectivity. It is in fact only the way in which these subjective facts are projected, only a form of the subjective itself. In both the systems, one of the terms which gives rise to the confusion is reduced to nil.

The Nature of Avidyā.

This gives a clue to the nature of Avidyā. Being itself unreal, it cannot exist by itself. In itself it is nothing.[31] It exists only through its function ; it is what it does. Its entire nature is falsification of the Real[32]. It exists only by exploiting the latter. It is essentially parasitical in its nature. Though objectivity is an illusion, it can yet be nourished only by the Real, the subjective itself. It is a mistake on the part of the Real, due to ignorance of its own nature. It is the Real which suffers under the illusion of objectivity, by negating itself. Avidyā exists only in and through the self-forgetfulness of the Real.

Objectivity is unreal ; there is only the idea of objectivity which governs all empirical experience. This idea being a subjective fact, there arises a misunderstanding regarding the nature of the subjective. The subjective is the real, and yet the idea of the object being also subjective is again unreal. This is due to a confusion of the two senses in

31. svayam asad api yad ākāreṇa pratibhāsate sā bhrāntir māyāvat ; MVSBT, p. 18.

32. MVSBT, p. 29.

which the term 'subjective' is used. First, the subjective means the epistemic, i.e., the knowing of a thing, not the thing itself. Secondly, the subjective is taken to be the false, as it imports to the objective what is not there. In the Vedānta, these two meanings are equated : what is subjective is false, and vice versa. The Yogācāra keeps these two separate. The subjective is the only reality ; it is epistemic, and yet exists ontologically. It is at the same time the locus of unreality, since Avidyā cannot exist anywhere else. The subjective thinks itself to be something other than what it is ; this thinking itself is subjective. In this sense there is a subjectivity in the subjective, and the former is the falsification of the latter.

There is however no contradiction involved in this. Avidyā has this peculiar nature that it exists in the Real, and yet is nothing. The two are in fact not of one order, but belong to different planes altogether. They cannot be put side by side, and compared. Avidyā exists only so long as the Real is not known. This apparent contradiction exists in the Vedānta as well. Subjectivity is unreal ; universal objectivity or the pure Being is the only reality. But since subjectivity is nothing in itself, and yet must somehow exist, it can exist only in the Pure Being, i.e., in the objective. It seems that there are two objectives then, one ontological, and the other epistemic. The contradiction can arise, only when they are on a par. But the epistemic, in the sense of falsification, is a fact in neither of the two systems. It is, as we have said, parasitical, and can exist only by exploiting the reality of the Absolute. The difference becomes clear when we contrast the idea of objectivity with other ideas. Both are subjective, but the former can exist only through the projection of the real subjective facts. There is no idea of objectivity as such, comparable to the ideas of blue or yellow. It is in fact only the form of the appearance of the latter. The distinction is that of the transcendental function and its empirical product, the objectifying tendency and the object 'blue'. This appearance being unreal, the form also must be denied.

What is the genesis of Avidyā ? How is it that the Absolure forgets its pristine purity, and gets phenomenalised ? It is difficult to conceive how the Absolute becomes ignorant all at once. There is no reason why it should change its natural unruffled existence for a defiled one. If it was not ignorant at any one time, it can never be so. Ignorance must be posited as already defiling the Absolute. There is no conscious falling into illusion. Avidyā is therefore beginningless, but can be cancelled. The progression is invariably from the unreal to the real, and never the other way. If the real becomes involved in unreality without being so beginninglessly, the realisation of freedom, would be futile; the possibility of bondage again will always be there.

Absolute and Phenomena

Phenomena are the defiled existence of the Absolute. It is the empirical world precipitated by the subject-object duality. Owing to the idea of an illusory other, the pure Will acquires the subject-function, and this duality constitutes the empirical world. The reality of the latter is the Absolute, which shines forth when the negation limiting it is removed. The way in which the Absolute is implicated in phenomena must be indicated.

The Absolute, as we have said, is defiled by the subject-object duality, which constitutes its negation. The two terms of this duality are however not on a par. The subject is not unreal. Only its relation to the object is negated. The object is utterly unreal, and is therefore subject to total rejection. The subject is the result of this illusion, but is not itself illusory. Here the speculative bent of the Yogācāra is exemplified. He is aware that the Absolute is free from any relativity, and cannot even be called the subject; yet in the phenomena themselves he distinguishes two aspects, one absolutely unreal, the other real. He has not the heart to condemn the whole of phenomena as illusory. He is interested in showing the Absolute as working in phenomena. The Absolute itself is beyond Reason, and as such is neither the subject nor the object.[33] But the two are not equally foreign to it. The Absolute becomes the subject, when infected by the idea of objectivity. The two elements of our empirical experience are not both phenomenal. The subject is in phenomena, but has its root somewhere else.

The Absolute is reached by the negation of phenomena. This negation operates in two ways. The object is totally rejected ; it is absolutely unreal. The subject on the other hand is real, and as such cannot be negated. It is only purified, i.e., purged out of the idea of the unreal object. The subject, when not confronted by an 'other'

---

33. Cf. MSA, p. 55.

to it, is the Absolute.[34] The pure subject is no subject. In the phenomena themselves, one aspect is retained and purified, though however it will not remain phenomenal. This provides an easy transition to the Absolute ; it does not remain utterly dark to us.

The Advaita Vedānta provides another speculative approach to the Absolute. He also distinguishes aspects in phenomena themselves, though he will not call one aspect of it phenomenal. The Pure Being is the implicate of all phenomena; it is the pure object. It is not however an object, but its approach is through the realistic analysis of the object. The subject is real only as identical with the object. When it becomes distinct from the latter, and claims to *know* it, it is unreal. The knowing of the object is rejected[35]; the object when free from all knownness is the Absolute.

The Vedānta analysis of knowledge being realistic, the Absolute is never affected by phenomena. The object of knowledge is indifferent to the knowing of it; it remains identical (kūṭastha). Hence the Absolute is never really objectified. What appears before knowledge is largely subjective; the pure object is only the "thatness" (sattā) of things which never appears. The Absolute is not really the object, but the implicate of it. It does not become the object. The appearance of the object is superimposed upon it ; it is an ascription (vivartta). In the Yogācāra idealism the Absolute is really involved in phenomena. It actually becomes the subject; its diversification (pariṇāma) into different knowledges having different forms is a fact. The reason has already been indicated. The Will cannot remain neutral in willing its content. The content is identical with it, and constitutes therefore its determination. But in spite of its evolution being ontological, it does not militate against its absoluteness, since the change is not integral to it.

In any form of absolutism the relation between the Absolute and phenomena can be understood in two ways. The Absolute can be wholly immanent in phenomena, so that it is nothing apart from the latter. Hegel may be taken as the representative of this view ; the Hegelian Idea is merely the totality of phenomena. It is not the deni-

---

34. yadā tvālambanam vijñānam naivopalabhate tadā, sthitam vijñāna-mātratve grāhyābhāve tad agrahāt ; VMS, p. 43.

35. It is avedya (unknown), though aparokṣavyavahāra-yogya (the implicate of all knowledge.).

zen of an Olympic realm, looking down upon the mundane world below. The Absolute Idea *is* the world as viewed with all abstractions removed. Other thinkers hold that in this hypothesis the Real will be subject to all the defilements characteristic of the empirical world. In their attempt to keep the purity of the Absolute intact they contend that it is wholly transcendent to phenomena, that one has nothing to do with the other. In the so-called dark period of the Western philosophy this controversy raged high. This is based bowever on a misunderstanding of the nature of the Absolute and its relation to phenomena. The Yogācāra is aware of the fact that not only these two do not militate against each other, but both are even necessary for an adequate comprehension of the Absolute. They are in fact different aspects of the same relation which phenomena bear to the Absolute. The Absolute is both immanent as well as transcendent to phenomena. It must be immanent,[36] because it is the reality of the latter. Were it an other to phenomena, the two would lie side by side, and one would not constitute the falsity of the other, and the other its reality. Absolutism is not a two-layer metaphysics. If the two are different, the negation of phenomena cannot yield the Absolute. Phenomena cannot even be negated; since, if they are other than the Real, they would exist in their own right, and would no longer be parasitical. Difference therefore cannot be maintained between the Real and the illusory. But nor can they be identical.[37] If the Absolute is nothing other than phenomena, it would itself become illusory. In this case also, phenomena cannot be negated ; they are deemed unreal only because of some norm or standard which itself is not phenomenal. In a total immanence this norm cannot be had. The Absolute must transcend phenomena ; otherwise it will not be Absolute at all.

There is however no contradiction involved in this. This is the peculiar nature of the relation that the false bears to the real ; it can neither be identical with nor different from the latter. In the Advaita Vedānta this concept presents no problem, since the Real is never involved in phenomena ; it always transcends the latter, though phenomena are nothing apart from it. But in the Yogācāra system it would seem that the transcendence of the Absolute cannot be main-

---

36. Cf. *Nirvāṇa*, p. 34.

37. ata eva sa naivānyo nānanyaḥ paratantrataḥ ; VMS, p. 40.

tained, since its defilement is ontological. The Absolute becomes phenomenal, and this becoming is factual. Still however, the transcendence is there, since this change or becoming is not an integral part of the Absolute ; it can be helped. The change itself may not be illusory, but it happens because of the transcendental illusion. Once this illusion is dispelled, the Absolute regains its transcendence.

We have said that the negation of the phenomenal gives us the Absolute. Yet so long as one thinks of having realised the reality of pure consciousness with no trace of an other to it, the negation of phenomena has not been complete.[38] There can be no self-consciousness, i.e., the consciousness of freedom, in the pure Will. This consciousness can arise only by contrasting it with the empirical consciousness ; along with the total negation of the latter even the consciousness of freedom must go.[39] It can be accepted only during the process of realization, not in the realised state. Self-consciousness of phenomena is inherently unstable. It must be distinguished from the ordinary consciousness, where the notion of falsity finds no place ; yet it cannot be separated from the latter, since it is the consciousness of the phenomenal itself, viewed as illusory. This consciounsess cannot be dispensed with, because the quest for the Real will not even arise without it. It is not however ultimate ; in the Absolute, even the consciousness of having achieved it cannot remain.[40] It is an absolutely non-dual consciousness, pure Will, enjoying itself with no disturbing presence of an 'other', even if that other be its own reflex. There being no 'other', the contingency of turning back upon itself, which is implied in the consciousness of freedom, is precluded. It is Tathatā or Vijñaptimātratā *par excellence*.[41]

Doctrine of Truths

All forms of absolutism are necessarily committed to the doctrine of a plurality of Truths. An absolutistic metaphysics cannot stop with

38. MSA, XI, 47 ; also 48 ; VMS, p. 42-3.

39. MVSBT, p. 23-24.

40. tathatānimittaparivarjanam tathateyam ity api ābhoganimittaparivarjanāt ; MSA, p. 191 ; MSA, XI, 47 ; MVSBT, p. 23 ; VMS, p. 43.

41. VMS, p. 42 ; MVSBT, p. 41.

the empirical experience ; it must make a distinction between what *is* and what *appears*. What exists is real ; what appears to exist has only a semblance of reality. In itself it is naught. This distinction between phenomena and noumenon, between the relative and the Unconditioned, is the very essence of absolutism. The acceptance of a plurality of Truths—the real (paramārtha) on the on hand and the apparent (samvṛti) on the other—is therefore common to all systems other than rank realism. The realist identifies these two ; for him the apparent is the real.

For the Yogācāra what appears is an illusory duality ; the Real is non-dual consciousness. The Real is invariably obscured by appearance.[42] There are therefore two orders of existence, one empirical, the other transcendent. Empirical existence is conditioned by the subject-object duality, while the other is free from the least trace of it. These two orders of existence constitute the so-called plurality of Truths—the paramārtha and the samvṛti.[43]

A possible misconception must be avoided here. If there are two orders of existence, it may be objected, these would constitute two reals, and this militates against the absoluteness of the pure Will, which does not allow an other to stand out against itself. Both the realms cannot be true simultaneously. There is no common factor present identically in these two which can make both of them true. The objection would not arise if the relation between samvṛti and paramārtha were correctly understood. These two do not constitute different realms of existence, each independently real. There is only one Truth ; paramārtha is the only reality. Samvṛti is only empirically real ; it suffices so long as one is rooted in phenomenal activities. With the dawn of philosophic consciousness, the superficial texture of phenomena is torn asunder, and the inner core, the essential reality of dharmas (dharmatā), is revealed. Samvṛti is truth by courtesy. Strictly speaking, it is mere appearance, unreal like a dream or a mirage. It is called a Truth because it is taken as such by the ordinary folk, for whom it is the only truth. Paramārtha is not another reality along with samvṛti, but is the essence of samvṛti itself.[44] Phenomena, freed

---

42. tattvam sañchādhya bālānām atattvam khyāti sarvataḥ ; MSA, XIX, 53.

43. MSA, XI, 16. 44. MSA, XI, 13.

from the false notion of objectivity, are the paramārtha or the Absolute.

This also disposes of the question as to why samvṛti need be considered at all? If it is a mere naught, its discussion is an idle task; one should confine one's attention to the transcendentally real. Dreams as they are, phenomena should not engage one's serious notice. The objection would have been pertinent, were the objector already consicous of the falsity of phenomena. For him its consideration is futile enough. But for the phenomenal beings, samvṛti is not a mere naught. It does appear and create a problem. Dreams are realised to be nothing only on waking. Moreover there is no other way to realise the Absolute than by being aware of the nothingness of phenomena.[45] It is only by a serious and sustained consideration of phenomena that the paramārtha is known. There is no other mysterious access to it. Samvṛti may be nothing in itself—in fact it is nothing—it needs to be realised as such nevertheless. The negation of samvṛti is the dawn of paramārtha. Since the negation is to be significant, the consideration of samvṛti cannot be avoided.

To denounce all phenomena as samvṛti is however an extreme position. For a system which is all criticism and has no view about the real, as the Mādhyamika[46] is, there is nothing to pick and choose in phenomena themselves. Since he offers no account of his own for the explanation of phenomena, he is not interested in preferring any particular aspect of it to another. He can therefore relegate the whole of empirical existence under one category, viz., samvṛti and condemn it as unreal. But the Yogācāra is a speculative system, and professes to give a constructive interpretation of all experience. He leads to the Absolute (paramārtha) through a particular approach ; he shows that the Real is working within phenomena in a particular way. The whole of empirical experience is therefore not equally despicable. In phenomena themselves there are two aspects—the one utterly unreal, and the other real, though infected by the former. Samvṛti must be split into two,

---

45. tathyasamvṛtisopānam antareṇa vipaścitaḥ tattvaprāsāda-śikharārohaṇam na hi yujyate ; quoted in *Abhisamayālaṅkārāloka*, p. 150. Cf. also MVSBT, pp. 11-12 ; 47.

46. For the Mādhyamika conception of Two Truths, see CPB, p. 243. ff.

the subject and the object. These two factors of all experience are not of an equal status. There are thus three, and not merely two, Truths. First, there is the paramārtha which is called *pariniṣpanna* in this system. This is the Absolute. Secondly, there is the phenomenalized aspect of the Real. This is known as the *paratantra* which denotes the subjective. The third is the object, which has no reality whatsoever, apart from the consciousness of it. It is merely imagined to exist ; it has no intrinsic existence of its own ; it is therefore only *parikalpita*. The paratantra and the parikalpita together constitute our empirical experience (samvṛti), while consciousness as non-conceptual is the Absolute (paramārtha).

The Advaita Vedānta provides another speculative approach to the Absolute. It also has a constructive theory of phenomena, a norm of explanation for all things. Phenomena of themselves however do not indicate why they should be interpreted in a particular way. Different kinds of patterns are exemplified in our empirical experience. Speculative metaphysics stresses one at the cost of all others, and universalizes it to the extent of fitting all experience without exception to it. Identity as well as difference are required to make any knowledge possible. Why the Vedānta should prefer identity to difference and make it basic, while explaining the other away as illusory, is inexplicable. This much initial dogmatism is intrinsic to all speculative metaphysics.

The pattern which is thus universalized is therefore taken from the empirical experience itself. If the whole of phenomena is but an appearance, this universalization also must be shown to be an extension of a particular factor of empirical experience. The world-illusion is interpreted analogically, as illustrated by the parallel case of empirical illusion. Empirical illusion therefore must be distinguished from the transcendental illusion, since the latter is established on the strength of the former. Both the Vedānta and the Yogācāra employ the analogical argument, but their interpretaton of the empirical illusion itself is from radically opposite standpoints.

This gives us two degrees of the illusory which are known in the Advaita Vedānta as the prātibhāsika and the vyāvahārika. It involves no distinction of kind. The vyāvahārika is equally unreal as the other is; but it enjoys a relative stability, while the other is illusory even empirically. They must be distinguished because the prātibhāsika provides the pattern for explaining the vyāvahārika, i. e., the world-illu sion

Strictly speaking, there is no qualitative difference between the natures of the two. From the point of view of ultimate reality, even the vyāvahārika is tuccha.[47]

The Real, or the pāramārthika, as it is termed in this system, remains absolutely self-identical through all these gradations of the illusory. Everything phenomenal, as well as the prātibhāsika, can be equally rejected as illusory, because the Real is affected by neither. It is indifferent as to how many appearances are superimposed upon it—it remains neutral (kūṭastha).

There are thus three Truths in the Vedānta as well, viz., the pāramārthika, the vyāvahārika and the prātibhāsika. From the pāramārthika point of view, the latter two are of one category—the illusory. Their distinction is for the sake of procedure only.

Both the Vedānta and the Yogācāra are agreed in splitting up the samvṛti into two. The Mādhyamika is not interested in any constructive account of phenomena, and is not in need of any distinction between things phenomenal. But the two phenomenal Truths accepted both in the Vedānta and the Yogācāra are by no means the same in the two systems, and their difference is characteristic of their different metaphysical standpoints.

The paratantra and the parikalpita are distinguished by a different criterion than that by which the vyāvahārika is distinguished from the prātibhāsika. Both the paratantra and the parikalpita, as applied to the world-illusion, would be included in the vyāvahārika by the Vedānta, while even the prātibhāsika is analysed into the paratantra and the parikalpita by the Yogācāra. In the Vedānta the distinction is between the empirical and the transcendental illusion ; in the Yogācāra the distinction is one of two aspects of all illusion whatsoever. Both the vyāvahārika and the pratibhāsika can be rejected as illusory because the Real as kūṭastha is affected by neither. The Real never appears, but is the implicate of all appearance. But in the Yogācāra, vijñāna does get involved in phenomena ; it does appear. All appearance therefore cannot be rejected. Both the systems analyse the illusory into two elements coming from two different sources altogether, viz., the real, serving as the basis, and the apparent which appropriates the status of

47. tucchānirvacanīyā ca vāstavī cety asau tridhā jñeyā māyā tribhir bodhaiḥ śrautayauktikalaukikaiḥ.

the former. The real aspect in the Vedānta analysis is identical with the absolutely Real; the latter has suffered no change in being imposed upon. Since the pāramārthika is the Real *par excellence*, the two aspects in all cases of illusion, empirical or otherwise, need not be distinguished separately. The unreal aspect certainly admits of degrees—the vyāvahārika and the prātibhāsika. But in the Yogācāra the Real cannot remain indifferent to its appearance. Hence in spite of the real aspect of the illusion being essentially one with the Absolute (pariniṣpanna), it is yet a defiled form of the latter. There are thus two phases of existence of the Real—first, in its absolute purity (pariniṣpanna) and secondly, as defiled by phenomena (paratantra). The unreal aspect is the parikalpita. Though the doctrine of three Truths is common to the Vedānta as well as the Yogācāra, the Vedānta has only one real and two unreals, while the Yogācāra has two phases of reality, and does not analyse the unreal further. Appearance, whether empirical or not, has a common structure. Only the defilment (pariṇāma) of the Real need be noted.

The three Truths must now be explained individually.[48] (1) *Parikalpita* is that which has no authentic existence. It is only imagined to exist (kalpanāmātra). It is an object projected by the creative consciousness. This includes whatever confronts consciousness as an other to it, i.e., the external object, and the internal ideas[49], percepts, images, etc. which are no less external to consciousness. The object is unreal because causality does not operate in the objective realm. Causal interaction or efficiency (hetupratyaya-pratipadya-svabhāva) is the mark of reality. Whatever is not produced by causes and conditions is unreal.[50] The object is not a cause of the consciousness which is said to be caused by it. A post is perceived as a man by one person, while another mistakes the same for a ghost. One entity cannot generate so many perceptions at the same time.[51] These various perceptions are not caused by the post at all. Hence it is a mere construct, like a barren woman's son.

48. VMS, pp. 39-42 ; MSA, XI, 38-41 ;TSN; MVSBT, pp. 19-20; LAS, X.

49. VMS, p. 39.

50. VMS, p. 39.

51. PV, II, 356 ; VMS, p. 39.

Still its negation is not on a par with that of the barren woman's son. Though it is unreal in itself, consciousness does appear having this form. The negation of the external object must be significant. There is no consciousness of the barren woman's son, and its negation is therefore meaningless. The empirical object is identical with such fictitious entities in its essential nature, but with the significant distinction that it does appear in consciousness.[52] That is the peculiar status of the illusory, that though it is nothing, yet it is not an absolute blank. It must however be reduced to nothing, and that is possible only when it is ontologically nothing; i. e., it has no real existence, but is merely imagined to exist. Its existence is only through this constructive imagination. Negation pertains only to its apparent independence.

(2) *Paratantra* is that which appears as the subject-object duality. The form of appearance is unreal (parikalpita); but the stuff which projects the appearance is real. Paratantra is consciousness as diversified into the various forms.[53] It is called paratantra because it is caused by causes and conditions.[54] Causality operates on the subjective side. An idea is produced, not by any external cause, but by a previous idea. Pratītya-samutpāda[55] is the mark of reality. This functions between the various moments of consciousness themselves.[56] One idea generates another idea, because of its own inner dynamism. The moments of consciousness therefore are causally efficient and as such are real (pratītyasamutpannatvād vastusat). Paratantra is not an uncaused freak, like the barren woman's son, but is pratyayādhīna.

Paratantra includes the whole of phenomenal reality (cittacaittās traidhātukāḥ). The external object is unreal and is parikalpita. The

---

52. sa punar dravyato' sannapi vyavahārato' stīti svabhāva ucyate; MVSBT, p. 19.

53. LAS, X, 150.

54. VMS, p. 39.

55. This is in accordance with the Sarvāstivāda and against the Mādhyamika. For the latter pratīyasamutpāda is construed as logical dependence, and as such, the mark of unreality (śūnya). The Yogācāra restored its interpretation as temporal sequence, and as the characteristic of reality, thought not ultimate. See further Ch. I.

56. LAS, X, 60.

various forms of the subjective alone are real, all of which are designated by this Truth. It therefore denotes all the eight vijñānas, Ālaya, the Manas and the six pravṛttivijñānas. It is real but not ultimate, a paradox which can be resolved, as we have seen, by interpreting consciousness as will. It is a real diversification (pariṇāma) of the willing consciousness. As the seat of the creative imagination projecting the unreal object, it is called Abhūtaparikalpa[57] (abhūtasya parikalpo yasmin). That which is imagined is unreal. But consciousness itself, the basis of that imagination, is real, and this is paratantra. The constructive imagination is only the transcendental category of objectification which stirs consciousness into disruption.

(3) *Pariniṣpanna*[58] is the Absolute. It is pure Consciousness undefiled by the least trace of objectivity. When paratantra (the subjective) is purified of the false duality imposed upon it by the parikalpita (the constructed object), it becomes the pariniṣpanna.[59] It is called pariniṣpanna as it is not subject to the vagaries of the constructive imagination; it is ever the same (avikārapariniṣpattyā sa pariniṣpannaḥ). Consciousness gets modified only because of the presence of the illusory 'other'. Hence when the idea of this 'other', i.e., parikalpita, is eradicated out of the subjective (paratantra), it reverts back to its natural quiescence. To negate the object is not to experience it ; then the form of appearance of consciousness (paratantra) also is dissolved and its absoluteness realised.[60] This is the pariniṣpanna state of the Will.

No ultimate distinction can be drawn therefore between the pariniṣpanna and the paratantra. The pariniṣpanna becomes the paratantra due to the infection of the parikalpita; this last is utterly unreal. The subjective aspect of experience however is real. It is the Will itself that gets defiled. Were the paratantra (i.e., the subjective) different from the pariniṣpanna which is ultimately real, the former would then be unreal, and there would be no ground for distinction between the paratantra and the parikalpita (the object). Consciousness can never be freed from its objective entanglements, and the demand

---

57. MVSBT, I, 2.

58. MSA, XI, 41 ; LAS, X, 174.

59. yā abhūtaparikalpasya dvayarahitatā sa pariniṣpannaḥ svabhāvabhāvaḥ, MVSBT, p. 19 ; also MSA, IX, 78 ; VMS, p. 40.

60. TSN, 32, 33.

for philosophy as spiritual discipline would not even arise. The object cannot even be known as illusory, as it would invariably persecute consciousness by its persistent presence. So the paratantra cannot be held to be different[61] from the Absolute. But nor are they completely identical.[62] In that case, either the pariniṣpanna will always be defiled, or the paratantra would have all along been pure, so that there is nothing to purify; spiritual discipline would again be futile in both the cases. Hence it is said that the paratantra is neither identical with nor different from the pariniṣpanna. Essentially they are one. Their difference is because of an illusory infection. Once this false idea is got rid of, the paratantra completely lapses into the Absolute (pariniṣpanna).[63] To start with, the distinction between them must be made; without realising the pariniṣpanna the paratantra cannot be known.[64] There is no other way for being conscious of the difference in nature between the paratantra and the parikalpita, than by keeping in mind the norm (the pariniṣpanna) as the absolute reality of consciousness.

Hence it is that the same term Abhūtaparikalpa is applied both to pariniṣpanna and the paratantra. It is both the Absolute as well as phenomena. It is the Absolute, since śūnyatā, i. e., the negation of the subject-object duality (grāhadvaya), entailed by the sublation of the object, pertains to it. It is again phenomena, because Abhūtaparikalpa, construction of the false, defiles this śūnyatā,—i.e., the utter absence of the subject-object duality. If the stress be upon *parikalpa*, the creativity of consciousness, then it is phenomena (paratantra). But this construction is of *abhūta*, of what does not really exist, and as such the construction itself cannot inherently belong to consciousness. It is therefore the Absolute.

The paratantra therefore is real, being pratītya-samutpanna, and yet does not constitute a different order of truth than the pariniṣpanna (the Absolute). The Yogācāra would very strongly discountenance the so-called doctrine of "Degrees of Truth and Reality," advocated by Hegel and his followers. According to this the whole alone is wholly true ; nothing short of the Absolute Idea, the all-embracing

---

61. MVSBT, p. 40.
62. VMS, p. 40 ; ata eva sa naivānyo nānayaḥ paratantrataḥ.
63. LAS, CX, 151.
64. VMS, p. 40.

system of judgments, can claim complete truth. On the other hand nothing is completely false. No element in experience need be utterly rejected. Only its abstraction is removed and it takes its place in the total harmony. So each element is true to the extent it reaches to the Idea, and false in so far as it falls short of it. Thus a gradation is constituted of the varying "degrees of Truth," beginning from the most abstract and culminating in the whole Idea.

This is hardly the place for entering into a detailed consideration of this theory. It is clear however that the Yogācāra doctrine of the three Truths cannot be interpreted to mean degrees of Truth, and still less, kinds of Truth. Truth is one, and that is the Absolute. There cannot be more or less of Truth ; a thing is either wholly true or utterly false. If it is only partially true, it has a composite being then, and must be split up into the true and the false. Paratantra is not less true than the parinispanna; it *is* parinispanna, when divested of the illusory idea governing its pariṇāma. Nothing is added to or subtracted from vijñāna, in negating parikalpita, when it becomes parinispanna. Parinispanna is not *more* of paratantra ; it does not include the latter and something else, as the Hegelian Idea does the lesser truths. Because of the presence of the parikalpita, consciousness is diversified into the paratantra—into the willing of determinate contents. When the illusory infection is taken away, will becomes parinispanna and ceases to will any content. Strictly speaking it is no will. Consciousness (citta) becomes acitta. Yet it is vijñāna itself that is both. Hence it is stated that there is no difference between experiencing a content (upalabdhi) and ceasing to experience it (anupalabdhi)[65]; consciousness remains essentially the same, whether it be in its absolute purity (parinispanna), or be diversified into the willing of contents (paratantra). The two realities are not certainly completely identical, but nor are they absolutely different.

That which appears is then the Abhūtaparikalpa, and it appears into the form of the subject-object duality. When the former (paratantra) is freed from this illusory duality, it becomes the non-dual Consciousness, the essence of dharmas (advayadharmatā). The first is absolutely non-existent. As to the second (paratantra), only its form of appear

---

65. MVSBT, p. 23-4; tasmāc ca samatā jñeyā nopalambhopalambhayoḥ.

ance—the subject-object duality—is non-existent ; it exists, but not as it appears to exist. The third (parinispanna) is reached through the non-existence of this duality.[66] All the three are thus based on the same act of negation which culminates in the Absolute Consciousness.[67] The whole of empirical discourse (vyavahāra) is constituted by the parikalpita. The basis of it is the paratantra. The parinispanna is of the nature of the negation of this.[68]Abhūtaparikalpa is consciousness or the subjective, since this is the basis (adhiṣṭhāna) of the constructive imagination (avidyā). That which is constructed is the object which has no existence whatsoever, apart from the activity of its construction.[69]

The Absolute is reached through a process of negation. This negation applies differently to the three Truths. Each is declared void (niḥsvabhāva), but in different senses. All the three are sadasat ; affirmation and negation are both applied to each of them. The naive affirmation of the parikalpita and the paratantra must be sublated, while the affirmation of the parinispanna is reached through this negation alone. There are three kinds of nissabhāvatās (essencelessness) according to the three kinds of Truths[70]: (1) Lakṣaṇa-nissvabhāvatā, (2) Utpatti-nissvabhāvatā, and (3) Paramārtha-nissvabhāvatā. (1) The Parikalpita is unreal by its very nature. The object has absolutely no being. Its apparent characteristics (lakṣaṇa) only appear to belong to it ; in reality they are characteristics of the forms of consciousness. The object cannot be characterised by any real predicates. It is essentially void, like the sky-lotus.[71] Its naive affirmation must be sublated.[72] The parikalpita has therefore the Lakṣaṇanissvabhāvatā. (2) The case with the paratantra is different. It is as we have seen real. Only its form of appearance, its illusory infection, is to be negated.[7]

66. dvayābhāvabhāvaḥ; TSN, 25.

67. TSN, 26.

68. vyavahārasamucchedasvabhāva ; TSN, 23.

69. In the Advaita Vedānta also the illusory is pratibhāsamātraśarīrattva.

70. VMS, p. 41 ; Cf. also MSA, p. 95.

71. VMS, p. 40.

72. TSN, 11.

73. TSN, 12.

It appears to be produced because of its being confronted with an 'other,' whereas its real cause is its own inner dynamism. Its apparent production (utpatti) is unreal[74] and Utpattiniḥsvabhāvatā therefore pertains to it. (3) The pariniṣpanna is the essence of all reality (dharmāṇām dharmatā).[75] It is realised through the negation of the epistemological duality. Though it has the most positive existence in itself, the approach to it being negative,[76] it seems to be a bundle of negations. Only the means are negative, but its positive nature is not revealed in its phenomenalised state. No empirical predicate can be attached to it. Hence its very nature appears to be negative (pariniṣpannasya abhāva-svabhāvatvāt). This is its Paramārtha-niḥsvabhāvatā; it must be clearly understood however that this negation pertains to it only from the empirical point of view. Because of this it is called both existent and non-existent.[77] The content willed, as we have seen, constitutes the negation of that will. The negation of the content therefore is only the negation of a negation, resulting in the reinstatement of the previous affirmation.[78]

---

74. VMS, p. 41.
75. VMS, p. 41.
76. TSN, 13.
77. asti-nāstīti cocyate ; TSN, 26 ; Cf. also MVSBT, p. 39.
78. TSN, 16.

CHAPTER VIII

THE YOGĀCĀRA DISCIPLINE

Nirvāṇa is Freedom

Philosophy can have only a spiritual value. To think of it as serving any empirical purpose is grossly to miss its essential significance. It has been held that philosophy satisfies one's intellectual curiosity. But there might be other and better means of satisfying it. The demand to know the ultimate nature of things cannot be an empirical demand. No contingency ever arises in empirical discourse where ultimate questions must necessarily be asked. Our practical way of living would not be least affected one way or the other by the settlement of the question whether the world is made of atoms or is a construction of the subjective. And to suppose that philosophy is a display of intellectual gymnastic is to make little difference between a metaphysical system and a particular theory of chess. The very consciousness that the answer to the ultimate questions is highly pertinent, or that there are ultimate questions at all, presupposes a certain discontent regarding the empirical. The fact that the ultimate problems are insoluble and that the attempt to answer them gives rise to the antinomies of Reason is a different matter altogether. Here we contend merely that if philosophy, be it dogmatic or critical, has no spiritual value, it has no other value at all.

The value of philosophy as a spiritual discipline consists in freedom—freedom from pain or evil. Pain cannot be got rid of by mundane means[1]; it must be realised that pain is not one factor among others, constituting empirical experience, but that the whole of experience is pain.[2] It must be universalised. Just as, on the theoretical side, illusion is not taken as a stray case, but rather the whole of experience is condemned as illusory, so also on the practical side, existence as

---

1. dṛṣṭe sāpārthā cennaikāntātyantato' bhāvāt ; *Sāmkhya Kārikā*, 1.
2. duḥkhameva sarvam vivekinaḥ; *Yogasūtrabhāṣya*, II, 15, p. 77.

such is to be realised as pain. The first step to spirituality lies in being intensely sensitive towards the painful character of all experience.[3] The ordinary people do not feel pain where the developed susceptibility of the spiritually awakened person makes him experience it. Hence the former feels no necessity for philosophy; he thinks pain to be something particular and seeks empirical remedy. He has not even the faintest conception of the philosophic consciousness. Only he who perceives pain as universal realises the value of the philosophic discipline and yearns to embrace the philosophy that suits his spiritual temperament.

Why is pain realised to be all-embracing in its scope ? There are particular pains, and they can be avoided. The very awareness of something as painful arises only by contrasting it with something not painful. There is no necessity therefore for pain being universalised. This contention misses the true nature of the cause of pain. Pain is not something objective. *A thing* cannot be painful in itself. Pain is rather caused by the *attitude* mind takes towards the object. Pain is not in the object but in the reaction of mind towards it. The nature of the object is immaterial. Mind can be so trained as to like what was painful before and detest what previously gave pleasure. It is the wrong attitude of the mind therefore that is the root-cause of pain. And this is the reason why pain is universal. One particular painful object can be got rid of, but the basic attitude of mind persists. Pain arises because of the defilement of consciousness and consequently freedom consists in the purification of consciousness alone (cittameva saṅkliśyate cittameva vyavadāyate)[4].

Not only is pain a subjective experience, but its cause also lies in the subjective. The basic attitudes mind can take towards an object is attachment and aversion, and both generate pain. An object to which we are attached gives pain when separated from us and so does an object of aversion cause pain when we are forced into its contact. Freedom from pain is freedom from these two fetters of mind ; it is a balanced equanimity of mind, unruffled by any objective vicissitude.

Spiritual discipline is thus purely a subjective process. It is true that philosophy cannot change facts ; but it can effect the greatest of

---

3. akṣipātrakalpo hi vidvān ; ibid, II, 15, p. 76.
4. Cf. LAS, X, 145.

all changes ; it can change ourselves. A philosophic discipline has nothing to do with the objective world. Moreover, in the Yogācāra system, there is no such world at all. Consciousness is the sole reality. Both bondage and freedom therefore pertain only to consciousness.

What is the cause of bondage ? In agreement with the essential spirit of Indian philosophy, the Yogācāra holds that bondage is due to ignorance (avidyā)[5]. As to the nature and function of ignorance, systems differ in accordance with their different standpoints. In idealism ignorance consists in taking the apparently objective world as independently real. The object is not external to consciousness ; it is only a mode of the latter. Ignorance about the real nature of the object evokes attachment and aversion in mind, because of which it suffers bondage.

Bondage or suffering is therefore caused by the false idea of there being something external and real.[6] Dreams can move us only so long as the dream-contents are supposed to be external. On waking they are realised to be purely imaginary, subjective, and they lose their power of making us suffer. So long as a content is supposed to be something external to us, it constitutes a limitation of ourselves The acquisition of that content appears to be a real increase of the ego. If it is something obnoxious we would like to protect ourselves by avoiding it. When however the ideality of that content is realised, it becomes one with ourselves , and therefore no longer to be desired or feared. It can make us suffer only so long as it is supposed to be something external and foreign to us. Objectivity is therefore bondage. Owing to this false idea, consciousness becomes infected by the subject-object duality (grāhadvaya). It begins to project contents as though objective. The vicious chain of pratītyasamutpāda is started. Pure Will evolves into the three vijñānas, the root of which is the Ālaya. Ālaya is the Abhūtaparikalpa since it projects contents where they are not. Ālaya is samsāra and is bondage.[7] Because of the false projection of objective dharmas, an ego also is

5. MVSBT, p. 29.

6. kāmaśokabhayonmādacaurasvapnādy upaplutāḥ., abhūtān api paśyanti purato' vasthitān iva ; PV, II, 282.

7. MSA, XI, 32 ; also XIX, 49.

8. MSA, XI, 49.

at the same time posited.[8] This is kleśa, along with its attendant satellites.[9]

This is the defilement of Will. The object is a negation of will. When an object is projected by will-consciousness, it loses its hold over it. It becomes merely a passive spectator, helpless before the content which, though willed, is crystallised into a known content. The object is thus an obstruction or limitation of will. It ceases to be will, when confronted by the object.

Liberation is the regaining of the sovereignty of Will by negating the object and breaking down its obstinate externality. When will projects a content, it becomes limited by the latter. The consciousness of blue cannot be that of yellow at the same time. But when the blue is negated and its essential identity with consciousness established, the latter is no longer determined by the blue. Consciousness becomes universal.[10] It is not the consciousness of any particular content. This universal Will is the Absolute. Nirvāṇa is the realization of this universality.[11] It is the freedom of consciousness from the duality of the subject and the object.[12] It is the retracting of Ālaya from its forward movement (āśrayaparāvṛtti)[13]. Āśrayaparāvṛtti is the disappearance of the unreal object, and the realisation of Tathatā; and this is freedom (mokṣa)[14]. Impelled by the Transcendental Illusion of the idea of objectivity, it goes on projecting the forms of the so-called empirical objects, giving rise to various pravṛttivijñānas which, in their own turn, replenish it further. The Ālaya is thus the support (āśraya) of the entire phenomenal world. A vicious circle is started from which there is no escape. The Ālaya creates an 'other' to consciousness and the 'other' makes it create still further forms. Consciousness loses its equanimity and forgets its essential nature. This is samsāra. But when the unreality of the object is realised, there is nothing to govern the forward movement of the Ālaya.

---

9. Cf. MV BT, p. 34 ff.
10. jñānena jñeyam vyāptam; MSA, XX, 44.
11. sarvākārajñatāvāptiḥ sarvāvaraṇanirmalā, MSA, IX, 2.
12. Cf. VMS, p. 42.
13. MSA, XI, 44.
14. akhyānakhyānatā jñeyā asadarthasadarthayoḥ āśrayasya parāvṛttir mokṣo' sau kāmacārataḥ; MSA, XIX, 44.

Consciousness is no longer diversified into the moments of empirical forms. "Realising everything to be imaginary, the Bodhisattva ceases to imagine anything at all; this is Bodhi or Enlightenment."[15] Consciousness gets rid of the subject-object duality and rests again in itself.[16] This is nirvāṇa which is also supreme bliss (sukha). It is identical with the Tathāgata.

Nirvāṇa is not therefore the acquisition of anything new. It does not become anything what it was previously not. Nirvāṇa is only seeing things as they really are.[17] The object is not to be negated, since it is only imagined to exist. Only its ideality is to be realised. And to know the unreal as such is to get rid of it.[18] The defilement of consciousness is solely because of a false idea ; it is not intrinsic to consciousness. Freedom, as the eradication of this false idea, is not therefore to transform consciousness into anything else. It is simply the discovery of the sole reality of consciousness, the essence of everything (Tathatā). The purification is like that of the sky,[19] simply the removal of everything foreign to it.

The process of attaining freedom is real from the point of view of the subjective, though the cause of bondage is unreal. Consciousness is defiled ; this defilement is factual and so is its purification.[20] From the objective point of view however the entire process is unreal[21]. The object never existed ; hence its sublation also is a part of the illusion. The suffering generated by this illusion is subjective and is therefore real. It is consciousness which is defiled and consciousness again which is purified.[22] This fact distinguishes the Yogācāra

15. paśyatām kalpanāmātram sarvam etad yathoditam akalpa-bodhisattvānām prāptā bodhir nirūpyate ; MSA, IX, 81.

16. cittasya citte sthānāt ; MSA, XVIII, 66 ; VMS, p. 42.

17. nāpaneyam ataḥ kiñcit prakṣeptavyam na kiñcana draṣṭavyam bhūtato bhūtam bhūtadarśī vimucyate ; *Abhisamayālaṅkāra*, V, 21, quoted in MVSBT, p. 25.

18. Cf. MSA, p. 87.

19. MVSBT, p. 43.

20. This is implied by the similes given in MSA, XI, 33.

21. māyārājeva cānyena māyārājñā parājitaḥ ye sarvadharmān paśyanti nirmārās te jinātmajāḥ ; MSA, XI, 29.

22 MSA, XI, 34-5.

conception of the disciplinary process from that of the Mādhyamika and the Advaita Vedānta. For both the latter, the entire process is utterly unreal ; a thorough-going vivarttavāda can be maintained since the Real is never ontologically affected by bondage or freedom. The whole process is purely epistemic. But, for the Yogācāra the epistemic, as the subjective, is ontologically existent, and so is therefore the disciplinary process as well[23]. It can still be called illusory, being caused by the idea of an illusory content. From the point of view of the latter the process itself is a part of the nightmare, though its subjective aspect is real.

Freedom is not the peculiar privilege of any particular person. Freedom is the attainment of the ideal of Buddhahood. This is theoretically possible on the part of every human being. Everybody is potentially a Buddha, i.e., contains the potentialities of complete Buddhahood. Everybody is tathāgatagarbha[24]; this is the great advance the Mahāyāna made over the Hīnayāna. Everybody does not actually strive for freedom however because of the differences in the spritual attitude (gotra)[25] of different persons. People are not all alike in having parallel spiritual developments.[26] Only one in millions is aware of the intensity and universality of evil and misery, and for him alone is the spiritual discipline significant. The gotra has two aspects[27] : fundamental (prakṛtistha), existing in every living being from the very outset, and paripuṣṭa, that which undergoes the process of development. Since everybody is a potential Buddha, the former aspect is essentially identical in all persons. But there are very great differences indeed so far as the second aspect is concerned. It is this that distinguishes a layman who is not yet spiritually awakened from a saint who has attained the maturity of spiritual or philosophic consciousness. Along with the development of spirituality the gotra produces a metamorphosis (parāvṛtti) of the elements of a personality

---

23. tasmāt saṅkleśaviśuddhikālayoḥ śūnyataiva saṅkliśyate viśuddhyata iti ; MVSBT, p. 42.
24. MSA, IX, 37.
25. MSA, III, 2.
26. Cf. MSA, IX, 15-16 ; also 34.
27. Obermiller, *The Sublime Science*, p. 100.

(i.e., the eight vijñānas) into the elements of Buddhahood.[28] The gotra is a kind of force[29] or dynamism latent in man, which makes him strive for spirituality. This force is exhausted at the time of realisation of nirvāṇa.[30] The gotra is in fact identical with the Absolute[31].

The Spiritual Discipline

The various stages of the tortuous path of spiritual discipline have been discussed with a wealth of minutest details, born out of personal realisation, in texts like *Abhisamayālaṅkāra*, *Mahāyānasūtrālaṅkāra* etc. The details are out of place in a metaphysical essay. Only the broadest outline can be indicated here.

The initial stage is known as the *Sambhāramārga* (the Path of Accumulating Merit), and is only preparatory to the higher levels of the disciplinary path. Consciousness is defiled by the two obstructions which hide its real nature. These are kleśāvaraṇa and jñeyāvaraṇa.[32] The kleśas are pain and evil pertaining to the empirical level. The root of all pain is however intellectual. When the object is wrongly imagined to exist as it is not, it repels the will-consciousness. This is the primary obstruction, imagining that there is something to be known. This is jñeyāvaraṇa. These obstructions can be removed by the accumulation of merits and wisdom (puṇyajñāna-sambhāra).[33] Mere accumulation of merits is not sufficient, since the root of all evil is intellectual. The real antiodote is therefore knowledge, knowing things as they really are. This is the highest wisdom (prajñāpāramitā) and this alone can remove jñeyāvaraṇa by realising the nothingness of the object and consequently, the purification of consciousness. It is jñānasambhāra therefore that is the basic remedy for the evil of empirical existence ; puṇyasambhāra is only subsidiary.

---

28. *The Sublime Science*, p. 100-1.

29. Ibid, p. 102.

30. Ibid, p. 103.

31. *Abhisamayālaṅkāra*, I, 39. For a discussion of the different interpretations of the concept of gotra see *The Sublime Science*, pp. 97-102.

32. VMS, p. 44.

33. MSA, VI, 6.

Jñāna is philosophic wisdom. The root of all evil being theoretical, viz., ignorance, the antidote can only be philosophy, right knowledge of things as they are. At first this knowledge remains only verbal and mediate (śrutamaya). Mere intellectual knowledge is not however sufficient. This insight must be intensely meditated on (cintāmaya), and lastly, one must deeply concentrate on this theoretical understanding of things (bhāvanāmaya) so that it is immediately realised (aparapratyaya) as the ultimate truth. Complete realization comes however only in the subsequent stages.

Next comes the *Prayogamārga* (the Path of Training.) The Bodhisattva undertakes an intense cultivation of the philosophic wisdom, theoretically as well as practically. Realising that the objects are only subjective creations (manojalpa), he ceases to perceive any objective dharma (sarvadharmān na paśyati) ; he realises that they are only the two kinds of projections of the subjective imagination, viz., the svalakṣaṇa and the sāmānyalakṣaṇa. This is the *Uṣmagatāvasthā*[34] of the disciple. He obtains the first sparks of the spiritual enlightenment (dharmāloka) which he strives to make steady, and cultivates still more intense practices (dṛḍham vīryam ārabhate). This is the *Mūrdhāvasthā*.[35] With the intensification of the insight, the Bodhisattva realises the sole reality of consciousness (cittamātre avatiṣṭhate cittam etad iti prativedhāt). He sees everything only as appearances of consciousness (citta eva sarvārthapratibhāsatvam paśyati). Nothing is independent and external to consciousness. Thus the diversification of consciousness as the object to be known (grāhyavikṣepa) is removed ; there remains only the other diversification, viz., consciousness as the knowing subject (grāhakavikṣepa). This stage is known as the *Kṣāntyavasthā*.[36] The sublation of the object is comparatively easier than the realisation of the unreality of the subject ; the latter dawns only in the subsequent higher stages of the path. The former only paves the way for the latter (grāhakānupalambhānukūla) which is the real freedom of consciousness. After this there is the *Laukikāgradharmāvasthā*[37] in which the Bodhisattva enters into the Ānantarya-

---

34. MSA, p. 93, MVSBT, p. 23.
35. MSA, p. 93.
36. MSA, p. 93.
37. MSA, p. 93 ; MVSBT, p. 23.

samādhi. The trance is so-called because the deeper diversification of consciousness as the knower (grāhakavikṣepa) is removed immediately after this (anantara).[38] Realising the unreality of the object, even the awareness of the sole reality of consciousness ceases.[39] After this all the subsequent stages are transic. The Bodhisattva enters into higher and higher transic states.

The next stage is the *Darśanamārga* (the Path of Vision). The sage has an intuition of the highest reality, free from the false dualism of the knower and the known ; he has a non-dual, non-conceptual and pure (since the two obstructions have been completely destroyed) intuition of the ultimate and unique substance of the universe (sarvatragadharmadhātu), and enters into the first bhūmi, characterised by the withdrawal of the Ālaya (āśrayaparāvṛtti).[40] He realises the essential identity of every living being and thinks of them in terms of himself.[41] He acquires the characteristic excellences of the attainment of Enlightenment (Bodhi), like smṛtyupasthāna etc. Though he has no pain of his own, he grieves at the misery of suffering mankind.

The next and highest stage is the *Bhāvanāmārga* (the Path of Concentration) in which the Bodhisattva enters into the rest of the bhūmis. He obtains a complete mystic intuition of the Absolute. This intuition is twofold.[42] First is the nirvikalpa or the samāhita (transic)-jñāna.[43] "It is a mystic Gnosis, a direct supernatural intuition of the Saint (ārya)." It is immediate and entirely personal. The other is the pṛṣṭhalabdha-jñāna, the empirical (laukika) knowledge that arises in the wake of the first transcendental intuition. This knowledge is conceptual (savikalpa). "It is a logically constructed explanation of what has been perceived in trance, as far as it is capable of logical explanation."[44] Unlike the first, this can be communicated to others

38. MSA, XIV, 27.
39. MVSBT, p. 23 ; MSA, XI, 47.
40. MSA, XIV, 28-9.
41. MSA, XIV, 30.
42. MSA, XIV, 43 ; MVSBT, pp. 29-30.
43. The form of this non-conceptual intuition is the same in the Mādhyamika and the Yogācāra. cf. MSA, p. 191.
44. Obermiller, *The Doctrine of Prajñāpāramitā*, p. 20.

who are still ignorant. The transic culmination is reached in the Vajroapamasamādhi, which is so-called being impenetrable (abhedya) by any subjective construction (vikalpa)[45]. The process of the retracting of the Ālaya (āśrayaparāvṛtti) is completed. The intuition is absolutely pure, being free from any trace of the two obstructions (sarvakleśa-jñeyāvaraṇa-nirmalā). The disciple attains the universality of consciousness (sarvākārajñatā), which is no longer limited by particular objects. He rests in the absolute and ultimate reality (anuttarapada), and strives for the well-being of all humanity.

The different stages of the disciplinary process (yogabhūmis) are sometimes condensed into five,[46] viz., ādhāra, ādhāna, ādarśa, āloka and āśraya. Ādhāra is the reception of the verbal knowledge, taught by Buddha. Ādhāna is deep attention and meditation regarding the same. Ādarśa is the resting of consciousness in its own essence by the sublation of the object. Āloka is the correct vision of things as they really are by negating their externality and affirming their reality, viz. identity with consciousness. Āśraya is the consequent retracting of the Ālaya. This is nirvāṇa.

As already discussed in the last chapter, consciousness of freedom is incompatible with freedom. One can be self-conscious of one's freedom only by contrasting it with the consciousness of bondage, and this entails entertaining the idea of objectivity still. With the total sublation of this idea, even the consciousness of having attained freedom must go. To be aware of freedom is to allow something to stand out against consciousness, be it the idea of its own freedom, and this militates against the absoluteness of consciousness.[47]

Bhūmis and Pāramitās

No account of the Yogācāra discipline can be complete without some mention of the elaborate and detailed formulation of the pāramitā discipline and the minute description of the bhūmis. The details are out of place here, since the pāramitā discipline is nothing peculiar to the Yogācāra. It is found in a crude form in the early Hīnayāna texts ;

---

45. MSA, p. 96.
46. MSA, XI, 42.
47. vijñaptimātram evedam ityapi hyupalambhataḥ sthāpayan agrataḥ kiñcit tanmātre nāvatiṣṭhate ; VMS, pp. 42-3.

the Yogācāra simply accepted the entire doctrine elaborated in the Mahāyāna.

The traditional theory is the analysis of the disciplinary process into the six pāramitās,[48] viz., Dāna, Śīla, Kṣānti, Vīrya, Dhyāna and Prajñā.[49] The preliminary stages are more or less ethical rather than distinctively spiritual. The pāramitā discipline is not however the mere practice of morality. The guiding principle throughout is the Prajñāpāramitā, which informs and sustains the entire process from the very beginning. It is saturated by the philosophic wisdom regarding the ultimate truth. The discipline is intellectual through and through, being governed by the theoretical understanding of the nature of things. It is Prajñā alone from which the process takes its cue, and in which it reaches its complete fruition.

The pāramitā discipline is not peculiarly characteristic of the Yogācāra, since it can go along with any philosophy so far as the latter makes a distinction between the apparent and the real. The pāramitā discipline is common both to the Mādhyamika and the Yogācāra. The difference between them is purely theoretical ; it centres around the content of Prajñā, i.e., the standpoint from which intuition of the ultimate reality is obtained. Apart from this philosophic understanding of things, the pāramitā discipline is adopted by all the schools of Buddhism.

The conception of bhūmis also appeared early in the history of Buddhism. In the *Mahāvastu* are described[50] ten bhūmis, but the list differs totally from that given in the *Mahāyānasūtrālaṅkāra*, *Daśabhūmikasūtra* etc. The bhūmis are not physical planes of existence, but are stages of spiritual development of the Bodhisattva's career. The Yogācāra list of the ten bhūmis is[51] : (a) Pramuditā, (b) Vimalā,

48. MSA, XVI.

49. "The list of the first six appears to be original, as it ends with the attainment of full knowledge of wisdom, Prajñā. But the *Daśabhūmikasūtra* has four more, which make a list fitting imperfectly with the ten stages." E. J. Thomas, *The History of Buddhist Thought*, p. 211.

50. *The History of Buddhhist Thought*, p. 203.

51. Cf. MSA, XX, 32-8.

(c) Prabhākarī, (d) Arciṣmatī, (e) Sudurjayā, (f) Abhimukhī, (g) Dūraṅgamā, (h) Acalā, (i) Sādhumatī, and (j) Dharmameghā. The bhūmis are sometimes also described as vihāras. In the *Bodhisattva-bhūmi*, the number of vihāras is increased to twelve or (including the Buddha stage) thirteen.[52]

These are all scholastic elaborations which are not of any theoretical importance. The only point to be noted is that all through the career of the Bodhisattva run two motives, the aim of becoming a Buddha in order to save every human being (mahākaruṇā) and the attainment of absolute truth in Prajñāpāramitā.

52. E. J. Thomas, *The History of Buddhist Thought*, p. 210.

Chapter IX

THE CONCEPT OF THE TATHĀGATA

The Tathāgata occupies the same place in Buddhism as Īśvara does in Advaita Vedānta. He is the God of religion, an object of worship and veneration. He has also infinite compassion for the suffering mankind but for Whose grace their redemption would not be possible.

Can an absolutism have any place for a personal God ? He must be distinguished from the Absolute ; the latter is not a person but a principle. Nothing can be predicated of the latter, it being the negation of all thought-categories. The Tathāgata however is conceived of as having infinite good qualities, supernatural powers etc. Moreover the Absolute can tolerate no other to it. It is a non-dual principle. The Tathāgata on the other hand is posited only to lend succour to the ignorant humanity. If there were no finite persons, struggling in a finite world, a God would be utterly superfluous. He cannot therefore be simply equated with the ultimate reality, as is done in theistic systems and religions. But nor can He be anything phenomenal, since in that case He would be merely one among other phenomenal beings, and subject to the same sufferings for the removal of which a God was admitted. A being under the sway of Avidyā is not free ; when he attains freedom he becomes one with the Absolute. A *person* who is yet free is an absurdity.

The argument for the existence of Tathāgata has two aspects, viz., its metaphysical necessity in the system and secondly, its logical tenability. The Yogācāra represents a particular line of approach to the ultimate reality. This latter is conceived by him as the Absolute of Will. This entails a particular explanation of phenomena, based on the fundamental doctrine of consciousness as creative. The question is: how does the Yogācāra become aware of this fact ? The knowledge of the illusoriness of the object is not an empirical one.[1] The object does not proclaim itself to be illusory. The obvious answer

1. Cf. Ch. 7.

that the total failure of all devices to render the object intelligible sets the norm of explanation is not satisfactory : this presupposes a prior prejudice in favour of the subject. Once this basic concept is *given* the rest of the dialectic of idealism can be worked out by reason : but what reason cannot account for is how this basic concept or pattern itself is given. This problem as to why one particular Analytic is chosen in preference to other possible Analytics equally plausible is inherent in all speculative metaphysics. It indicates an alogical source though working by means of logic. A being rooted in phenomena can have no inkling even of the existence of the Unconditioned[2]; or, if the demand for the Unconditioned be a natural disposition of mind, as Kant would have it, he cannot have the faintest conception of the positive content or character of the Unconditioned. That can only be revealed by a *person* already in the possession of such a knowledge. That person can certainly not be any one of us; the problem as to how he comes to know of it would remain unsolved. The person can only be that who was never ignorant, who is not phenomenal at all. God or the Tathāgata is such a person.

But the necessity for the Tathāgata in the Yogācāra metaphysics would be of no avail if the concept were inherently unstable. The next step in the argument is to show the logical tenability of the concept of Tathāgata. Consciousness, as we have already seen, is creative. This creativity has two aspects[3] ; first, when it is governed by the idea of objectivity, it goes on projecting an 'other' ; the 'other' is in reality only the form of consciousness, but is yet invariably perceived as something objective. This is the Cosmic Illusion under which the will suffers. When the illusory 'other' is sublated, Will reverts back to its natural state of pure Act, where it wills only itself. This is the second aspect of its creativity. But the possibility of an intermediate state between those two aspects must be recognised, where the Will is self-conscious of itself. Here the 'other' is still present, but its apparent externality is realised to be illusory. It is a transitional stage from ignorance to knowledge. It is neither pure Will nor again defiled will.[4] It is not pure since it is still a consciousness of the 'other'. Nor is it defiled

2. CPB, pp. 276 ff.
3. Cf. Ch. 7.
4. Cf. MSA, IX, 22.

as it does not mistake the 'other' as something objective, is not taken in by it. The self-conscious Will can be neither identical with nor different from the defiled will. If it is identical with the latter, it cannot be the consciousness of it, it cannot analyse and correct it. But if it is different from the latter, it would not be relevant to it. It will simply be another consciousness but would not be self-consciousness. In that case also it cannot analyse or correct the defiled will. This state of self-consciousness is obviously unstable as the two aspects in it cannot be reconciled with its unity[5]. It cannot be made ultimate. Nevertheless, it cannot be denied. It is that state where Will has become free from its objective entanglements, but is yet short of the Absolute in that it is conscious of its freedom.[6] The personality of Tathāgata is constituted by such a self-conscious Will, and this concept lies at the basis of Īśvara in the Advaita Vedānta[7]. It cannot be denied since that would entail the denial of any consciousness of the hollowness of objectivity. Such a consciousness must be accorded a third place as it refuses to be identified either with the contentless Will, i.e., the Absolute, or with will as petrified by the idea of objectivity, i.e., will suffering under Avidyā. The Tathāgata is the cosmic counterpart of this consciousness of the illusory object, i.e., the consciousness of freedom. He is not, and cannot be, ultimate. He condescends to be still confronted by an 'other' out of his boundless compassion for the suffering mankind. He is not bound by it, since the corrective self-consciousness of the illusoriness of the 'other' is always present. He perceives the 'other', but always as a creation of consciousness and is therefore never taken in by it. He enjoys an amphibious status. Though He is in phenomena and is Himself but

5. Cf. Ch. 7.

6. Cf. VMS, p. 42-3.

7. This concept is even stabilised and raised to an ultimate status in the Pratyabhijñā system (Kashmir Śaivism). In this system there obtains an inexpressible and non-relational identity between the principle and the person, i.e., between the Absolute and its creativity (between Śiva and Śakti). Its creativity is not therefore due to Avidyā as in the Yogācāra, but ensues out of its consciousness of freedom itself. Śiva is free to create or not to create. Here the Absolute and God are identified.

phenomenal, He yet knows the true nature of phenomena and therefore transcends it at the same time. These two aspects of His being are very aptly put in *Mahāyānasūtrālaṅkāra* where it is said that the Bodhisattava has two kinds of sambhāras[8], viz., puṇyasambhāra and jñānasambhāra. Because of the former He does good to the world, but by His jñānasambhāra His existence here is not defiled by the kleśas.

The Buddha therefore, though essentially one with the ultimate reality, is yet not absolutely identical with it. Because of this, speculation about His personality, i.e., about His mode of existence after the mahāparinirvāṇa, is condemned. It is treated as avyākṛta. He is a person, though a free one.

The free descent of the Tathāgata into the world is therefore a temporal event from the phenomenal point of view. It has a before and an after. He appears to take birth and die; and yet all this is part of the cosmic illusion which it is His mission to dispel. It is therefore said that He is neither pure nor impure.[9] He cannot be said to be pure because He appears in time and is therefore pratītya-samutpanna. But as He is free from the two obscurations (kleśāvaraṇa and jñeyāvaraṇa), He cannot be said to be impure. He is like the sky[10] which pervades everything, not excluding the human beings and yet is affected by nothing. He is essentially identical with all dharmas[11] and yet He cannot be defined in terms of any dharma, as He transcends all of them. Strictly speaking, He can be said neither to have existence nor not to exist.[12] As He is Himself phenomenal, which latter has no real existence, He cannot be said to exist ; nor can He be said not to exist as He is identical with the Absolute itself. Again, it is said that He is neither one nor many.[13] From the phenomenal point of view He is not one, since He has taken innumerable births. Each incarnation is an individual Buddha. In fact, as has been said in the last chapter, every one of us is a potential Buddha (Tathāgatagarbha) and it is

8. MSA, XVIII, 38, p. 139.
9. MSA, IX. 22, p. 27.
10. Ibid, IX, 15, p. 36.
11. Ibid, IX, 4, p. 34.
12. Ibid, IX, 24, p. 38.
13. Ibid, IX, 26, p. 38.

this fact alone that lends significance to our spiritual aspirations. But, speaking from the ultimate point of view, He is not many because He has no body. That is to say, He never identifies Himself with the particular body that He has freely assumed for the time being. He is one like ākāśa.

All the usual powers and excellences associated with the notion of God-head are ascribed to Him. But His most important aspects are two, viz., Prajñā and Karuṇā. The first makes Him one with the Absolute while the latter keeps Him in phenomena. The first is spoken of under four heads:[14] 1. Ādarśajñāna, 2. Samatājñāna, 3. Pratyavekṣājñāna and 4. Kṛtyanuṣṭhānajñāna. The first is the basic one and is invariable while the other three depend upon it and are variable.

(a) *Ādarśajñāna* is that knowledge which is not limited to any personality (amamam). It is spatially undifferentiated and temporally all-comprehensive. That is to say, this knowledge extends to everything existing in all three times. It is not therefore obstructed by anything knowable, as it is free from all obscurations. Such a knowledge is infinite because it is indeterminate, and not because it depends upon anything knowable. All other knowledges spring out of it; it is their fountain as it were, because it reflects the Tathāgata and His knowledge like a mirror.

(b) *Samatājñāna* is the knowledge of the essential identity pervading all existence.

(c) *Pratyavekṣājñāna* is that knowledge which perceives all things without confusion. That is to say, it is by virtue of this knowledge that the Tathāgata has a correct knowledge of each individual thing without confusing one with the other. It indicates the vibhūti of the Lord, i.e., His omniscience, and removes all doubt.

(d) *Kṛtyanuṣṭhānajñāna* is the knowledge meant for the projection of His apparitional bodies, infinite in number and variegated in nature, for the purpose of benefitting mankind. Such a projection cannot be rationally worked out ; it depends on the different purposes to be served by it ; hence the number to be projected and the place where it is to take place cannot be determined *a priori*.

---

14. Ibid, IX, 67-76. In some Mādhyamika texts a fifth, viz. Advayajñāna, is added. Cf. Obermiller, *The Doctrine of Prajñāpāramitā*, p. 45 (*Acta Orientalia*, Vol. XI) ; CPB, p. 281.

All knowledges are but the different expressions of the highest wisdom of the Lord, ensuing out of the realisation of His identity with the Absolute. The second aspect in the conception of the Tathāgata is His Karuṇā, infinite compassion for the suffering of people. It is because of this that He freely consents to continue as a phenomenal Being. That compassion is not however on a par with the love, say, of a father for his son. The love that the Tathāgata has is neither impure nor mundane.[15] Love that is tainted with attachment and craving cannot be pure. But the love that the Tathāgata has for people struggling in the tempestuous sea of misery and passion, groping in the darkness of ignorance, is of a different kind. It is absolutely disinterested and hence is pure. He is not affected by any consideration of 'I' and 'mine', but purely by that of finding a way for their rescue. Nor can such compassion be termed mundane. The conception of a more loving god could hardly be found.

The Three Kāyas

The concept of the Tathāgata is constituted by different metaphysical principles. This fact is illustrated in the theory of the three kāyas of the Buddha. It is one of the most important doctrines in the whole of Mahāyāna religion[16] and it is nothing peculiar to the Yogācāra who accepted the traditional doctrine.

There are three aspects of the God-head, technically known as the three kāyas of the Tathāgata. They[17] are : 1. The Svābhāvika kāya, 2. the Sāmbhogika kāya and 3. the Nairmāṇika kāya.

1. The *Svabhāvakāya* of the Buddha is the principle of pure Will (viśuddhā Tathatā)[18] which is the ultimate reality. As such he is identical with the Absolute. It is also called Dharma-kāya, being the dharmatā (essence) of things.[19] Its essential character (lakṣaṇa) is āśrayaparāvṛtti,[20] i. e., the withdrawing or retracting of the Ālaya.

---

15. MSA, XVII, 43-44, p. 127.

16. See for further details Dutta, *Aspects of Mahāyāna Buddhism*, p. 96-128 ; CPB, pp. 284 ff.

17. MSA, IX, 59, p. 44.

18. MSA, XXI, 60, p. 188-189.

19. MSA, IX, 4.

20. MSA, p. 45.

When under the influence of Avidyā, the illusion of objectivity, the Ālaya is compelled into a forward movement. It goes on creating forms of objectivity which in their turn further replenish it. On the sublation of this disturbing illusion a retracting movement of this Ālaya is started. It no longer posits an 'other' but rests in itself. This is the state of Vijñaptimātratā, of consciousness as pure Act. It is the Dharmakāya of the Buddha and is His natural aspect.

Being essentially identical with the Absolute, the question of the number of Buddhas[21] has no meaning. Certain arguments,[22] it is true, are offered for the plurality of Buddhas. Every person being a potential Buddha (budhagotrāḥ sattvāḥ) it cannot be maintained that only one out of that infinite number attains liberation ; since, in that case, the accumulation of merit and wisdom (puṇya-jñānasambhāra) in the rest of the Bodhisattvas would be futile. Moreover, the Buddhahood itself cannot be established on the hypothesis of there being only one Buddha. There is no one original Buddha who is to reveal the doctrine to others and yet, without this revelation, the attainment of Buddhahood on anyone's part is inconceivable. The tradition of revelation is therefore beginningless and this can be accounted for by positing an infinite number of Buddhas. All these considerations, it will be seen, are relevant to the fact of a Buddha appearing among ourselves for an infinite number of times. They are by no means pertinent to the ultimate metaphysical status of the Tathāgata. The Dharmakāya of all the Buddhas is identical, as all are identical with the Absolute.[23] It is also beyond thought as this identity cannot be grasped with mere concepts.

2. The second aspect of the Buddha is His *Sāmbhogika Kāya*—His body of Bliss. It is this body with which the Buddha enjoys His creation (dharmasambhoga)[24]. Strictly speaking, this is the concept of God *par excellence*. All the glorified descriptions of the Buddha found in the scriptures, e. g., rays emanating from the innumerable pores of His skin and penetrating to the remotest corners of the universe, pertain to this kāya. The Buddha dwells in the Akaniṣṭha

21. MSA, IX, 26, p. 38.
22. MSA, IX, 77, p. 48.
23. MSA, IX, 62, p. 45.
24. MSA, IX, 60-1, p. 45.

Heaven, surrounded by a host of Bodhisattvas and other minor personages. Sambhoga kāya is the personality of the supreme God, associated with all powers and excellences.[25] It is comparable to the concept of God in the Brāhmanical systems which finds the best illustration in the Eleventh Chapter of the *Bhagavad Gītā*.[26]

3. The *Nairmāṇika Kāya* is the apparitional body of the Buddha. Hence one is explicitly warned that the human form which the Lord might temporarily assume should by no means be mistaken for His real body. This assumption is solely for the purpose of lending succour to mankind.[37] The forms assumed can be infinite in number (aprameyaprabhedam buddhanirmāṇam). Whereas the body of Bliss characterises the Divine qualities of the Buddha existing for Himself (svārthasampattilakṣaṇaḥ), the assumed body characterises such qualities existing for the sake of others (parārtha-sampattilakṣaṇaḥ).[28]

In short, the human Buddha who is ordinarlity seen in the various worlds and exemplified in different individuals is the Nirmāṇakāya of the Buddha. It is of this kāya that any historicity can be ascribed. That body which is visible to some heavenly beings is His Sambhogakāya which obviously has no historicity. But both the kāyas are His free assumptions. The utter invisibility (sarvathā-adṛśyamānatā) of any form is His Dharmakāya.[29] This is His real essence. The Sambhogakāya is the supreme God while the Nirmāṇa kāya is the Śākyamuni who actually took birth amongst us.

The difference between the conceptions of the Tathāgata and Ïśvara in the Advaita Vedānta is apparent[30]. In both the systems the necessity for positing an omniscient person is realised who provides the cue for negation. In the Advaita Vedānta, Ïśvara, though phenomenal, yet acts always from above. The Tathāgata on the other hand actually takes birth as man and undergoes all the discipline necessary for realising the truth. Though He is the impersonation of truth itself, He yet acts as an ordinary person in order to breed confidence in others. They

---

25. *Abhisamayālaṅkārāloka*, p. 526.
26. See Otto, *Idea of the Holy*, pp. 101-3.
27. yena nirmāṇena sattvārtham karoti ; MSA, IX, 60, p. 45.
28. MSA, IX, 63.
29. MSA, pp. 188-9.
30. See CPB, pp. 288-9.

also feel that it is possible to acquire freedom. The ideal is actually illustrated and exemplified in the phenomenal.

As this aspect of the God-head, viz., His functioning as a guide and mentor in the tortuous path of disillusionment, is more emphasised upon, the other aspects are ignored. To Īśvara are ascribed the cosmic functions as well ; He is the creator and the sustainer of the world. In the Yogācāra however, as indeed in all Buddhism , the notion of a god is vehemently opposed. The governing principle in the world is not any alien personage, but the Karma[31] itself. This is the famous theory of Pratītyasamutpāda. The Tathāgata is merely a spiritual preceptor. He cannot, or rather does not, interfere with other cosmic functions. In this respect the concept corresponds to that of the Īśvara in the Yoga system.

31. karmajam lokavaicitryam.

CHAPTER X

THE YOGĀCĀRA AND SOME OTHER FORMS OF ABSOLUTISM

A comparative study between the Yogācāra absolutism and some other forms of absolutism is profitable, not because it will establish the superiority of the Yogācāra system over the latter, but because it will serve to distinguish between the various approaches to the Absolute. Though it will not materially add to our knowledge of the Yogācāra system, it will yet make it more precise. A thing is never known in its fulness until it is known in its entire setting. The value acquired is not regarding the logical clarity of the system, but only its aesthetic clarity. For this purpose two other systems, thoroughly analysed to their last details, are selected, viz., The Advaita Vedānta and the Mādhyamika.[1]

Some misconceptions are to be carefully avoided in this connection. Some thinkers hold that there cannot be alternative forms of absolutism.[2] They interpret the apparent divergence between these systems in two ways. The first line of interpretation is that their differences are only at the surface ; in reality they are essentially identical and are kept separate only by partisan motives. The second line is to insist that some of them are, strictly speaking, not absolutisms. As to which system represents the true type of absolutism, there is no unanimity, the preference depending upon individual idyosyncrasy. We have however reasons to believe that this line of interpretation is

---

1. The selection of both of these from Indian Philosophy is not accidental. In the West, though forms of absolutism are present, they are never consistently systematic, so that one cannot be sure about their exact significance. Hegel we refuse to call an absolutist; he stops at idealism.

2. CPB, pp. 311 ff.

neither logically sound nor does it do justice to the essential spirit of Indian Philosophy.

I

Advaita Vedānta

The Advaita Vedānta is, as already discussed above, realistic in its epistemology.[3] It tries to explain entire phenomena from the knowledge-standpoint.[4] The real is what is independent of the knowing act. Knowledge does not create or in any way distort its content. Its function is just to reveal the object existing in its own right. The content known asserts its own existence irrespective of the fact of its being known. In the presence of the object, consciousness cannot pick and choose or in any way domineer over it. The object irresistibly stamps its existence over consciousness. Knowledge does not depend upon the individual caprice of the knowing subject (puruṣa-buddhyapekṣam) but must faithfully reveal the object (vastutantra) existing independently.[5]

Śaṅkara adduces certain arguments to establish the independence of the object. The object is experienced in all knowledge and as such its existence cannot be gainsaid.[6] The idealist may urge that the actual experience of the object is never questioned ; what is sought to be refuted is its apparent independence apart from its being known. Śankara answers that, from the very nature of knowledge, its distinction from the object is proved. Knowledge is invariably the cognition *of* an object, and none of the terms can be done away with. The awareness of this 'of'-relation is not possible without granting the real existence of the object. What obtains in the knowledge-situation is never mere consciousness, but consciousness *of* the object. Consciousness itself is never apprehended as the post etc. The latter are rather cognised as the *objects of* consciousness.

Were no external object ever cognised, it can never be asserted that the content appears 'as though external' to consciousness

3. See supra Ch. 7.
4. CPB, p. 315 ff.
5. BSSB, I, 1, 2.
6. BSSB, II, 2, 28.

(bahirvad avabhāsate).[7] This indicates that the idealist is in fact aware of the distinction between the object and its consciousness, and yet his whole endeavour is to obliterate this very distinction. The given element in all knowldge cannot be doubted without endangering the very possibility of knowledge.

Again, when two objects are successively cognised, there arises the distinct knowledges of the form 'I know A' and 'I know B'. Here the objects known are different and yet there is no difference in the two acts of knowing themselves.[8] Knowledge is common, or both would not have the same form, viz., 'I know'. Hence it is different from either of the objects. The changing element must be distinguished from the unchanging one.

If an independent object were not accepted, which confronts consciousness and is cognised by it, then strictly speaking there is no knowledge, as there is nothing to be known.[9] Consciousness reveals and as such cannot itself be the object of revelation. An act can never be identified with the content known by the act. If consciousness were to know itself, it would be in the same predicament as that of fire burning itself. Nor can it be said that one moment of consciousness is known by a succeeding moment, since, being momentary, they are not available together.[10] Fire of yesterday cannot burn today's faggot. Moreover, the succeeding moment would itself stand in need of being revealed and so on *ad infinitum* so that ultimately nothing is revealed. Again, the two moments are not disparate in nature and it remains unintelligible why one moment should reveal whereas another should be revealed.

The ideality of empirical objects is sought to be proved on the strength of the dream-contents being ideal. But one is not a justification for the other, the two having nothing in common. The dream-contents are sublated upon waking ; this implies that the objects of waking experience supply the norm or standard of reality. Moreo ver, objectivity (sattā) of things is never cancelled.[11]

---

7. BSSB, II, 2, 28.
8. Ibid.
9. Ibid.
10. BSSB, II, 2, 32.
11. BSSB, II, 2, 29.

Without the acceptance of the object the variety of the contents appearing in consciousness cannot be accounted for. There is no extraneous factor to consciousness, and there is no reason why a particular content 'A' should be apprehended at a particular time in preference to all other possible contents. The hypothesis of the innate vāsanās, latent in consciousness and giving rise to these contents in a determinate order, cannot be accepted since the variety of these vāsanās themselves cannot be established without positing an objective variety as its cause.

Śaṅkara concludes that the distinction between consciousness and its content is too patent to be explained away by any dialectical jugglery.[12] The fact of their being available invariably together (sahopalambhaniyama) proves nothing more than that the object is the cause of the forms of consciousness. The object is the primary condition of the possibility of any knowledge.

These arguments are sufficient to delight the heart of the most fastidious realist. This is not however a complete picture of Advaita Vedānta. Śaṅkara should not be branded as a realist on the strength of these contentions. The discovery of the object as it is is the true function of knowledge : this doctrine is common both to Śaṅkara as well as the realist. The further step in the Advaita analysis marks a radical departure from realism. Knowledge can also be invalid, and this contingency is not and cannot be recognised in realism. The real is pure Being[13] whereas what appear in knowledge are the empirical objects. Hence empirical knowledge is not pure revelation. There is some extraneous factor involved which vitiates this revelatory function. Knowledge *qua* knowledge can never be invalid. In mere revelation the possibility of mistake is precluded. The presence of some non-knowledge factor is therefore to be suspected.

This factor is the contribution of subjectivity. When something appears in knowledge which has no objective counterpart, it is to be supposed that it is merely in knowledge ; it is a creature of the subjective. It is exhausted entirely in the knowing of it and has no existence apart from its appearance in knowledge.

---

12. BSSB, II, 2, 28.

13. This thesis is presupposed and not proved here.

All our empirical knowledge is thus not *merely* knowledge. There are two factors functioning together whose synthesis is called knowledge. If we stick to the purely knowing function of consciousness there can be no illusion. Revelation cannot err. The other function of consciousness we have called the will-function. Here there is construction instead of revelation. But there is nothing in the nature of willing itself either to make it false. Falsity of a content lies in *mistaking it*, taking it as other than what it is. Illusion is the confusion of these two subjective functions, viz., knowing and willing. Knowing is the discovery of the objectively given; willing is the subjective construction. Illusion takes place only when the content willed is mistaken for a known content, i.e., what is in reality merely subjective is judged to be given : what is exhausted in the consciousness of it is mistakenly thought to be independently real. All illusion is misinterpretation, importing to the given what is not there.

This can be illustrated in the case of an empirical illusion. In the stock-example of the illusory rope-snake, the appearance of a unitary content must be analysed into its ingredients. Illusion is confusion, and confusion presupposes the existence of two factors of which one is confused with the other. What obtains in reality is the rope ; it is the given. It exists independently and is absolutely indifferent to the knowing of it. When the snake appears in its stead, the rope does not evaporate. Its existence remains unimpaired even in its unperceived state. And when it comes to be known subsequent to the sublation of the snake, its ontological status does not gain in any respect. Knowing or its absence does not make or unmake it.[14] The case with the snake is entirely different. Though it appears as objective, it refuses to be incorporated along with the objective order of things. It exists only so long as it appears to exist ; after cancellation it simply melts into naught. It cannot be related to other objective things. This is because it is not objective at all. Its existence lies solely in the perception of it (pratibhāsamātraśarīratva). It is a content willed, constructed by the subjective and projected as though outside. Being projected is its life ; when it ceases to be projected, it ceases to be.

---

14. If a content is destroyed because of knowledge, it is illusory. jñāna-nivarttyatvam vā mithyātvam ; *Advaitasiddhi*, p. 160.

The snake enjoys no unknown status, whereas the rope does. The rope did exist even at the time of the appearance of the snake, though it was not percieved as such.[15] But, the idealist objects, unknown existence is a contradiction in terms. How can a thing be *known* to exist when, *ex hypothesi*, it is *not known*. This "egocentric predicament" which is really fatal to naive realism is escaped by the Advaita Vedānta transcendentally. There are certainly no empirical means of knowing the existence of an unknown thing. But such existence must necessarily be conceded when it is the primary condition for the very possibility of knowledge. The rope is not *known* to exist during the appearance of snake and this is all that the egocentric predicament requires. But, had it not existed, the snake could not have appeared.[16] The snake, as we have seen, has no objective existence, and yet it appears as though objective. If it did not, it would be robbed of all its sting as an illusory content. Hence this existence, which it does not really possess and which it yet appears to have, must be a borrowed one. The existence belongs in fact to the rope and the snake appropriates it as its own. The rope therefore must have existed even in its unperceived state and had lent its objectivity to be imposed upon.

The Advaita Vedānta is thus strongly realistic, but is nevertheless not realism. Realism cannot accept subjectivity in any form ; illusion is rather to be explained away than be squarely faced as a stubborn fact. The Advaita Vedānta recognises that into the composition of empirical objects a large amount of subjectivity enters.

The acceptance of subjectivity in one form or other is the common form of all systems other than rank realism. Hence this fact by itself should not be construed as idealism. In idealism there are two principles employed ; first, everything without exception is under-

---

15. "etāvantam kālam mayā na jñāto' yam idānīm jñāta" ity anubhavāt, *Advaitasiddhi*, p. 562.

16. This is the implication of the famous statement of the *Vivaraṇa* : sarvam vastu jñātatayājñātatayā vā sākṣīcaitanyasya viṣaya eva. When the snake is sublated, how do we know that the rope existed even during the time of appearance ? This is possible only if there is a way of knowing the unknown rope. This knowledge is not indeed that of the pramātā, but is of the sākṣī-consciousness.

stood as the creation of the subjective, and secondly, the subjective itself is understood as real, the substrate, where the unreal constructs are imagined. These two are closely interrelated, though the latter need not follow from the first.

Can the two factors, which, when synthesised, are called knowledge, be separately real ? Illusion is, as we have seen, the confusion of these two functions. There is no mistake in knowing a willed content as willed. The rope-snake is analysed into the objectively given and the subjective construction, both of which are actual facts and as such are to be understood as separately real. This contention is based on a misconception of the nature of these two functions and their relation. If both were separately real, they would exist merely side by side. The possibility of their being confused with each other would be utterly precluded. One would not constitute the falsity of the other. Mere differents are not confused with one another. They belong in fact to different planes altogether. While the one (object) is ontological, the other is not. The subjective is mistaken for the objective only because it is nothing in itself. Its whole force is entirely exhausted just in being mistaken. It cannot exist but as exploiting the other, as the falsification of the other. When the snake is sublated as an objective thing, it is not reinstated as the subjective fact. The centre of interest shifts towards the real objective, the rope. The subjective nature of the snake is cognised, but it is realised at the same time that it has only a sort of vampire-like existence. Analysis not only clears the confusion, it reduces the subjective to naught.[17] The subjective is parasitical in nature; it is nourished only by a mistake, only as superimposed on the object.

The Advaita Vedānta is thus by no means an idealistic system. If it is called idealism at all, it is so in the same sense in which Kant or the Sautrāntika is an idealist. It is a species of transcendental or critical idealism. The presence of the subjective factor is recognised ; but this subjectivity creates falsity and is itself false. For Kant and the Sautrāntika, the given is the unique particular (svalakṣaṇa), the pure difference; subjectivity consists in unifying, relating, synthesising what is utterly discrete. In the Advaita Vedānta the situation is

17. pratipannopādhau traikālika-niṣedha-pratiyogitvam vā mithyātvam ; *Advaitasiddhi*, p. 94.

exactly reversed. It is the universal Being, the pure identity, that is given ; the function of the subjective is to import difference and particularity to the undifferentiated universal. Both are agreed however in making the given the prius of knowledge, but for which knowledge would not be possible. Empirical knowledge is in large measure a contribution of the subjective, but that is because it is not all knowledge. The will-factor should also be taken into account, with this proviso, that it makes for the falsification of given. For a true idealist there can be nothing given, and the subjective cannot be false. It is the givenness of the content that is illusory whose negation reveals the reality of the subjective. But Kant and the Sautrāntika on the one hand, and Advaita Vedānta on the other, insist on the given element in knowledge on which the thought constructions take place. The Advaita Vedānta detects the presence of the will-factor in knowledge, but the will is here understood as creating falsity and as itself being false. The demand is to know the given in all its purity, just to discover it and not to interpret it in any way ; in short, to annihilate the will-function.

it is thus not naive realism, since it denies the reality of empirical objects ; nor is it pure idealism, as the reality of the subjective is denied with equal vehemence. It is in fact that aspect in the constitution of empirical objects which is the contribution of the subjective that is condemned as unreal, and the reality of the pure given, the bare thing-in-itself as unrelated to the knowing act, is upheld. Unless the subjective itself is understood as the basic reality, and the independence of the content known as merely apparent, there is no idealism in its precise sense.

In the orthodox school of Advaita Vedānta the emphasis is on the given, the thing-in-itself. The real is what is in itself—the unrelated—unrelated to the knowing act. It is the pure object, the thinghood (sattā) of things, i.e., that essential nature of things (sanmātra) which remains unaffected when their willed aspect is negated. But since the creativity of the subjective is accepted, it is capable of bearing an idealistic interpretation and this is what the author of *Vedānta-Siddhānta-Muktāvalī* does.

This school is commonly known as dṛṣṭi-sṛṣṭi-vāda, and is the only idealistic school on the Brāhmanical side.[18] According to it, things exist only so long as they are known[19]; they are created by the knowing of them. Since empirical objects contain a large amount of subjectivity in their constitution, this statement might be true of the orthodox school as well. Their difference centres round the conception of what a thing is. For the orthodox school, though empirical objects may not exist when unknown by anybody, yet they have an inner core which is their reality and which remains entirely unaffected. This essential reality is the Kūṭastha-nitya. Dṛṣṭi-sṛṣṭi-vāda however denies the existence of any unknown sattā whatsoever.[20] Things are as they appear, with nothing underlying at the back of them. They are wholly the creatures of the subjective. The distinction between knowledge and the known can be maintained neither by perception nor by inference.[21] To exist and to be known are identical. Their being is all on the surface; unknown existence (ajñāta-sattā) is a contradiction in terms.

The substrate (adhiṣṭhāna) is not the objective Being on which the falsity of empirical things is superimposed, but is rather the subject itself.[22] Vijñāna itself appears as though objective, as in dreams. That there is something in the content which does not owe its being to knowledge is not brought out and this fact makes the argument idealistic. The "Being"-aspect of Ātman is ignored and its consciousness-aspect (i.e., creativity) is emphasised.[23] The substrate of unreality is supposed to be the subject and not any objective or universal Being.[24] The Sākṣī is in both the schools the reality of the subject, but whereas in the orthodox school it is identical with the reality of things, it is the sole reality in the school under consideration, as other objective things have no reality whatsoever apart from their being willed. Will is

---

18. Exception is made of the definitely idealistic teachings of the *Yogavāśiṣṭha*, but they remain mere suggestions and are not articulated into a full-fledged system.

19. VSM, p. 43 (Acyuta Edn.).

20. VSM, pp. 26-7 ; Cf. *Advaitasiddhi*, pp. 533-4.

21. VSM, pp. 43-48.

22. VSM, p. 54.

23. VSM, p. 55.

24. VSM, p. 56.

certainly false, and to this extent it agrees with the orthodox school as opposed to the Yogācāra, but it is so only because it imagines things as though objective. When these latter are sublated, will itself ceases and only the substrate, pure consciousness, remains. It does not admit change in consciousness, as pure idealism of the Yogācāra type does; but its approach to the Real is nevertheless by way of the subjective. The phenomenal world is explained after the pattern of the dream-experience where the emphasis is on subjective, rather than after the illusory rope-snake where the reality of the objective dominates.

Since all experience is reduced to so many ideas in the mind of the knowing consciousness,[25] the other minds also suffer a similar fate. The plurality of egos cannot be maintained,[26] as their existence outside *my* consciousness of them is denied, because of the same consideration that the existence of real objective things is denied. Consequently there can be no intra-subjective world and we have an extreme form of solipsism (ekajīvavāda). Īśvara, whose existence is accepted in the orthodox school in order to sustain the intra-subjective world, is similarly denied, and the vyāvahārika sattā of things goes along with this. There are only two truths, viz., the prātītika and the pāramārthika.[27]

This excursion should serve to make the realistic epistemology of the orthodox school more evident. We are now in a position to differentiate the respective standpoints of the Advaita Vedānta and the Yogācāra. Both the systems are agreed in admitting that knowledge is not a unitary affair but is the synthesis of two factors, or rather, two functions of the subjective, viz., knowing and willing. Knowing is the revelation of the given, while the other is the projection of its own construct. Illusion is the confusion of these two functions and analysis not only clears the confusion, it also demonstrates that at least one of them is parasitical in nature, so that when left to itself it just evaporates into naught. They belong in fact to different orders altogether and both cannot be said to exist in the same sense. One of them is unreal, the whole being of which is totally exhausted in being superim-

25. dṛṣṭimātram jagattrayam ; VSM, p. 56.
26. VSM, p. 24, Also p. 19.
27. VSM, p. 27.

posed upon the other, and which, apart from the latter, is simply nothing.

This logical outline of the nature and structure of illusion[28] is common to both the forms of absolutism. Their unanimity ceases however when they come to the details. The general principle that illusion is a false relation, and that a relation cannot be false without at least one of the terms being so, is employed by both. But as to which of the two terms should be retrieved as real and which other be condemned as unreal, there is a world of difference between them. For the Vedānta it is the knowing function of the subjective which is real, that is to say, which reveals reality. The real is the given, the thing-in-itself. But all our empirical knowledge is vitiated by the other factor, viz., the will-function which makes for falsity and is in itself false. It is in fact the relatedness to the knowing subject, when this relatedness becomes essential to the thing known, which is false. Noting can be real which is merely *in* knowledge and is exhausted within that relationship ; for a term which is made by a relation can be nothing in itself and is therefore false. In the Yogācāra however, as already seen, the situation is exactly reversed. It is the *knownness* of the content that is merely apparent, is false. Objectivity is unreal and it is the independence and externality of the content known that is to be denied. The givenness of things is false, since there is nothing given to consciousness. Consciousness is self-legislative and depends upon nothing other to it. If anything is to be real at all, it can be so only as being identical with consciousness. The will alone is real and knowing is its falsification. The content as a willed construct is perfectly real, but when it appears as though objectively outside, it becomes false.

The difference between these two standpoints can be illustrated in the case of an empirical illusion. In the familiar example—"That is a snake,"—the Vedānta analysis makes the snake unreal for the reason that it is peculiar to this particular situation. Being is prior to being known and cannot be dependent upon the latter. The snake however is posited in its being known and is not to be independently had. The other term is the 'this'. The this-ness of the snake does not really belong to it ; it is borrowed from another order of existence. It is not made by being related to the snake, nor is it unmade when such relationship is cancelled. It is real because it enjoys an independent exis-

---

28. For this and other allied problems, see CPB, Ch. 13.

tence of its own. For the Yogācāra it is precisely this independent existence which is unreal ; what is to be denied is just this "this-ness" of the snake. The existence of a real content lies in the fact of its being known. The snake is perfectly real as a subjective fact ; cancellation merely reinstates its identity with the subjective.

Applied to the Transcendental Illusion, the difference between the two standpoints means that Reality for the Yogācāra is Avidyā for the Vedānta. For the latter the real is the pure object ; no empirical object however is pure as it has invariably a compounded being. Hence the real is rather the implicate or the substrate of the object and is one identical universal principle. When it is brought into relationship with a knowing subject, it gets determined and particularised and consequently falsified. The real is the object which is never objectified, i.e., never related with the knowing subject.[29] The function of Avidyā is thus to relate it. For the Yogācāra, its function is to posit the content as objective and independent. Consciousness is the sole reality and any content is real only as within consciousness. There is no being which is not being known. A thing is real only as essentially related to consciousness. To objectify it is to falsity it.

The difference persists right upto the notion of the Absolute. The Vedāntic Brahman is realised when knowing is purified of all traces of the will. The Absolute is an ever-accomplished fact (pariniṣṭhita vastu) which is revealed in knowledge, but need not be revealed : in fact it cannot be revealed in empirical knowledge where the will plays a large part. Brahman is not objectified in any actual knowledge, but is rather the ideal of pure knowledge. The bare given, untainted by any trace of subjectivity, is the Absolute. Since it is eternally neutral (kūṭastha), there is no change or process in it. Strictly speaking it cannot be said to be known ; the knower is so absorbed and engrossed in the contemplation of it that he is not even aware of his knowing ; he loses his individuality as a particular perspective and becomes merged as it were in the all-embracing Universal. Pure knowing of a content is being it.[30]

---

29. vṛttikāle vṛttirūpeṇa dharmeṇa śuddhatvāsambhavāt śuddhasya vṛttiviṣayatvam na sambhavati ; *Advaitasiddhi*, p. 242.

30. brahma veda brahmaiva bhavati.

Vijñaptimātratā of the Yogācāra, on the other hand, is the Absolute of pure Will. It is the pure subject—the subjective purified of all objective infection. When objectivity is cancelled the creativity of the subjective is so purified as to create nothing, or rather, nothing particular. The subject acquires all its meaning and significance only as contrasted with the object : with the sublation of the latter the subject itself vanishes. There is no knower when nothing is there to be known. We still persist in calling the Absolute the subject, because it is nothing other than the latter. It is pure Consciousness, untainted by any trace of the given, whereas for the Vedānta, it is the pure given itself.

From the point of view of the object, the illusory never existed ; it is simply naught. But it appeared nevertheless before the subject ; the subject therefore cannot so easily dismiss it. The Absolute of the pure object is thus ever neutral (Kūṭastha); it is subject to no change or process. The Absolute of the pure subject however cannot be indifferent to getting entangled in the meshes of objectivity. The process is real here. Hence Vijñaptimātratā is realised only after a real process which is involved in the progression from the willing of a determinate content to the willing of no content at all. This has been made clear in the previous pages.[31]

Both are agreed in making the Absolute inaccessible to the categories of empirical thought. No empirical object is the Brahman of the Vedānta ; no empirical subject is the Vijñāna of the Yogācāra. It is realised only in an intuitive state, called aparokṣānubhūti by the former, and lokottarajñāna by the other. In consonance with this contention it seems hardly possible to maintain a distinction even in that stage ; it has to be made notwithstanding, in view of the fact that the two approaches are so radically apart. Simply because both are unthinkable pure Will does not become one with Pure Being. We may not assert any actual difference between them, but this does not amount to an assertion of their identity, since the ways leading to them are so sharply contrasted.

There is a possible misconception in this connection which is to be avoided very carefully. Both the forms of the Absolute are invariably referred to as Consciousness. But though consciousness is said to be

31. See supra Ch. 7.

the Absolute in both the systems, it has by no means an identical meaning. For the Vedāntin, the Real is not the knowing act, but rather the underlying principle of identity because of which knowledge is possible.[32] Consciousness is not the subject, but is that basic principle, superimposed upon which the drama of the subject-object duality is enacted. Both the terms of this duality are equally false, the creations of Avidyā. The Real is the objective implicate of all things empirical, including the subject. When it is said to be the self, it should be clearly understood that there is nothing subjective about it. It is the reality of both the subject and the object alike. Self is that by virtue of which things are what they are—their sattā. The knowing subject (paramātā) is itself illusory ; it is one thing among other illusory things and as such has an underlying reality which over-reaches the knowing act and is identical with the reality of the object. The knowing act merely reveals this essential identity. For the Yogācāra, consciousness is understood as the knowing act itself. The object is identical with it in the sense that it is a form (prakāra) of consciousness, constructed and projected by it as though outside. This act is real and it alone is real. Consciousness is nothing if not creative ; it can certainly be so purified as not to create an 'other', but it does not thereby cease to be will. The Vedāntin on the other hand holds that consciousness is an eternally quiescent principle, entirely indifferent to the knowing act. Any activity is foreign to its nature and can only be falsely superimposed upon it. It is the intelligibility of things by virtue of which things are revealed. Since a dead and innert matter (jaḍa) cannot reveal anything such a principle is said to be consciousness (jaḍa-vyāvṛttatvāt).

This can be illustrated by another difference characteristic of the two standpoints. Since consciousness is creative for the Yogācāra and is actually bifurcated, it can be said to know itself (svasamvedana), as it is itself both the knower and the known. It may not be maintained as an ultimate position, but empirical knowledge cannot otherwise be explained on the idealistic principle. The saving feature is that consciousness never knows that it knows only itself, that it never goes beyond itself. It is ever governed

32. Perception is accordingly described as abhedābhivyakti or āvaraṇābhibhava.

by the false idea that it knows an 'other'. With the sublation of this idea, it ceases to know at all. But that it did objectify its own form, and consequently itself, is a fact. But consciousness for the Vedāntin is never objectified at all. Svayamprakāśa does not mean that consciousness is its own object known by itself. It is defined as that which, itself remaining unknown, is yet immediate (avedyatve sati aparokṣa-vyavahāra-yogyatvam). It is self-evident because it does not stand in need of being evidenced by another. This criterion is satisfied by the substrate of the illusory, which is itself not known and yet is immediate, in the sense that it is this that is immediately confronting the knower. The idantā of the content known belongs to the adhiṣṭhāna. Hence self-evidence means unrelatedness ; that is self-evident whose reality its unknownness is unable to suppress. Consciousness is self-evident, and it alone can be self-evident, because it is unrelated to or independent of the knowing act, but is its substrate. This distinction between the doctrines of svasamvitti and svayamprakāśa is indicative of the distinction between the two senses in which consciousness is said to be the Real in the Vedānta and the Yogācāra systems.

II

The Mādhyamika

The Yogācāra analysis of experience is thus antipodal to that of the Advaita Vedānta. The Real for one is Avidyā for the other, and vice versa. But how is such a state of affairs possible or permissible? Of two rival explanations, both claiming to be the only true one and yet opposed to each other at every conceivable point, which one is to be preferred and why ?

In the case of empirical theories the matter is not so serious. Any opposition arising in the course of scientific enquiry is resolvable, theoretically at least, by an appeal to sensuous experience. There can be no other way of refuting a scientific hypothesis, nor is any other needed, than by pointing out a discrepancy between it and the facts given by the senses. An appeal to the testimony of the senses is the last tribunal for testing the truth or otherwise of an empirical theory. In the language of Logical Positivism, the meaning of any proposition is the method of its verification. The verdict of experience is final.

But such a procedure is, from the very nature of the case, not possible in metaphysics. Here we are not interested in explaining a particular phenomenon ; our ambition is rather to interpret the totality of phenomena as such. In claiming absolute universality for a particular explanation, the possibility of an appeal to the senses is necessarily precluded. Any system of metaphysics claims to interpret the totality of phenomena, hence there remains no neutral fact which can decide between two opposed systems. And the opposition is so total and absolute as to make it impossible for them to be synthesised in a higher system, without losing their individual identity. The consciousness dawns that the opposition is not due to any other cause than the inherent conflict in Reason itself. Speculation claims to be universal, and yet it can never be universal, so long as it sets up, as the norm of explanation, one category in preference to all others. A combination of categories is no solution, since that itself becomes one more complex category along with the previous ones. This consciousness marks the transition from construction to criticism.

Criticism entails dialectical consciousness. Dialectic means,[33] first, the awareness of the conflict in Reason and secondly, an attempt to resolve it. The resolution is possible only in one way—by rejecting Reason as such. It sees all systems as merely so many views about the Real. The categories, when enlisted in the service of metaphysics, are merely empty and formal and become Ideas of Reason, to use the Kantian terminology. Dialectic exposes this emptiness of views, by splitting up each in turn and convicting it of self-contradiction.

Metaphysical systems are then all deductive structures. Once grant the initial selection of one pattern in preference to all others, the rest follows as a matter of course. The procedure is guided from beginning to end merely by the laws of self-consistency, and not by the laws of reality (if there be any such laws at all). But this requisite self-consistency is not available. One set of facts cannot incorporate affirmation and negation with regard to itself at the same time. Not can any one single attitude of thought be accepted ; no one attitude of thought can be employed without bringing its opposite also into play.

---

33. CPB, Ch. 6.

The basic attitudes of thought are two, viz., affirmation and negation.[34] Their ontological counterparts are identity and difference. All metaphysical views can be grouped according to these two and their two derivatives, formed by conjunctive affirmation of the basic attitudes, and the disjunctive denial of them. Criticism exposes the fundamental self-contradiction inherent in each of them, and proves their utter incompetence to give reality. All views of the Real are merely views and, as such, false. Thought is relative and relativity is the mark of unreality.[35] A depends upon B for its own reality and B in its turn is itself not established without A ; both are therefore to be rejected.[36] The rejection of thought entails the rejection of all metaphysical systems constructed by thought-categories.[37]

The Mādhyamika is the champion of pure criticism. For him criticism itself is philosophy.[38] Criticism of systems is itself not a system; negation of a fact is itself not a fact.[39] It is the self-consciousness of thought, thought become self-aware of its own unreality.

Both the Advaita Vedānta and the Yogācāra are, as contrasted with the Mādhyamika, speculative systems. They give constructive accounts of phenomena, each from its own standpoint. The Mādhyamika is, in this sense, not a system at all. The two speculative systems interpret the world as an illusion, but they understand the Cosmic Illusion analogically; the theory of this illusion is modelled after their interpretation of the empirical illusion. But in this procedure there are two dogmatic elements involved, viz.—first, as regards the analysis of the empirical illusion, and secondly, the applicability of this analysis to the world as a whole.

As there are two, to leave the rest for the time being, interpretations of the empirical illusion, each thoroughly self-consistent, and yet

---

34. astīti nāstīti ubhe'pi antā...quoted in MKV, p. 135 ; CPB, Ch. 5.

35. CPB, Ch. 5.

36. ekībhāvena vā siddhir nānābhāvena vā yayoḥ na vidyate tayoḥ siddhiḥ katham nu khalu vidyate ; MK, II, 21.

37. śūnyatā sarvadṛṣṭīṇām proktā nissaraṇam jinaiḥ; MK, XIII, 8.

38. CPB, p. 209 ff.

39. CPB, Ch. 6.

each being the exact converse of the other, there is nothing to decide between the two. Each analysis is satisfactory from its own point of view, but both cannot be the truth about this illusion. The conflict in Reason, characteristic of dogmatic metaphysics, is present from the very beginning. The analysis is not punctuated by the facts themselves, but is motivated by the speculative tendency of Reason. The preference of one over the other depends upon one's initial prejudice ; this is dogmatic to the core.

But the application of a particular analysis of the empirical illusion to phenomena as such is still more dogmatic. The world does not proclaim itself to be illusory ; the awareness of the Transcendental Illusion remains an unsolved enigma. The empirical illusion is resolved with its consciousness, as the consciousness of the illusory is incompatible with the existence of the illusory. And there the matter should end. A stray case should not be held as the pattern for all cases ; an accident cannot be generalised ; an exception must not be mistaken for a rule. The colour-blindness of one individual does not prejudice the vision of the rest. The world might be an illusion ; that is not in question. What is not accounted for is how one becomes *aware* of this. Neither the illusory nor the world itself supply this information.

The cue for this extension comes from elsewhere. Here is shown the strength of the Vedānta metaphysics, which is supposed by many to be its weakness. Here the procedure is not first to analyse the empirical illusion and then to universalise it. The illusoriness of the world is rather known beforehand and the empirical illusion is offered merely as an illustration. We start with the knowledge of the Real, and because of this knowledge our empirical experience is accounted as false. The Real is not arrived at as the conclusion of any enquiry ; it is given as the starting-point, but for which the enquiry would not have arisen. Rooted in phenomena as we are, we could not have even an inkling of anything transcending it. The knowledge of the Real can therefore only be *revealed*.[40] The cue is alogical, not logical.

---

40. Puruṣa (Brahman) is Aupaniṣada, revealed through the Upaniṣads. The first step in the disciplinary path is śravaṇa, i.e., revealed knowledge. This is the importance of the concept of Iśvara in the Advaita Vedānta; it is He who reveals. See further Ch. 9 ; CPB, Ch. 13.

The same predicament is present in the Yogācāra also. The cue cannot be a logical one. There is nothing in the nature of things to declare the world illusory, and that too in a particular way. It would appear that the Yogācāra is even aware of this, for he makes[41] affirmation (knowledge of the Real) logically prior to negation (of the illusory). The Yogācāra asserts that in the highest transic states, though the object is certainly not present, consciousness itself cannot be denied.[42] It is illustrative of the dogmatic character of these speculative systems that the same state of nirvikalpa samādhi would be interpreted by the Vedāntin as identity with Brahman (i.e., *being* Brahman) without any trace of subjectivity. The difference does not pertain to the transic state itself but rather to the approaches leading to it. The Mādhyamika makes capital of this opposition, ensuing, not out of the conflict in things—since it pertains to the same state of consciousness—but out of the conflict in Reason.

The Mādhyamika is therefore not interested in empirical illusion at all. His concern is with the Transcendental Illusion alone as exemplified in the opposition of views. This illusion consists in the fact that the empirical categories or predicates are wrongly ascribed to the Unconditioned, giving rise to the various systems of metaphysics. All the categories are of merely empirical value ; when pressed home, as in metaphysics they must be, they are invariably found to be riddled with self-contradiction. Unlike the Yogācāra or the Vedāntin, he does not offer any constructive explanation of phenomena. For him, the illusion is, not to import difference to the Pure Being as in the Vedānta, nor to view pure Will as infected with an 'other,' but the illusion consists rather in interpreting phenomena thus in a particular way according to a particular view. He has therefore no theory of illusion, or rather, for him all theories are illusion. He has no theory of Avidyā; Avidyā is the theorising or the speculative tendency of Reason.

System-building in any of its forms is thoroughly denounced. No aspect of phenomena is retrieved and exalted as the thing-in-itself.[43] For both the Vedāntin and the Yogācāra the negation of phenomena is not complete. All is not phenomenal that appears in phenomena. For

---

41. TSN, 36.
42. VMS, p. 19.
43. CPB, p. 237.

the former only the subjective aspect of things is false. But the "thisness" (sattā) of things is not false ; only its relation to the subjective need be negated (samsargato mithyā, not svarūpataḥ). For the other, it is the apparent independence of things that is false. Consciousness as the creative will cannot be false. In both the systems there is one factor which, though working within phenomena, yet transcends them and is not exhausted in its relationship to the phenomenal. The other aspect however is so exhausted and is therefore illusory.

For the Mādhyamika there is nothing in phenomena whch is not phenomenal.[44] He does not countenance any theory of thing-in-itself; he does not believe in any two-layer metaphysics. Even at the last stage, he urges, one meets with opposed views, and the thing-in-itself is therefore not beyond the categories of Reason. As long as there is speculation about the nature of the Real, the Real has not been reached. What is opposed in its stead is only a view.[45] The Yogācāra's quarrel with the Vedāntin does not stop even when discussing the notion of the Absolute ; hence none of their views can be said to be ultimate, as none is beyond the pale of predication. The Absolute is not residual in its nature, precipitated when one aspect of phenomena is sublated. The consciousness that all views about the Real are unreal is itself the Absolute.[46] That is to say, the Absolute is Reason itself become self-conscious. To know the emptiness of Reason is to transcend it. What is required of Reason is not speculation about the Real, but rather the exposition of its own hollowness. The real is the utter silence of Reason (paramārtho hy āryāṇām tūṣṇīmbhāva eva).[47] Philosophy is not the construction of thing-in-itself, but is pure criticism. It is not an exercise of the inveterate philosophising tendency of Reason, but rather its condemnation, resulting ultimately in its suicide. The Real is not anything beyond Reason, but is the self-criticism[48] of Reason itself. To speak in Kantian terminology, it is reached, not through Analytic but through Dialectic. Any Analytic, i.e., the elucidation of the con-

---

44. CPB, p. 237.
45. buddher agocarastatvam buddhiḥ samvṛtir ucyate; BCA,IX,2.
46. aparapratyayam śāntam prapañcair aprapañcitam nirvikalpam anānārtham etat tattvasya lakṣaṇam; MK, XVIII, 9.
47. MKV, p. 57.
48. CPB, pp. 209 ff.

cept of thing-in-itself and the reconstruction of experience on the basis of it, which both the systems—the Vedānta and the Yogācāra—indulge in, has alternate possibilities and consequently smacks of Reason. It is still entangled between 'is' and 'not-is' and cannot be ultimate.[49]

According to the Mādhyamika therefore, all speculative systems are dogmatic and the Yogācāra is no exception. It must have a constructive theory of phenomena according to which it interprets all experience ; but there are other constructive theories in the field and the dogmatism lies in its thinking itself to be the only possible explanation. The Yogācāra is blind to the Vedānta approach because of its initial dogmatic presupposition, and so is Vedānta insensitive as regards the idealistic analysis. The arguments serve no purpose ; they come afterwards and follow logically from the basic metaphysical presuppositions.

According to the Yogācāra there can be no object independent of consciousness ; consciousness however is not so dependent and can exist even without any object. The Mādhyamika sets against this the Vedāntic contention that the object can exist even without the knowing of it, as in the case of the ground of appearance, e.g., the rope in the rope-snake illusion. In the knowledge-situation, the Mādhyamika urges, one of the two terms cannot be made transcendent at the cost of the other. The identity of the non-implicatory term with its counterpart inside the knowledge-relation can never be proved, there being no means of comparing it in its two states. One can never know whether the object is the same inside the relation as outside it ; this is the "ego-centric predicament" (sahopalambhaniyama) of the idealist. But nor is there any means of asserting the independent existence of the subject. It acquires all its significance only as confronted with the object ; it cannot even be known to exist when it is not knowing anything. The two terms are in fact correlative ; they become meaningless when torn from their relational context. One term, when divorced from the other, is not purified, becoming the Absolute ; it becomes simply nothing.[50] None of them can be established without the other.

49. catuṣkoṭivinirmuktam tattvam mādhyamikā viduḥ ; quoted in BCAP, p. 359.

50. viṣayam vinā jñānasya durniścayatvāt; MA, p. 47 : CPB, Chs. 5, and 13.

If there can be no object without the subject, nor can there be any subject without the object.[51]

It is not a plea for accepting the reality of both ; when one term makes the other meaningful but is itself not established without the latter, both of them should be rejected as false.[52] It certainly means that in phenomena themselves we cannot pick and choose. No element in it can be preferred to any other. Empirically speaking, both are real ; or rather, the question of their reality does not arise. Transcendentally speaking, both are equally unreal. Their empirical reality is not incompatible with their transcendental ideality. The position is the same as that of Kant in his "Refutation of Idealism" where he strongly denounces the idealists' contention that the existence of the subject is in any way more certain than that of the object.

On the idealistic hypothesis of the sole reality of consciousness, the diversity of empirical experience cannot be accounted for. The Mādhyamika vehemently criticises the theory of consciousness turning against itself (svasaṃvedana). Consciousness cannot act upon itself.[53] The knowing agent and the content of knowledge cannot be identical. One entity cannot have manifold aspects, and if it has, it can no longer be called one.

It must not be supposed that the hypothesis of a real external object fares any better. Is consciousness different from its object, or is it not ?[54] If it is not, there is no knowledge, as there is nothing to be known. A sword cannot cut itself, nor can a finger be touched by its own tip. If it is different from its object, then we shall require two consciousnesses, viz., one to cognise the object and the other to know that the former is different from the object cognised.

If consciousness cannot be cognised by itself, nor can it be known by any other consciousness.[55] It cannot be known by a previous one, as it has not yet arisen ; nor by a subsequent one, as it has already pe-

---

51. MKV, p. 61 ff.

52. yo'pekṣya siddhyate bhāvaḥ tam evāpekṣya siddhyati yadi yo'pekṣitavyaḥ sa siddhyatām kamapekṣya kaḥ ; MK, X, 10.

53. BCA, p. 392 ; CPB, pp. 317 ff.

54. BCA, p. 393 ; Cf. also MKV, p. 62.

55. BCA, p. 398.

rished by then. Hence the reality of consciousness, whether known or unknown, cannot be established in any way, and it is only phenomenal.[56]

It cannot be said that consciousness is not really objectified and that it is only the idea of objectivity that is present, since this idea is itself epistemic and as such cannot be distinguished from real subjectivity. Consciousness is subjective, but so is Avidyā, and no distinction can be drawn between them.

Much of the force of this criticism is lost when we remember that the position refuted here is not the ultimate position of the Yogācāra. He recognises the fact that the subject is essentially correlated with the object and that it is reduced to nothing without the latter.[57] He therefore explicitly warns one against calling the Absolute the subject. With the sublation of the object the subject lapses of its own accord. No separate effort is required for its negation.

Nor is the theory of svasamvedana an ultimate position. There is svasamvedana only so long as consciousness continues to project an 'other'. That one and the same entity cannot have a double aspect is accepted by the Yogācāra. If it were not so, he would not be an absolutist. The form of consciousness which is objectified as an 'other' is not inseparable from the latter. The sole reality of consciousness is incompatible with svasamvedana. But the denial of the latter does not entail that of consciousness itself. Pure Will is the Absolute, but it does not cease to be consciousness. The internal diversity in consciousness is because of the presence of an illusory 'other'.

When all is said however, the fact remains that the Yogācāra represents a speculative approach and cannot be said therefore to be a pure form of Absolutism. If the ultimate reality is neither the subject nor the object, why not begin the analysis by negating the whole relational complex ?[58] The texture of phenomena is such that no element in it can be tampered with without bringing down all the rest of it. Strictly speaking the subject is never negated by the Yogācāra ; it is simply purified of its false entanglements. This indicates that he does have a bias in favour of it which he maintains to the last.

---

56. BCA, p. 398.
57. Cf. Ch. 7.
58. MVSBT, p. 23.

We are now in a position to understand and assess the respective values of the different forms of absolutism. As said before, both the Vedānta and the Yogācāra employ the analogical argument ; they understand the structure of the empirical illusion in a particular way and then universalise it. This extension of what is true only within a limited sphere is unwarranted and imports an element of dogmatism into these two systems.

This dogmatism is inherent in all speculative metaphysics, since there is invariably an one-sided employment of Reason. Both the Vedānta and the Yogācāra use the apagogic proof, characteristic of all such metaphysics. The Yogācāra seeks to establish idealism by making the concept of objectivity unintelligible, whereas the Vedānta bases its realistic epistemology on the refutation of subjectivity. Both these contentions, viz., the refutations of objectivity and subjectivity, would have been perfectly valid had they been free from any further implications. But such is not the case. For the Yogācāra, criticism of realism is by itself tantamount to the acceptance of idealism ; in the Vedānta a similar procedure is adopted. Criticism is not pure and unfettered here ; it is motivated. What both of them fail to see is the fact that these two criticisms supplement each other. Each system is blind to the dialectic of the other. The Mādhyamika is just the awareness of this fact. His dialectic is therefore not the adoption of any particular standpoint by refuting any other, but is the refutation of all standpoints without exception ; it is the criticism of Reason as such.

Self-consciousness of Reason itself is the Mādhyamika Absolute. The approach is purely negative here.[59] Negation is not complete in the Vedānta and the Yogācāra ; it is in the service of an affirmation, which is really the guiding principle of these systems. Negation is simply the removal of the outer husk at it were, which hides the inner core, the affirmation. For the Mādhyamika, it is bare negation, total and absolute, so far as thought goes. The Absolute is identified with nothing within thought, i.e., within phenomena. Though the Absolute in both the other systems is said to be beyond thought, the transition is yet made easy by indicating something within phenomena themselves which is not exhausted in it

59. CPB, Ch. 8.

and has a transcendent existence. The gulf between phenomena and noumenon is not frightfully abrupt in these systems.[60] It is bridged by that which is itself not phenomenal but can yet be shown to work within it. This reality is pure Being in the Vedānta and pure Will in the Yogācāra. But, for the Mādhyamika, it is not anything within phenomena. His interest in phenomena is indirect ; primarily he criticises the various views ; but, as in metaphysics there can be had no neutral fact which is not coloured by one view or another, that is, which is not the subject of any predication, affirmative or negative, his criticism of all views amounts to the rejection of phenomena *in toto*.[61] It is not merely one aspect of it that is negated, the other being preserved and exalted as the Absolute. No aspect is preferred to any other ; criticism is complete here. Avidyā is not viewing things as objective which are really identical with consciousness, nor viewing things as different which are in reality identical, but it is "viewing" as such, Reason itself.

The argument of both the other systems is that illusion is not possible without a substrate reality. For them the Mādhyamika is an extreme position where there is an illusion without any underlying reality which alone makes it possible. This substrate is Consciousness for the Yogācāra and Being for the Vedāntin. The Mādhyamika does not deny the necessity of a substrate; his contention is that it cannot be identified with anything within the context of the illusion itself[62]; in that particular context everything is relative to each other and is therefore equally false. The substrate is the critical consciousness itself, which, when diversified by the views, becomes false. Remove all thought categories and the basic reality, the Dharmatā or Tathatā of things, shines forth. It has not to be led to in a particular way ; it is just the cancellation of all ways.

The Mādhyamika Absolute is therefore epistemic. At first sight it might seem to be utterly transcendent, but a closer inspection reveals the fact that it is nothing outside thought, not a thing-in-itself. The Vedāntic as well as the Yogācāra Absolute are both ontological. In

---

60. CPB, Ch. 9.

61. yadā na bhāvo nābhāvo mateḥ santiṣṭhate puraḥ, tadānyagatyabhāvena nirālambā praśāmyati ; BCA, IX, 35.

62. CPB, pp. 237; 324 ff.

the Vedānta it is one reality without a second, the only existent; it is rather existence itself. In the Yogācāra also it has no other than itself, being the only reality. In the Mādhyamika however, what is negated is not any second reality other than the Absolute, as in the former two systems, but rather any view about it. As has just been said, the Absolute is purely epistimic here. Contrasted with this, the Vedantic Absolute may be said to be ontological and the Yogācāra Absolute psychological.[63]

The form of all the three Absolutisms is, however, common.[64] All agree that the Absolute cannot be realised within thought; that is something transcendent. All the same it is the reality of phenomena and is therefore immanent in it. The knowledge of the Absolute is possible only in a non-discursive intuition, where there is no difference between the Absolute and the knowing of it. Strictly speaking it is not knowledge; knowledge *of* the Absolute is a misnomer. Again, duality is negated by each, duality of things by the Vedānta and the Yogācāra and the duality of views by the Mādhyamika.

The Real being realised in a non-conceptual experience where the diversity of perspectives lapses, one cannot draw any distinction between the different Absolutes. If one is unable to assert an identity, nor can one positively maintain any difference between them. That is to say, though the form is common, we cannot say anything regarding the identity or otherwise of their contents. But as it is beyond thought in each case, it is futile to speculate about it. The general norm is set once for all by the Mādhyamika, which, if anything, is wider than the other two, being more universal and more indeterminate.

---

63. CPB, pp. 217 ff.
64. CPB, pp. 320 ff.

Chapter XI

YOGĀCĀRA AND SOME OTHER FORMS OF IDEALISM

In the previous chapter a comparative study was attempted between the Yogācāra absolutism on the one hand and the Vedānta and the Mādhyamika forms of absolutism on the other. In the present chapter a comparison is attempted between the second aspect of the Yogācāra metaphysics, viz., its idealism, and other allied forms of idealism. For this purpose two distinctive systems are selected as representing idealism in its various aspects, viz., the systems of Berkeley and Hegel.[1] A section on Italian Idealism, as represented by Gentile, is added as an appendix to the account of Hegel.

I
Berkeley

Nothing has done more injustice to the Yogācāra than the line of interpretation which makes it an Indian edition of Berkeley. It has been labelled subjective idealism, sensationism, impressionism and what not.[2] We have however reasons to believe, not only that the doctrine of flux is not the last word of the Yogācāra idealism, but also that its own inner logic cannot let it stop anywhere short of absolutism. This fact should carefully be borne in mind when entering into a comparison between these two forms of idealism.

Berkeley also holds that the empirical world cannot be independent of the perceiving consciousness *Esse est percipi* : the essence of things lies in their being perceived.[3] What are actually perceived are the sense-

---

1. The selection of both of them from the history of Western philosophy is significant. By implication it means that no other system of Indian Philosophy can be called pure idealism, though an idealistic strain is present in some of them.

2. Cf. *Indian Realism* by J. N. Sinha—a book which is otherwise very valuable.

3. *Principles of Human Knowledge*, p. 114 (Everyman's Ed.).

data. What we call an 'object' or a 'thing' is only "a certain colour, taste, smell etc., which having been observed to go together, are accounted one distinct thing, signified by a name,"[4] "These various sensations or ideas imprinted on the sense, however blended or combined together (that is, whatever object they compose), cannot exist otherwise than *in* a mind perceiving them "[5]. This is the same argument as that of sahopalambhaniyama employed by the Yogācāra. The utter impossibility of thinking a thing, when *ex hypothesi* it is not thought of, gives weight to the contention that such a thing is non-existent ; even granting its existence, there is no way in which this existence could be known. We cannot know without knowing : we cannot know therefore an unknown thing Senses give testimony to the content only as within consciousness ; "but they do not inform us that things exist without the mind, or unperceived, like to those which are perceived "[6].

The doctrine of a substance, supporting the various sense-data but itself not sensed, is the most pernicious form of an abstract idea.[7] That which is merely a name is given an ontological status as an 'I know not what'. Of this substance nothing more can be said than that it exists. A substance however is nothing but a collocation of sensa. It cannot be said that some of the latter are ideal, while the rest are independently real, and it is to support these latter kind of sensa that a substance is posited ; no such distinction between the so-called primary and secondary qualities of a thing can be drawn.[8] It is obvious that a sense-datum is only an 'idea'; its existence is to be perceived. A coloured thing is nothing but the colour itself along with extension, and it is inconceivable how a colour can exist even when unperceived by anybody. There are two steps in the argument. First, the so-called object is resolved into a collection of sensa-data ; and secondly, these sense-data are transported into the ideal realm, are made mere "ideas in the mind." The second step follows by no means from the first.[9]

---

4. Ibid, p. 113.
5. Ibid, p. 114.
6. Ibid, p. 121.
7. Ibid, p. 115.
8. Ibid, p. 117.
9. e.g., in the Sautrāntika analysis the object is explained away as a construct, but that does not entail the ideality of the dharmas.

If the object perceived be conceded an independent status, apart from what it enjoys as a content of consciousness, we shall be "led into very dangerous errors, by supposing a two-fold existence of the object of sense, the one *intelligible*, or in the mind, the other *real* and without the mind."[10] We have no access to the latter sort of existence, without making it at once known. Nor can we ever know whether an object remains identically the same in both its states, "for how can it be known, that the things which are perceived are conformable to those which are not percieved, or exist without the mind" ?[11]

Berkeley employs also the analogical argument. The creativity of consciousness is evinced in dreams and other illusory objects. "It is granted on all hands (and what happens in dreams, frenzies, and the like, puts it beyond dispute) that it is possible we might be affected with all the ideas we have now, though no bodies existed without, resembling them."[12] The hypothesis of an independent object therefore, existing outside, is unintelligible and superfluous whose rejection affects not an iota of experience.[13]

The whole of the empirical world is thus reduced to so many ideas in the mind. Concrete experience can be analysed into two factors—the ideas and the mind. Ideas are inert, passive, inactive ; their existence lies solely in their being perceived. They are the contents of consciousness and have no meaning apart from this relation. Mind on the other hand is essentially active. Its essence is, not to be perceived, but to perceive. Of every conceivable thing we can have an idea, but there can be no idea of a mind, for the simple reason that the subject perceiving the ideas cannot itself be perceived like an idea.[14]

From the passivity of ideas it follows that one idea cannot produce or be the cause of another. Only an active being, i.e., the spirit, can be the author of ideas. "All our ideas....are visibly inactive ; there is nothing of power or agency included in them. So that one idea or object of thought cannot produce, or make any alteration in another".[15]

---

10. *Principles of Human Knowledge*, p. 156.
11. Ibid, p. 156.
12. Ibid, p. 121-2.
13. Ibid, p. 122.
14. Ibid, p. 186.
15. Ibid, p. 125.

Ideas are not a substance ; the only substance that exists is spirit which cognises the ideas. Ideas can be produced only by an active spirit.

Though the activity of consciousness is thus established, the apparent fact that the objective world perceived in our waking experience is in no way dependent upon our perception of it cannot be denied. It must not be supposed that when I go out of my room, all the things there go out of existence, I not being there to perceive them. Since they are not independent, and yet since they do not exist in the mind of any created spirit, "they must subsist in the mind of some spirit."[16] "When in broad daylight I open my eyes it is not in my power to choose whether I shall see or no, or to determine what particular objects shall present themselves to my view ;...the ideas imprinted on them are not creatures of my will. There is therefore some other will or spirit that produces them."[17]

A distinction therefore must be drawn between the creation of productive imagination, and the ideas constituting the empirical world, between "ideas" and "real things." But they are nevertheless alike in that none of them can exist without the mind. The distinction is between different orders of creativity. Objectivity in general cannot be my individual creation. Hence the activity of an eternal and universal spirit must be posited. This spirit is God, who is creative *par excellence*. The mundane spirits are themselves created, and their creativity is of a limited extent.

This in brief is the form of idealism as Berkeley presents it. Its affinity to the Yogācāra idealism is obvious. The impasse of thinking a thing when it is not thought of is made much of in both the systems. Sahopalambhaniyama is the main plank on which any form of idealism must rest. To assert the existence of an object outside knowledge is to transcend the given data ; the assertion will necessarily remain dogmatic.

In Berkeley's argument however there lurks some confusion. His main interest is apparently to deny something which does not enter the knowledge-situation at all. Matter as an 'I know not what' is never perceived through any sense ; it lies at the back of everything known without itself being ever known. It is a kind of thing-in-itself, not only

---

16. *Principles of Human Knowledge*, p. 116.
17. Ibid, p. 127.

because it is existent by itself, but also because it is the unknown and unknowable. Sahopalambhaniyama is applied to banish this abstraction. But the denial of object is a different matter altogether. Berkeley imagines that as soon as an unknown material substratum of sensible qualities is denied, everything sensed becomes ideal. His argument in fact is based on a confusion between "matterism"[18] and realism. The realist would welcome Berkeley's contention that a matter which can never be brought within the ken of knowledge is a fiction. This doctrine of matter entails the acceptance of the theory of representative perception and a three-term theory of knowledge, which is as repugnant to the realist as to Berkeley. Berkeley however starts with the assumption that what are actually experienced are only the sensible qualities. He takes for granted that his denial of "matter," in the Lockian sense, is the same thing as the denial of substance. But the realist, though agreeing with Berkeley in rejecting an unknowable matter, would very much insist on the reality of substance. Reality has no secrets from knowledge. Substance must be accepted to account for the sense of unity in the object, but it is not an unknown something. Substance is as much perceptible as are the sensible qualities. A self-conscious realist would hold that it is perceived by the same sense as cognises the respective sense-data.[19] Against this theory of a perfectly transparent object Berkeley's criticism loses all its force. According to realism, though the object need not be known, yet when it is known at all, it is theoretically capable of being known in its entirety, leaving no residual 'I know not what.'

Granting even that Berkeley's argument is applicable to the doctrine of substance also, and that there is no substance apart from the particular sense-data, that does not make the latter subjective. It makes the sense-qualities, if anything, still more objective. It would be the substance which is subjective construction imposed upon the objective sense-data. This theory is certainly not pure realism, but nor is it in any way idealism. Berkeley makes both substance and attributes subjective, but does not make out the fundamental distinction between their respective orders. According to him, substance is a mere name, having no reality whatsoever ; the sense-qualities are on the other hand

18. This word has been coined in the absence of a better one.
19. This, for example, is the Nyāya theory of perception.

real "ideas" existing solely for mind. But this is not enough. Even though the substance be a mere name, the fact that the content perceived is cognised as an "object" or a "thing" cannot be gainsaid. The substance therefore is a subjective form or category under which the attributes, which are real subjective ideas, are necessarily perceived. Substance is the form of the objectification of sense-data. There are thus two orders of subjectivity, as already discussed above.[20] The sense-data are real subjective facts ; but they are realised only as objectified, and substance is this category of objectification. It has no ontological status at all ; it can be called subjective because consciousness is its basis on which it functions. It is the Avidyā, or Transcendental Illusion of the Yogācāra, of which illusion Berkeley has not even an inkling.

In spite of his premises being faulty Berkeley's real intention is obvious enough ; it is to deny the object as such. He raises all this dust about "matter" because he takes his cue from the Lockian realism which is not a basic type of realism at all. All the contents of experience are reduced to so many "ideas" whose essence is to be perceived. The status of an idea is however far from being clear. That its existence lies solely in its being perceived does not make much sense. Berkeley strongly insists on the distinction between the preceiving mind and the perceived idea.[21] If the one is creative, active, dynamic, the other is dead, passive, inert. How this sharp distinction is to be reconciled with the utter dependence of an idea on mind remains unintelligible. Difference can be maintained only between distinct existents. The separate existence of an idea is however vehemently denied. If the idea is different, why should it not enjoy an independent status ? Whatever is distinct from consciousness is an 'other' to it, and once this distinction is factually admitted, there is an end of idealism as such. Although the Yogācāra does not deny the idea of an 'other'—in fact no theory of knowledge can do that—still it stops with the mere idea. The distinction itself is within consciousness, and not between consciousness and something other than it. The *esse* of an idea is *percipi* only because it is identical with the perception of it, is only a form of consciousness.[22] Its apparent otherness is the way in which conscious-

20. See Supra, Ch. 7.

21. *Principles of Human Knowledge*, p. 186.

22. Berkeley explicitly denies this. Ibid. p. 136, "not by way of mode or attribute, but by way of idea."

ness appears. The bifurcation is not a factual one. Were it so different from consciousness, it may as well be taken as objective, for aught we know. Matter may be rejected, and no self-conscious realist would accept it, and yet the various sense-data may be taken as objectively confronting consciousness. No ultimate distinction can be maintained between consciousness and something outside it, be it an idea or an object ; this is the fundamental principle of the Yogācāra idealism. The apparent distinction is projected by consciousness itself, and exists only as its form.

The distinction therefore between consciousness and the ideas cannot be maintained. Berkeley distinguishes between an idea and a creative act for which alone the idea exists. For the Yogācāra the idea itself is the creative act. An idea is nothing but will as determined by the presence of an illusory 'other'. Consciousness is not a transparent revelation ; it posits its own content. The ideas are precipitated in this creative act and they can have no separate existence than that of being posited. Their apparent otherness is itself ideal. If an idea is a real 'other', then it is difficult to understand in what respect is it different from an independent object, and why it should owe its existence to the fact of its being related to consciousness. This relation can be intrinsic to it only when the absolute distinction between it and its author, viz., the creative will, is given up.

The Yogācāra is cautious enough to discern the other side of the argument. If he denies an object apart from the consciousness of it, nor does he accept any "spirit" or "mind" at the back of the ideas. Ideas are not distinct from consciousness : this means that they have no separate existence, they are not objects before consciousness. Nor is consciousness distinct from ideas : this means that, behind the creative act, there is no agent or "creator." Berkeley's distinction between the spirit and the ideas can be interpreted in either of these two ways. The first view makes the ideas more or less objective as against the subject ; the second view is to understand the ideas as subjective facts existing *for* a mind. The distinction is practically the same, being merely one of emphasis. For the Yogācāra however the ideas are in themselves self-sufficient. An idea exists for itself, and not for some other mind. The idea of an ego is certainly there, but it is only a synthesising category, imparting the sense of unity of discrete ideas; it is the work of Kliṣṭa Manas.[23] The ego as well as the object are both mere forms of consciousness; just as there is no object apart from the idea of it, so also the ego has no real existence apart from the idea of it. Consciousness is creative, and it creates the ego as also the object, though the creation remains always ideal.

So also Berkeley's contention that the spirit is known in a different way than the ideas are is not acceptable to the Yogācāra. Berkeley holds that a spirit is not known by way of idea, and that we can have only a "notion" of it.[24] For the Yogācāra, consciousness is diversified into the various ideas, each of which is a unique and individual unit (svalakṣaṇa) of consciousness. An idea knows itself in knowing the content; no separate act of knowledge—in the way of notion—is required to make it known.

The reason as to why Berkeley does not have an inkling of svasamvitti is obvious. All knowledge is constituted by the ideas, which are the contents of a mind. The mind, being the knower of the ideas, cannot itself be known in the way of an idea, as that would require another mind to cognize the new ideas and so on *ad infinitum*. The Yogācāra escapes this regress by abolishing once for all any distinction between consciousness and something other than it. Consciousness, if it is to be known at all,[25] can be known only by itself.

The Yogācāra would contend that any "spirit" over and above the ideas cannot be accepted, since the latter are consciousness itself split by the category of objectivity. Ideas play a double role in Berkeley's system. They are the immediate sense-presentations before the mind, and as such are distinguished, first, from an independent and external object which has however no real existence ; in this sense they are more or less subjective facts : secondly, the ideas are distinguished from the subject, i.e., are objective contents before it. They are thus both subjective as well as objective facts in the same breath ; the Yogācāra would urge that one cannot thus play fast and loose with the ontological status of a thing. If the distinction between the ideas and

---

23. See Supra, Ch. 5.

24. *Principles of Human Knowledge, pp.* 186-7

25. The Advaita Vedānta holds that consciousness in itself is never revealed (avedya). It cannot turn back upon itself, and make it its own object.

the spirit were made rigid, no scope is left for the creativity of consciousness. It is by virtue of this creativity that an idea is precipitated, which has no separate existence at all, not even a "passive" existence. The distinction is within consciousness. If ideas enjoy a distinct existence, consciousness becomes then helpless before them, and idealism is done away with. The content created cannot be absolutely separated from the creative act.

The creativity of consciousness is the basic bed-rock of idealism. That Berkeley is not sufficiently aware of the implications of this doctrine can be shown by some other fundamental considerations. Though Berkeley makes much of the activity of consciousness, he gives it up at the most crucial points. In spite of consciousness being essentially creative, the apparent fact that the external sense-data seem to force themselves upon us cannot be denied "When in broad daylight I open my eyes, it is not in my power to choose whether I shall see or no, or to determine what particular objects shall present themselves to my view. . . .the ideas imprinted on them (the senses) are not creatures of my will." This apparent independence of the content experienced militates against the idealistic epistemology. Metaphysics consists in explaining all phenomena according to a consistent pattern. The idealistic solution of this realistic predicament should be the acceptance of a different order of creativity. That will, which projects the world of our waking experience, is not empirical at all. This is the Transcendental Subjectivity of the Yogācāra. But instead of arriving at this proper conclusion, Berkeley gives it such a twist, that it practically ceases to be idealism. His argument for the existence and activity of a supreme spirit, viz., God, is very much realistic. If the contents of my experience are not the creation of my will, they are independent of my will, whatever their ultimate origin might be. My consciousness has no jurisdiction over them; for me it is realism pure and simple. The contention that the activity of consciousness is evinced in dreams goes for nothing ; it can be made acceptable even to the realist. The relation that consciousness bears to the contents of its waking experience is the vital issue at stake. And here Berekeley is tragically one with the realist. Whether the ideas are imprinted by an independent and external God, or they are produced by an independent and external object, it does not make much difference. The one hypothesis is not nearer idealism than the other. Once grant that the object is not created by me, it matters little by whom else it is created.[26] If my knowledge is not creative, another one can no more be so, if knowledge has the same meaning in the two cases.[27]

A God can be admitted in Berkeley's system only by giving up his idealism. His contention was that the existence of the object is inconceivable apart from the knowing of it. Here he urges just the reverse of it. It is only because the object *can be* conceived as existing independent of my will, that we arrive at God. He gives his whole case for idealism away by this admission. In fact his argument is exactly the same as the realistic one for the existence of an objective and independent world. The ideas may not be ultimately independent, but it curbs the creativity of individual consciousness very seriously. The creativity that Berkeley assigns to particular minds is very limited in its extent—it is active only in dreams and fantasies—and this is hardly sufficient to establish idealism. Consciousness being essentially active, it can allow nothing to be imparted to it from outside.

Berkeley's God can be interpreted as a different order of creativity, as the Transcendental creativity of consciousness. Since our empirical will is not potent enough to account for the whole of experience, another order of subjectivity is admitted over and above the empirical one. God is only a name for this subjectivity. This explanation would purge his idealism of all those shortcomings discussed above, but is unfortunately not acceptable. Though the transcendental subjectivity is a different order of creativity, it cannot function independently of our individual consciousness. Consciousness is one, and the plurality of orders must so pertain to it as to be essentially correlated to each other. As the transcendental will feeds the empirical consciousness with its contents, so the latter in its turn impels the other to further acts of creation. In Berkeley this correlation is signally lacking. The created spirits have absolutely nothing to do with the creativity of the supreme Spirit ; they can only bow submissively before it. God is a different kind of creativity altogether; it bears no comparison to the creativity of empirical will. But transcendental subjectivity is transcendental only in the sense of being deeper in its functioning and

26. Cf. A. C. Ewing, *Idealism*, p. 21.
27. Pringle-Patison, *The Idea of God*, p. 192.

wider in its scope. It is ultimately the same consciousness which has all the orders of creativity.

Consciousness must create its own world ; the latter cannot be given to it. When a particular content is not being experienced, it has no other existence. It certainly deposits its seeds in the Ālaya, to give rise to further contents, but that individual content disappears once for all. Even when we are ordinarily said to perceive a so-called identical content, this process of incessant recreation goes invariably on. But since Berkeley's idealism is not so fully worked out, this point need not be stressed. But outside my individual experience, the contents belonging to it can exist in another manner. Each centre of experience has its own private world of contents. The identity of the intra-subjective world is only apparent.[28] Once this is accepted the necessity for God disappears. Berkeley himself raises this point of "perpetual annihilation and creation"[29] and he rightly contends that there is nothing objectionable in this doctrine, but that, on the other hand, it is a correct appraisal of idealism. After this significant admission, the hypothesis of God seems to be quite superfluous. The inner motive of Berkeley is however obvious enough. Though he perceives that the phenomenal objects can have no unknown existence yet, since he assumes the initial dogmatism of an intra-subjective world, he has to make room for an all-comprehensive consciousness, in order to sustain the continued existence of those objects.

The further consequence of the abolition of the distinction between the created idea and the creative act is to make meaningless the contention that one idea cannot cause another. An idea is not a mere passive sensum waiting meekly to be cognised by the active spirit, but is identical with the activity of the latter, is only the form in which that activity expresses itself. It is not correct therefore to assume that an idea is a dead thing, having nothing to do with another idea, except in the fact of their both being eternally present before a Universal Mind. Says Berkeley, "The connection of ideas does not imply the relation of cause and effect, but only of a mark or sign with the thing signified."[30] If it means merely that an idea cannot bodily

---

28. See Supra Ch. 4.
29. *Principles of Human Knowledge*, p. 134.
30. *Ibid*, p. 145.

give rise to another, being itself exhausted in its being projected, the Yogācāra cannot find fault with the statement. All ideas being momentary, the concept of causality is here radically modified. An idea is merely an occasion for the occurrence of another. Though an idea dies an instantaneous death, it yet deposits its seed in the Ālaya, which produces further ideas in its turn. The governing factor is not an external God sitting above, but transcendental subjectivity impelled by the category of objectivity. This requires an elaborate constructive theory about the different strata of consciousness of which there is not a trace in Berkeley.

The most fundamental divergence between the two systems lies however somewhere else. However ill-worked out Berkeley's idealism may be, that his real intention is to demolish objectivity cannot be doubted. But since he is not aware of the full implication of this doctrine, he can by no means arrive at the logical conclusion to which idealism tends, viz., absolutism. Any form of idealism which is not an absolutism cannot even be a consistent idealism. The negation of the object cannot be complete there, and an incomplete negation is no negation. In Berkeley we find that the ideas take the place of the objects. If objectivity is to be totally rejected, the first step is to make it a form of the creativity of consciousness ; this, as we have seen, Berkeley has failed to do. The second and more important step is to realise that the 'other' cannot be retained even as a form; the creativity of consciousness must be so purified as to be purged out of all traces of an 'other', be it its own form.[31] Berkeley has not even the faintest notion about the Absolute of pure Will. His system can at best be regarded as containing some idealistic suggestions, but it is not pure idealism. Since he makes an absolute distinction between spirit and its ideas, the creativity of the former is very seriously checked; and the question as to whether the ideas themselves, even as mere forms of consciousness, can be ultimate, does not even arise in Berkeley. His idealism itself is half-hearted and can by no means yield an absolutism. The Yogācāra however, as we have already seen, is nothing if he is not an absolutist.

---

31. See Supra Ch. 7.

II

Hegel

Hegel has been called the "prince of idealists." He is generally supposed to represent the most perfect type of idealism in comparison to which other types of idealism are all found to be defective in some respect or other. It is incumbent to see how the Yogācāra compares with Hegel and what are their spiritual affinities and differences. Our account of Hegel is necessarily very summary and is therefore somewhat arbitrary. But in a comparative account not only is it excusable, it is arther inevitable.

The key to the understanding of the Hegelian system is provided by the logic of unity-in-difference. Neither identity by itself nor pure difference is sufficient to render a thing intelligible. If a thing is supposed to be constituted by bare identity of the form 'A is A,' it is hardly distinguishable from its negation. A thing must be a determinate something, and "all determination is negation" as Spinoza said long before. It must contain therefore negation as well as affirmation in its constitution, and its complete explanation cannot dispense with either. To posit a thing, it must be differentiated from all other things in the universe ; otherwise, it would not be able to maintain its identity. Identity, if it is to be significant, must be supported and defined by difference. The norm of explanation is this identity-in-difference; it is not abstract identity, but rather unity mediated by difference, identity as expressed in and through difference.

This logic is realised in the concept of the 'concrete universal.' Truth is the whole, but this whole is not to be had apart from the parts which constitute it and whose organic totality is the whole. Ordinary consciousness perceives things as merely different : scientific consciousness at the level of "understanding" perceives things as relative to each other where one essentially depends upon another for its reality. But even "understanding" is not the complete truth of things: it leaves things in an unreconciled contradiction. Understanding is to be transcended by Reason or the philosophic consciousness. Here things are not merely particulars relative to each other, but rather particulars permeated by this universal, the unity underlying at the back of the differences, and which is the reality of the partciulars. This universal is however concrete. A universal, which is realised apart from the particulars of which it is the universal is an abstraction and defeats its very purpose of functioning as a universal. It cannot be different from its particulars. Nor is it completely identical with them ; it enjoys a mediated identity, or unity in difference.

If relativity is the nature of things by which their apparent opposition is to be resolved, still more is it true of the most fundamental opposition, that of the subject-object duality. A complete explanation of a thing is not furnished until it is shown to be essentially related to the knowing subject for which it exists. The hypothesis of an independent object existing unrelated to consciousness is refuted by the logic of relativity. This has two implications. First, there can be no irreducible surd, no unknown and unknowable thing-in-itself outside knowledge, which cannot be made transparent to knowledge. Secondly, even the known object is shown to be necessarily known ; being known enters into its being but for which fact it would not be what it is.[32]

But the other aspect of the concrete universal is equally true. The subject is as much relative to the object as the latter is to it. If there can be no object without the subject, nor can there be a subject unrelated to the object. Pure will is an abstraction. To will only itself is to will nothing at all. There cannot be a knower without there being something to be known.

Thus the opposites, thought and its content, are not left apart but are reconciled as being relative to each other. But this is not enough to establish idealism. An essential interrelation between the subject and the object does not give the subject a preference over the latter. At best it would be a philosophy of indifference. All difference presupposes a basic unity which alone makes the differents intelligible. The subject-object opposition also must therefore be resolved and transcended in a higher unity. But this unity is not one of the opposites. It has no nearer affinity to the subject than it has to the object.

Hegel escapes this objection by making the ultimate reality, not indeed bare consciousness, but self-consciousness. The two terms of the epistemological duality are not on a par. Though the subject is

32. This is technically known as the theory of 'internal relations'.

apparently just one of the terms as the object is the other, it has this peculiar nature that it is at the same time *conscious* of the opposition. The distinction between the subject and the object is a conscious distinction ; its opposition to the object is an opposition for itself. The subject therefore transcends or 'overreaches' the opposition. The full elucidation of the nature of self requires that its opposition to the not-self also be included in itself. It is one of the terms of the opposition and also its spectator, the opposed term as well as the reconciled unity.

The distinction between these two aspects of consciousness is not a factual one ; it is purely logical. The subject as one of the opposed terms does not exist in its solitariness ; it is an abstraction. All reality is mediated ; hence the reality of consciousness is self-consciousness, where it is not asserted by itself but has been made concrete by over-reaching all opposition to itself. The object is therefore just a moment in the life of the subject. It is necessary for the latter to go out of itself only in order to return to itself with all possible richness. As has been said before, the awareness of the objective is the necessary condition for consciousness to pass into self-consciousness.[33]

The relation between the subject and the object is not pure identity; it is one of identity-in-difference, the most ultimate form of which is illustrated in self-consciousness. The unity of consciousness does not do away with the reality of the object. If the object were not an existent, consciousness would not be mediated self-consciousness and would cease to be even consciousness. The difference between the subject and object is to be maintained. It remains to be seen in what sense they are identical.

The object is a determinate existent among other determinate objects. Hegel accepts the Kantian analysis that all determination is categorisation by the intelligence. The object has two aspects, viz., one is its apparent discrete existence, and the other is its organic existence where it shades off as it were into other objects. The first is its particularity as the second is its universality. The latter is its essential nature and here consciousness recognises its own counterpart. Reflection penetrates through the external surface to the inner reality and finds this to be ideal in nature.

33. See Supra Ch. 5.

So also in the case of the subject itself the two aspects must be carefully distinguished. The merely subjective is constituted by the ideas peculiar to each individual. It may be quite important in the history of a particular person but it is important in that respect alone. Unless consciousness rises above the subjective and accidental associations and takes the objective attitude it must bid farewell to all real intellectual discourse.

The unity to be discovered between the subject and object is made possible by the dual nature of each of them. When it is recognised that the categories and forms of thought which constitute mind are also the categories determining the object, the consciousness dawns that the reality of the object is spiritual. It is only necessary to remove the external accidents which hide this spiritual core and the unity would be revealed in all its concreteness. Mind can take an objective attitude only because it finds itself in the object. "Nature is the extreme self-alienation of spirit in which it yet remains one with itself." And the object is a necessity in the life of the subject because "the reality is the universal, which goes out of itself, particularises itself, opposes itself to itself, so that it may reach the deepest and most comprehensve unity with itself."

The Absolute is the most concrete "Idea" where all oppositions are reconciled. It necessarily breaks forth into the subject-object duality in order to attain self-consciousness. The object is not a creation of the individual consciousness. It is given to it, and consciousness is not creative in the ordinary idealistic sense. Its creativity consists in striving to make the object its own. What is really creative is the Idea, the universal Reason, which enters into the utmost opposition to itself and yet maintains its identity. The subject is not simply identical with the object. Their distinction is to be scrupulously maintained and the Idea realises itself only through this distinction. Its creativity is an expression of self-determination. What is not determined is indistinguishable from nothing and yet the ultimate reality cannot be determined by an 'other,' for the simple reason that it includes all oppositions within itself ; it is therefore determined by itself, and in all its determinations it cannot go out of itself. The object is proved to be a determination of spirit by the fact that what necessarily exists *for* intelligence must be a manifestation *of* intelligence.

The Idea could not be the Absolute if it did not exist for itself.

There are other unities exemplified in nature, e.g., life, which cannot yet said to be ultimate as they exist for another, for a conscious subject. It is only self-consciousness that exists for itself and it is by the light of this that we must explain itself and all other things. It is by virtue of self-consciousness that all-individual subjects partake of the being of the universal Reason, the Absolute, whose creativity is renewed in every conscious subject.

Hegel therefore is not an idealist in the ordinary sense of the term, unless the term be so defined as to rob it of all definiteness as a specific theory. The Yogācāra is a true idealist. For him reality is the subjective, the creative consciousness. Hegel however aspires to go beyond the merely subjective and penetrate to the core of it which is a universal. Creativity does not belong to the individual and discrete moments of consciousness but to the objective Reason. But here the Yogācāra would urge that either thought is creative or it is not, and if it is not my thought which is creative it matters little what else is. If the Yogācāra is called a psychological idealist, the Hegelism system can by contrast be termed logical idealism ; it is the system of logical categories, culminating in self-consciousness, which is creative. Creativity is interpreted as differentiation and integration in a higher level. But this differentiation must be on the part of my thought. Hegel however would brand this theory as subjective idealism.

These difficulties arise because Hegel would not accept the reality of simple consciousness. For him all reality is mediated, hence consciousness must pass into self-consciousness in order to be real. Though the Yogācāra also accepts self-consciousness (svasamvedana), it is so only because it cannot be helped. When consciousness itself is the sole reality, it must take the place of both the knower and the known. But he is conscious of the instability of the position. The object, though only an illusory one, is still present there, and hence the illusion on the part of consciousness of knowing something other than itself persists. With the sublation of this illusion the emptiness of self-consciousness is exposed, and consciousness again rests in itself (cittasya citte sthānāt). But Hegel accepts self-consciousness as the highest reality, even higher than consciousness itself. The latter is merely a moment, as the object is another, for the realisation of this reality. For the Yogācāra, consciousness is necessarily self-consciousness as there is nothing else to be known. For Hegel, the latter is a return to consciousness, from the simple 'abstract' unity of the mere subject to the mediated unity transcending the subject-object duality.

Hegel's insistence on concreteness as the mark of reality would be utterly unintellgible to the Yogācāra. It is all very well to say that reality must be mediated. A thing must be something in itself to be mediated even. The necessity for conceiving the unity or universal as concrete is felt, since it cannot be realised apart from the particulars. This however is not a correct appraisal of the Yogācāra or the Vedānta position. How is such a universal to be related to its particulars? That it cannot be different from them has been proved by Hegel himself. Nor can it be identical with the latter, as it would cease then to be their universal. But identity-in-difference fares no better. The differents cannot be reconciled with the identity. What is the relation between the differents when they are opposed to each other and when they are reconciled in the identity? How to trace their identity in these two states? It is said that in the latter position their abstraction is removed. But abstraction is the very soul of a particular. With the removal of this it is changed beyond recognition. Hence it cannot be asserted that the same particular enters into the unity even when without its abstraction. The conclusion is that the universal can in no way be reconciled with the particulars if the reality of both be insisted upon. The universal can be retained only if the particulars are given up. Particularity is an illusion and the universal is their reality.[34] It is realised, not through the particulars, but by negating the particulars.

This brings us to the fundamental difference of approach in the Hegelian and the Yogācāra analyses. The Yogācāra bases his absolutism on the negative judgment. The object is negated totally and absolutely; it is not retained even as a form of consciousness. In Hegel the object is a necessity; without it the subject would not be a subject. Negation finds no place in Hegel, in the sense that nothing is rejected in his system. The negation that is there is better called difference; it is simply on a par with affirmation. Difference—it is not even an absolute opposition—is merely a prelude to a greater and more perfect affirmation. But negation,

---

34. The other solution is to accept the reality of the particulars and to make the universal a thought-construct, as the Sautrāntika, Hume and Kant do.

i.e., a self-conscious rejection of a mistake, totally and absolutely, cannot even be conceived of by Hegel. For the Yogācāra the projection of an 'other' is a negation of will[35]; hence this negation is to be negated, and he arrives at the concept of an undifferentiated consciousness. Hegel however welcomes the diversification of the (universal) Reason as a necessary moment for achieving a more 'concrete' unity with self, i.e., self-consciousness.

That is to say, no element of experience is false. Even to appear, a thing must exist, and whatever exists must be incorporated in reality.[36] An absolute non-entity cannot even appear. The only falsity that there is is abstraction or one-sidedness. No theory of Avidyā is worked out. His system admits of no cancellation, but only of rearrangement. Any illusion that might exist is to be resolved by removing its one-sidedness, i.e., self-existence. He has no conception of the Transcendental Illusion in the Yogācāra sense. For the latter the subject-object relation is something inherently unintelligible. There is no way to render consistent the notion of the object. It can be understood neither apart from the subject nor along with it. The Yogācāra way of resolving the difficulty is to make it, and consequently the whole relation, unreal. The relation is unintelligible because the object is naught; there is no way of relating the unreal to the real. For Hegel, both the terms of the relation are self-discrepant so long as they are kept apart ; once make them relative to each other and the inner unity, which manifests itself in both, reveals itself.

There is thus no necessity to go beyond thought. Thought, containing all possible differences, is itself the reality. For the Yogācāra also thought is reality, but he finds no way of reconciling the manifold differences that diversity it. With the negation of the object, the diversification of thought also comes to an end. Hegel would not countenance any such theory. For him whatever exists, exists for thought and only a definite thing can so exist. An undiversified entity is indefinite and is therefore equivalent to nothing. But to swallow a contradiction is not to resolve it. The self-existence of the object must be given up ; is this not tantamount to giving up the reality of phenomenal experience altogether ? Can an object be experienced which is not conceived as

35. See Supra Ch. 7.

36. Cf. Bradley, *Appearance and Reality*, pp. 120, 123, 404.

an independent 'other'? The sublation of its independence amounts to the cancellation of the object as such. Hegel must concede at least this much that the viewing of things as external to thought, i.e., in their abstraction, is an illusion. If even this be not granted the philosophic enquiry would be utterly devoid of any value. When thought is disinfected of this illusion, its character is radically and fundmentally altered; to persist in calling it thought even then is to fail to appreciate this important fact. Hegel asserts that there can be no higher knowledge which quarrels with the ordinary consciousness of things, or rather this higher knowledge is only in continuation with the latter. This again indicates that Hegel has no conception of the Transcendental Illusion. Illusion and its negation cannot be put on the same footing or be only quantitatively distinguished.

Since Avidyā finds no place in his system, it cannot, strictly speaking, be said to be an absolutism. Though he apparently tries to go beyond the merely phenomenal, his attempt is vitiated by the fact that this entails no rejection of phenomena. The transmutation of phenomena can be rendered intelligible only when the resultant is itself not phenomenal. But that would mean that an object in its transmuted state has been mutilated beyond recognition, so much so that it cannot be said to be the same object that has been transmuted. This amounts to a total rejection of its pre-transmuted existence, in fine, to a transcendence of the empirical. But abhorring all forms of transcendence Hegel tries to perform the impossible, viz., to make the Absolute something more than the sum-total of the empirical differents and yet it can be nothing apart from the latter. The Yogācāra solution is easy: the Absolute is the reality of appearance, i.e., of the illusory; it is the illusory itself perceived in its true form. It is not the mere ilusory and at the same time not another existence different from the illusory. But without positing the illusoriness of appearance the 'of'-relation in "reality *of* appearance" cannot be made intelligible. Is the Absolute exhausted in its manifestations or not? If it is, it would cease to be something distinct from and higher than the latter; it would be the empirical itself. But if it is not so exhausted, it must have a transcendent existence unaffected by the difference and this would militate against its concreteness. In short, there can be no Absolute whose relation to phenomena is not both transcendence as well as immanence.[37] To insist upon

37. See supra Ch. 7.

one at the cost of the other is to fail to understand the true nature of the Absolute. It is the reality of phenomena, itself not being phenomenal, which can never be realised without making phenomena an illusion. To retain pheomena without their abstraction is unmeaning. When two differents are reconciled in a unity, does the removal of their abstraction effect any change in them or not ? If not, they remain still unreconciled, and their unity is a chimera. But if it has, can we still speak of the same differents being present in the unity ? Some other thing is concerned then, and the former have been totally cancelled. Again and again Hegel stumbles against the fundamental fact of illusion, but in his attempt to retain all the differences he refuses to profit by it. Notwithstanding his violent protest to the contrary, his Absolute remains just a system of relatives ; it cannot realise its absoluteness without giving up being involved in the latter, i.e., without ceasing to be 'concrete.'

III

Gentile

Gentile comes nearer to the Yogācāra in his theory of the mind as 'pure Act' than Hegel. Hegel as we have just seen is hardly a true idealist in the strictest epistemological sense. His system is better termed logical or rational idealism. In Gentile we again meet with a full-fledged idealism, pleading for the supremacy of the subject, and doing full justice to its creativity.

Reality is conceived by Gentile as process or act. "Nothing but the constructive process is."[38] Though thought is reality for Hegel, there is yet a very important difference between him and Gentile. Hegel concentrates on the objective thought, i.e., the logical content of thought, its meaning ; the actual process as to how this is being thought is dismissed by him as inessential. Gentile restores to thought its idealistic prerogative. There is no thought apart from thinking. In Hegel the dialectic "is understood as a dialectic of thing thought," whereas the true dialectic "can only be conceived as a dialectic of the thinking outside which there is no thought."[39] When reality is conceived as being a thing thought of, it becomes abstract and loses

---

38. *Theory of Mind as Pure Act*, p. 18.
39. Ibid, p. 55-6.

its dynamism. The thought in Hegel is like the Platonic Idea from which "it is impossible to redescend to the individuals of nature."[40] Hegel cannot solve the problem of individuation.

"Idealism is the negation of any reality which can be opposed to thought as independent of it and as the presupposition of it."[41] No better definition could be given by the Yogācāra even. "Speaking strictly, there can be no *others* outside us, for in knowing them and speaking of them they are within us. To know is to identify, to overcome otherness as such."[42] Again, "we know an object when there is in that object nothing *immediate*, nothing which our thought finds there already before we begin to know it, real therefore even before it is known."[43]

How do we know that the object cannot exist independent of the knowing consciousness ? We again meet with the sahopalambhaniyama (ego-centric predicament) which is *the* argument for idealism. "Because, whatever effort we make to think or imagine other things or other consciousnesses outside our own consciousness, these things or consciousnesses remain within it, precisely because they are posited by us, even though posited as external to us. The without is always within."[44] It is impossible to offer a better statement of the Yogācāra position. It is remarkable that Gentile does not fight shy of solipsism. Like a true idealist, he is wise enough to perceive that the other minds also sail in the same boat as the other objects do.[45]

But the positing of the 'other' does not alienate it from mind. That is because it is never posited finally, once for all. Spiritual activity continues in the actuality of positing it. It is never posited but always is to be posited.[46] It is posited afresh in every moment.

If the object is a creation of the constructive process, the subject is not less so. Nothing is real other than the actual act of thinking. "Mind according to our theory is act or process not substance."[47] It is not the subject of an activity of which it is independent. "Mind

40. Ibid, p. 67.
41. Ibid, p. 18.
42. Ibid, p. 13.
43. Ibid, p. 16.
44. Ibid, p. 28 ; also pp.90-2
45. Ibid, p. 41, 138, 275.
46. Cf. Ch. 4, supra.
47. Ibid, p. 20.

has no existence apart from its manifestations." Thought itself, not less than the object, cannot be conceived "as a reality existing apart from its developing process."[48] "Idealism is the denial of being either to a mind or to mind, the denial that a mind *is*, because "being" and "mind" are mutually contradictory terms." "The process is constructive of the object just to the extent that it is constructive of the subject itself."

Reality is thus to be understood not as a being or a state, but as a *constructive process*. The spiritual reality is not strictly speaking a fact or a deed but a doing. "In the world of mind nothing is already done, nothing is because it is finished and complete; all is always doing".[49] "The true is what is in the making." This act of thinking must not be conceived of as thought in the Hegelian sense. It is not the finished product, but the actual process, that matters. And this process is constructive of the product. "For if the idea is the idea or ground of the thing, the thing must be produced by the idea. The thought which is true thought must generate the being of what it is thought."[50] Or if thought is distinguished from the content of thought as form and matter, "matter is posited by and resolved into form. So that the only matter there is in the spiritual act is the form itself, as activity."[51]

The Hegelian dialectic is inert and passive compared to the dialectic of incessant Act. Here we deal, not with a system of thought, but with the thinking itself. That reality for Hegel is thought and not thinking is revealed by another important difference. The Hegelian dialectic starts with the thought having the poorest content, viz., pure being and ends with the thought having the richest content—the Absolute Idea. It is obvious that what are important are really these contents. If we concentrate on thought itself or rather on thinking which goes on creating its own content, the richness or otherwise of the content would be immaterial. In such a dialectic we can find no beginning ; no stage can be conceived in the evolution of mind when it all at once becomes active, becomes *to do*, as though hitherto it was only *being*. Nor can it ever come to an end where the activity would cease to be.

48. *Theory of Mind as Pure Act*, p. 18.
49. Ibid, p. 20.
50. Ibid, p. 100.
51. Ibid, p. 243.

The process is an incessant going-on-ness, and the question of its becoming richer does not arise. "From this theory that the mind is development, it follows that to conceive a mind as initially perfect, or as becoming finally perfect, is to conceive it no longer as mind. It was not in the beginning, it will not be in the end, because it never is. It becomes. Its being consists in becoming, and becoming can have neither antecedent nor consequent without ceasing to become."[52]

The doctrine that the spiritual world is only conceivable as the reality of my own spiritual activity would be absurd if it referred to my empirical activity. A distinction must therefore be drawn between this mind and the empirical ego. "Applied to the empirical ego the doctrine is meaningless." Its limitations are obvious. The creativity that is the reality of the spirit must therefore be referred to a deeper level of consciousness. This transcendental ego is the fundamental reality. It is the Absolute. It however does not exclude the reality of the empirical ego but even implies it.

A closer parallel to the Yogācāra could hardly be found. The negation of the independence of the object, the assertion of the supremacy of the subject, the conception of the subject as being essentially process or creative act, these are all the fundamental doctrines of idealism and as such are common to both these systems. This parallel is so close as to refer the creativity of consciousness to a transcendental level in both the systems, to the transcendental ego in Gentile, and to the Ālayavijñāna in the Yogācāra.

The difference however between these two is no less fundamental, and that because of the strong Hegelian tendency in Gentile. The difference is no less than between bare idealism and absolutism. Like Hegel, the latter also conceives the ultimate reality as self-consciousness. "The self-concept, in which alone mind and all that is is real, is an acquiring consciousness of self."[53] It is not a consciousness of self, but rather the process itself, that is consciousness, become self-conscious. "It is realised in the position affirmed when the self is subject and that identical self is object....It duplicates itself as self and other, and finds itself in the other."

52. *Theory of Mind as Pure Act*, pp. 39-40.
53. Ibid, p. 248.

The necessary implication of this is that the 'other' can never be dispensed with, as it is only the diversification of consciousness that makes self-consciousness possible. "The self which would be self without other would clearly not be even self because it only is in so far as the other is."[54] He accepts the Hegelian principle of identity-in-difference and does not countenance therefore the concept of pure will realised through the negation of the 'other.' The positing of multiplicity is a necessity for consciousness. As it is creative it must go on creating. "The very word development includes in its meaning both unity and multiplicity." "Multiplicity is necessary to the very concreteness, to the very dialectical reality of the unity. . .Its infinity is realised through the multiplicity, for the multiplicity is nothing but the unfolding which is the actualising of the reality."[55]

For the Yogācāra, as we have seen, positing of an 'other' constitutes a negation of will. The idea of an 'other' is the Transcendental Illusion but for which consciousness would not be diversified. Gentile, a Hegelian as he is, has no conception of Avidyā. The 'other' is not imposed on consciousness by any illusion, but it is the very nature of consciousness to create an 'other'. And because of this he perceives no possibility of consciousness ever being freed from its objective entanglements, the process ever coming to an end. The Yogācāra however, for reasons already discussed, arrives at the notion of pure Will or pure Act, which is just willing without there being anything willed, or rather, which wills itself. This entails viewing the object as an illusion, the cancellation of which is not complete by merely denying its independence. The object, when it is perceived no longer as an 'other', ceases to be perceived as a form of consciousness even. Externality is its very essence the negation of which leaves nothing to prevent consciousness regaining its absolute unity.

54. Ibid, p. 248.
55. Ibid, p. 40.

Idealism is one of the greatest philosophies of the world, and the Yogācāra system, it has been the contention of this essay, represents idealism in its pure epistemological form. It cannot be stigmatised as merely subjectivism, since absolutism is its inevitable logical goal. In spite of being absolutism however it does not give up its idealistic bias. This shows its speculative character. It is subject to the inherent contradictions latent in all dogmatic metaphysics. This defect, common to all constructive systems, is to be found in the Yogācāra too. The other contradiction however, viz., that of inconsistency, of making an assertion which as idealism it cannot make, does not vitiate the system. Inconsistency arises because of the lack of awareness of the implications of one's own position. The Yogācāra is, as is indeed all Indian philosophy, free from this grave error. The other contradiction cannot be removed, being ingrained in speculation. The Yogācāra philosophy is, from this point of view, a perfect example of coherent construction. It is not to be challenged by other constructive philosophies ; one dogmatism is not refuted by another dogmatism. If one refuses to accept idealism, one can do so, not by embracing another speculative philosophy, but only by ceasing to have any speculation at all. Dogmatism can be refuted only by pure criticism which analyses its inner self-contradictions. The Mādhyamika is, in this sense, the philosophy of philosophies. The Yogācāra is only one constructive system amongst other such great systems, no better and no worse.

Glossary

abhūtaparikalpa : imagining the object to exist as independent of consciousness.

ālambanapratyaya : the object as a condition of its consciousness.

ālaya : 'storehouse consciousness', where the fruits of actions are stored.

anātma : soulless, unreal.

anitya : transient.

arthakriyākāritva : causal efficiency.

āśrayaparāvṛtti : transformation of the 'storehouse consciousness' when it ceases evolving and merges into pure Consciousness.

ātman : soul.

avidyā : ignorance.

avyākṛta : the inexpressible.

caitta : the 'mentals', factors inhering in consciousness and introducing distinctions in it.

citta : consciousness.

dharma : element of existence.

dharmatā : reality of things, the Absolute.

dṛṣṭi : view; speculative or discursive thought, which can grasp reality only through concepts.

grāhadvaya : the subject-object duality.

jñeyāvaraṇa : ignorance, hiding the true nature of consciousness, and positing an unreal object instead.

kalpanā : imagination, construction.

kleśāvarana : ignorance of reality due to passions.

kliṣṭa manas : consciousness as defiled by the sense of 'I' or ego.

kṣaṇika : momentary.

madhyamā pratipad : the middle course, avoiding two extremes.

nairātmya : unreality.

neyārtha : teaching which is true only of the phenomenal world.

nirākāra : contentless.

nirvāṇa : freedom; Absolute.

nissvabhāva : essenceless, unreal.

nītārtha : teaching about the ultimate reality.

paramārtha : ultimate reality.

pāramitā : infinite excellence; perfection.

paratantra : consciousness as dependent on its object.

parikalpita : imagined, unreal.

parinişpanna : the Absolute; pure Consciousness without duality.

prajñāpāramitā : highest wisdom.

prajñaptisat : apparent existence.

pramāṇa : instrument or source of knowledge.

pratītya samutpāda : the law of dependent emergence, according to which one moment emerges upon the cessation of another, though having no other relation to it.

pratyakṣa : perception.

pravṛttivijñāna : empirical consciousness.

pudgala : substance or soul; a constructed whole.

sahopalambhaniyama : the availability of the object invariably along with its consciousness, thus refuting its independence.

sākāra : having a form or content, determinate.

samanantarapratyaya : the preceding moment of consciousness, as a condition for the emergence of the succeeding moment.

saṁvṛti : appearance, phenomena.

santāna : a stream-like succession of moments.

sārūpya : a peculiar relation between consciousness and its object by virtue of which the latter is grasped by the former.

satkāyadṛṣṭi : postulating a whole where there are only parts, including the postulation of the soul.

śūnya : phenomena as void of reality; also the Absolute as non-conceptual.

svalakṣaṇa : unique particular.

svasamvedana : consciousness cognising itself.

tathāgata : the Lord Buddha.

tathatā : essence of things, the Absolute.

trikasannipāta : the flashing together of three factors necessary for knowledge, viz. a content, an instrument of cognition and consciousness, each being momentary.

vāsanā : the motive force guiding the evolution of consciousness.

vijñāna : consciousness.

vijñaptimātratā : pure consciousness, the Absolute.

vikalpa : creativity of thought.

INDEX

Abhhidhammatthasaṅgaho, 16, 110.
Abhidharmakośa, 16, 36-37, 41.
Abhidharmasamuccaya, 31, 34.
Abhisamayālaṅkāra, 33, 161, 163.
Abhisamayālaṅkārāloka, 18, 70, 147, 176.
abhūtaparikalpa, 153 ff.
absolute, absolutism, 20ff, 92, 133ff, 143ff, 152ff, 169, 178, 189, 201.
and phenomena, 142ff.
Advaitasiddhi, 85, 138, 182, 183, 184, 186, 189.
Advaita Vedānta, 8, 47, 51, 97, 104, 137, 141, 143 ff, 148, 179ff.
Āgamaśāstra of Gauḍapāda, 43.
akhyāti, 56.
Ālambanaparīkṣā, 41, 45, 70, 76, 107, 110.
ālambanapratyaya, 16ff.
ālayavijñāna, 87, 88ff.
and prakṛti, 91ff.
and ego, 95.
and sākṣī, 96ff.
anumāna, according to the Sautrāntika, 6, 15.
anuvyavasāya, 68.
anyathākhyāti, 55.
apagogic proof, 73, 201.
Appearance and Reality, 82, 222.
arthakriyākāritva, 4, 74.
Āryadeva, 43.
Asaṅga, 31, 33ff.
Aspects of Mahāyāna Buddhism, 174.
āśrayaparāvṛtti, 160, 165.
A Study in Realism, 52, 53.
Aśvaghoṣa, 29 ff.
A Theory of Dircet Realism, 56.
ātman, 96ff.
atomism, 65ff.
Autobiography of Collingwood, 47.
avidyā, 136ff, 140ff.
avyākṛta, 26.
Awakening of Faith, 29.
Bendall, 34.
Berkeley, 52, 204ff.
Bhāmatī, 138.
Bhattacharya, B., 35, 44.
Bhattacharya, V., 32, 34, 42, 43.
bhūmi, 166ff.
Bodhicaryāvatāra, see under abbreviations.
Bodhisattvabhūmi, 34, 36.
bondage, 159ff.
Bradley, 82, 222.
Brahmasūtra-Śāṅkarabhāṣya, see under abbreviations.
Buddha-avataṅsaka-sūtra, 28.
Buddhism, three phases of, 2.
authenticity of the schools of, 24ff.
Buddhist Logic, 2, 4, 43, 81.
Buddhist Philosophy, 1, 13, 41, 43.
Buddhist Philosophy of Universal Flux, 4, 44.
Buston, 2, 27, 30, 32, 34, 38, 39, 40, 41.
caitta, 112ff.
Catuḥśataka, 70.
causality, 7ff.
Central Conception of Buddhism, 2,

3, 13, 17, 18, 22, 110.
Central Philosophy of Buddhism, see under abbreviations.
Chatterjee, D., 42.
Chatterjee, J. C., 70.
Collingwood, 47.
Conception of Buddhist Nirvāṇa, 29, 31, 40, 41, 91.
Concept of Consciousness, 52.
concrete universal, 216.
consciousness, according to the Yogācāra, 49, 109-10, 111-12, 127ff, 133ff.
darśanabhāga, 90.
Daśabhūmikasūtra, 28, 34, 39, 167.
Demieville, 30, 39.
dharma, 2, 7, 10, 11, 108ff.
  asaṁskṛta, 125.
  nairātmya, 10.
Dharmadharmatāvibhaṅga, 32, 39.
Dharmakīrti, 42-3.
Dhruva, A. B., 42.
Dignāga, 41-2.
Doctrine of Prajñāpāramitā, 2, 44, 165, 173.
dream, 60ff. 78ff, 140.
dṛṣṭisṛṣṭivāda, 185ff.
Dutta, N., 174.
ekajīvavāda, 187.
epistemic, 12.
Essays in Critical Realism, 58.
essences, theory of, 57ff.
Ethics of Spinoza, 118, 119.
Ewing, A. C., 48, 213.
Fragments from Dignāga, 41, 42.
Friedmann, 32.
Gaṇḍavyūhasūtra, 28.
Gauḍapādakārikā, 28, 43.
Geiger, 34.
Gentile, 67, 224ff.
Ghanavyūhasūtra, 28.
God, 169.
grāhadvaya, 153.
Hegal, 127, 216ff.
Hetubindu, 43,
Hetucakranirṇaya, 42.
Hindu Realism, 70.
History of Buddhism, see under abbreviations.
History of Buddhist Thought, 167, 168.
History of Indian Literature, see under abbreviations.
Holt, 52.
Hsuan Tsang, 39, 40.
Hume, 8, 9.
idealism, 131.
  subjective, 204.
Idealism, 48, 213.
Idea of God, 213.
Idea of the Holy, 176.
illusion, 47, 52ff, 182ff, 187ff, 194ff, 201.
  whether possible without reality, 76ff.
Indian Realism, 204.
intra-subjective, 80 ff.
Iyengar, H., 42.
Jha, G., 44.
jñātatā, 51.
kalpanā, 2, 6, 14, 72.
Kant, 9, 13, 14, 184, 185.
Karmasiddhiprakaraṇa, 39.
kāya, 174ff.
Keith, 1, 40, 41, 43.
Kemp Smith, N., 54.
Kimura, 36.
kleśa, 103, 118, 119ff.
kliṣṭa manas, 101ff, 211.

Krishnamacharya, E., 44.
kṣaṇikavijñānavāda, 86.
Laird, 52.
Lamotte, 28, 34, 88.
Laṅkāvatārasūtra, 27, see also under abbreviations.
Leibnitz, 81.
Levi, 5., 32, 33, 37, 38.
Lindquist, 39.
Locke, 12.
Madhyamakālaṅkāra, 44.
madhyamā pratipad, 22ff.
Mādhyamika, 7, 19ff, 147, 192ff.
causality, according to, 7.
self, according to, 9.
Mādhyamikakārikā, see under abbreviations.
Mādhyamikāloka, 44.
Madhyāntavibhaṅga, 32, 39, see also under abbreviations.
Mahāyāna, 25ff.
Mahāyānasaṅgraha, 34, 39, 88.
Mahāyānaśraddhotpādaśāstra, 28, 29ff.
Mahāyānasūtrālaṅkāra, 32, 39, 163, 167, see also under abbreviations.
Mahāvastu, 167.
Maitreya as an Historical Personage, 31.
Maitreya, as founder of Yogācāra, 31.
historicity of, 31.
Manual of Buddhist Philosophy 3, 111.
McGovern, 3, 111.
memory, 50ff, 85.
Mironov, 42.
Mukherjee, S., 4, 44.
Mukhopadhyaya, S., 39.
nairātmyavāda, 26.
negation, 126-27.
New Realism, 45, 46, 48, 68.
nimittabhāga, 90.
nirvāṇa, 160 ff.
nissabhāvatā, 155-56.
Nyāyabindu, 15, 42.
Nyāyakandalī, see under abbreviations.
Nyāyakaṇikā, 51.
Nyāyamañjarī, see under abbreviations.
Nyāyamukha, 42.
Nyāyapraveśa, 42.
Nyāyasūtrabhāṣya, see under abbreviations.
Nyāya-Vaiśeṣika, 8, 55, 66, 68, 208.
Obermiller, 2, 32, 33, 37, 44, 162, 165, 173.
object, objective, objectivity, 12, 15ff, 62ff, 90, 103ff, 127, 128, 140ff, 159, 179ff.
occasionalism, 18.
On Some Aspects of the Doctrines of Maitreya (nātha) and Asaṅga, 31.
Otto, 176.
Outlines of Mahāyāna Buddhism, 29.
Pañcaskandhaprakaraṇa, 39.
Paramārthasaptati, 38.
pāramitā, 166ff.
paratantra, 148, 149, 151, 153.
parikalpita, 148, 149, 150.
pariniṣpanna, 148, 152ff.
perception, distinguished from inference, 85.
Peri, N., 36.
permanence, 4.
Perry, 45, 48, 68.
Peterson, 42.
phenomena, 142ff.
Philosophy of Leibnitz, 81.
physical world, the reality of, 73ff.
Poussin, 28, 34, 38, 88.
Pradhan, P., 34.
prajñāpāramitā, 163, 167.

Prakaraṇapañcikā, 56, 74.
prakṛti, 91ff.
Pramāṇasamuccaya, 42.
Pramāṇavārttika, 41, 42, see also under abbreviations.
Pramāṇaviniścaya, 42.
Prameyakamalamārtaṇḍa, 43, 48, 68, 73, 79, 86.
pratītyasamutpāda, 21-2.
pratyakṣa, according to the Sautrāntika, 6, 13ff.
pravṛttivijñāna, 106ff.
pre-established harmony, 81.
Present Philosophical Tendencies, 45, 48, 68.
Principles of Human Knowledge, 204ff.
Pringle-Pattison, 213.
pudgala, 2, 7.
nairātmya, 10.
Rahder, 34.
Randle, 41, 42.
realism, 45ff, 73ff, 181, 183.
relation, 68ff.
rūpa, 123-24.
Russell, 81.
sahopalambhaniyama, 45, 48.
sākṣī, 96ff, 104, 105, 183.
Sambandhaparīkṣā, 43, 68.
samvṛti, 11, 140ff.
Sandhinirmocanasūtra, 28, 35.
Śaṅkara, 179ff.
Sāṅkhya, 8, 51, 91ff.
Sāṅkhyakārikā, 157.
Sāṅkṛtyāyana, R., 34, 37, 39, 42.
Santānāntarasiddhi, 43.
Śāntarakṣita, 43ff.
Santayana, 57.
sārūpya, 18.
Sarvāstivāda, 2, 3, 17, 18, 109, 113, 116, 118, 124, 125.
Śāstradīpikā, 85.
Sastri, A., 41.
Sastri, H. P., 31.
satkāyadṛṣṭi, 2.
Sautrāntika, 3, 4, 6, 7, 13ff, 36, 184.
Scepticism and Animal Faith, 57.
Siddhāntaleśasaṅgraha, 82, 98.
Siddhi and Abhīñña, 39.
Sinha, J. N., 204.
Six Buddhist Nyāya Tracts, 4.
skandha, 2, 25, 103.
Ślokavārttika, see under abbreviations.
Sogen, 30, 111.
solipsism, 82ff, 187.
Soul Theory of the Buddhists, 37.
space, 66.
Spinoza, 118, 119.
Stcherbatsky, 2, 32, 37, 39, 41, 42, 81, 91.
Sthiramati, 40.
Studies in the Laṅkāvatāra Sūtra, 28.
subjective, subjectivity, 1, 7, 11, 12, 13, 138, 140ff, 158, 184.
Sublime Science, 31, 44, 162.
substance, 4.
śūnyatā, 21.
Suzuki, D. T., 28, 29.
svalakṣaṇa, 4, 184.
svasamvedana, 83ff, 191ff, 199, 220.
Systems of Buddhist Thought, 30, 111.
Takakusu, 36.
Tārānātha, 35, 36, 41.
tathāgata, 169ff.
Tattvapradīpikā, 57, 82.
Tattvasaṅgraha, 43, 44, see also under abbreviations.
The Laṅkāvatāra Sūtra, Suzuki, 28.

Theory of Mind as Pure Act, 68, 72, 135, 224ff.
Thomas, E. J., 167, 168.
Three Dialogues, 53.
time, 66, 94ff.
Trikālaparīkṣā, 42.
trikasannipāta, 17, 114.
Trisvabhāvanirdeśa, 39, see also under abbreviations.
truths, doctrine of, 145ff.
Tucci, G., 31, 32, 35, 39, 42.
Turner, 56.
Twentieth Century Philosophy, 58.
Ui, H., 31, 32, 36, 39.
universal, 5.
Uttaratantra, 32.
Vādanyāya, 43.
Vādavidhi, 40.
vāsanā, 88ff.
two kinds of, 88-9.
vedanā, 123.
Vedāntasiddhāntamuktāvalī, 185ff.
Vijñaptimātratāsiddhi, 38, see also under abbrevations.
Vyākhyāyukti, 39.
whole, 4ff.
will, 13, 92, 134ff, 160, 170.
as contrasted with knowledge, 182ff.
Winternitz, 27, 29, 32, 34, 35, 39.
Wogihara, 34, 36, 37, 40.
Yamaguchi, 32, 41.
Yogācāra, idealism, 11ff, 19ff, 50, 55, 72, 126ff, 204ff.
and Mādhyamika, 19ff, 192ff.
the development of, 24ff.
whether taught by Buddha, 25ff.
two phases of, 30-1, 40-1.
Mādhyamika-Svātantrika, 44.
Yogācārabhūmiśāstra, 34.
Yogasūtrabhāṣya, 80, 114, 157, 158.
Yogavāśiṣṭha, 186.